To the Sportsmen of the World

THE BEAR HUNT

The three foremost figures are, left to right, Frederic
Remington, General Miles, and the Author. The hounds
are ahead and do not show in the picture. The dogs shown
are the fighting dogs

*From the painting by Frederic Remington
by courtesy of C. L. Maguire, Mount Pleasant, Michigan, U.S.A.*

MEET MR. GRIZZLY

A Saga on the Passing of the Grizzly Bear

By Montague Stevens

Originally published by the University of New Mexico Press, Albuquerque, 1943. This reprint, 2002, (our third reprint of this book) is, however, from the British Edition, Robert Hale Ltd., London, 1950. The British Edition contains six additional photographs and approximately 15 pages of additional text that the author added to the original volume. Additionally, High-Lonesome Books has added the story *"Front Name" Dick* to the original publication.

Library of Congress Catalog Card #87-82507
ISBN #0-944383-09-2
Introduction Copyright © 1987 by M.H. Salmon

HIGH-LONESOME BOOKS
P.O. Box 878
Silver City, New Mexico 88062

INTRODUCTION

Browsing that well known book store in the delightful village of Old Mesilla the other day I was struck by the number of grizzly books on the shelves. William H. Wright's classic *The Grizzly Bear* was available in a softcover reprint. David E. Brown's *The Grizzly in the Southwest* was there; it's due to be a classic. There were a couple of books on Alaska grizzlies, one on Yellowstone Park grizzlies. There was an anthology - *The Grizzly Bear: Portaits from Life.* I have another good anthology at home - *The Grizzly Book,* by Jack Samson. And I hear there is still another anthology in the works - *The Last Grizzly* - also by David E. Brown. It is sure to be interesting reading.

No wild animal in North America has as many enthusiasts and readers as the Grizzly Bear. This is quite remarkable in that almost no one today who buys books about the animal has ever seen one in the wild; and, in all likelihood, never will. The great bear is gone from all but a small percentage of its original range. It is gone from the entirety of its former range in the Southwest, including Mexico. Yet the myths, legends, stories and mystique remain. Even today, a hunter seated by the campfire in a range of mountains that haven't seen a grizzly in fifty years can't help but wonder what it was like when there was a bear out there who might weigh 800 pounds, who could bash in the skull of a grown steer or pull stumps with a roll of his paw. We've never seen one but we just *know* what he was like: big, brawny, smelly, mighty smart, and just unpredictable enough that some of those legends are true. There is a photo of an 800 pound grizzly facing page 161 in this book. That's him all right! Not surprising that such a creature would spawn a Western Myth all his own. There's something about Mr. Grizzly that keeps those books in print and readers eager for more.

And there was something special about Montague Stevens (1859-1953). Born in India, the son of an English Army General, he was a graduate (1881) of Trinity College, Cambridge University. Within six months of graduation the cultured British gentleman was in the Wild West when it was still worthy the name. Stevens never tells us why he chose what is now the Catron County area of southwest New Mexico for his ranching and sporting life. It is evident from a reading of his book that he had an intimate appreciation of a region that offers everything from desert to grasslands to chaparral to lush-timbered mountains. It was and is the least settled area of New Mexico, an area which, for all its awesome beauty, few people have wanted as a home. Even today less than 3,000 people inhabit a county easily larger than the state of Connecticut. But the self-described iconoclast and lover of the wild chose well.

Stevens also has little to say about an 1888 hunting accident that cost him his left arm. This accident he describes as "unfortunate." The shock of a serious hunting accident has brought more than one confirmed nimrod from the pursuit of game down to the likes of birdwatching, gardening, or reminiscing in a tavern. Certainly an accident which maims would be expected to at least tame the pursuit. Evidently, Stevens simply decided that he would continue to live his life as he liked. In 1889 Stevens began hunting bear, horseback with hounds.

In my first reading of *Meet Mr. Grizzly* I can recall quietly criticizing the author for not giving me more of Stevens. This was a supreme character writing a book and I wanted more of that character, more revelation, more philosophy, more of the man. I wanted less British understatement. I think now, that Stevens provides the reader with about as much as a good reader ought to have. That the author went on to pursuit of the grizzly *after* he lost his arm tells us all we need to know about the courage of Montague Stevens. That he broke ranch horse with a threshing machine and considered spurs "an insult to a good horse" confirms his iconoclastic character. As for Stevens' philosophy of life, Stevens does give us a hint of that, during the course of a chess game. Like the rest of us, Stevens' life was a series of problems and obstacles requiring resolution. Rather than shirking those problems, be it managing a life with one arm, or training hounds to catch grizzlies with "reasonable certainty," Stevens found his best pleasure in figuring those problems out. With Stevens it wasn't so much success but the *road to* success that counted. Stevens knew that in life, as in chess, there is always a right move offering a simple solution; one merely has to find it. The setting for the obstacles the author faces is the American wilderness. The cast of mind which confronts them is the result of a classical education.

The modern reader is more apt to criticize Stevens for all the killing. We are witness to dead bears, dead bobcats, dead mountain lions, dead dogs. Stevens writes with precision and considerable skill; but the descriptions are in a sense unvarnished. In another sense they are true to life. When the great grizzly, Susie, cuts her feet to ribbons running across the rocks we are made to know of it, vividly. Today the hunting of any sort of game for sport is under attack from an increasingly urban society which is rapidly losing its roots in the natural world. So one is tempted, as usual, to go on the defensive. One can point to Stevens' closing chapter wherein, upon seeing the severe decline in the grizzly population, he becomes ..."a zealous convert to their preservation, to prevent so noble an animal from becoming extinct." All to the good of course, and notwithstanding that his efforts, and those of many others, were in vain, at least in the Southwest. Also, it must be noted that it wasn't sportsmen like Stevens who extirpated the Southwestern grizzly but, rather, the organized and well funded efforts of a government/livestock industry coalition. As a rancher,

Stevens knew how the grizzly could cut into profits. He had an interest in control and in sport, but never in extermination. Stevens' place as a sportsman/conservationist can best be put into perspective by considering the essence of his hunting. And that essence is found in his relationship with hounds and horses.

In *A Sand County Almanac*, Aldo Leopold, another avid hunter, discusses at length the value of hunting in building character and a sense of ethics and fair play. During that discussion he comments that..."hunting generally involves the handling of dogs and horses, and the lack of this experience is one of the most serious defects of our gasoline-driven civilization." Stevens used hounds and horses to hunt the most magnificent and arguable the most challenging game animal on the continent. The patience, kindness, and intelligence evident in his training of his hounds and horses is portrayed in the best writing you'll find in this book. Eventually, hunting in concert with hounds and horses, he became extremely successful in the pursuit of the Grizzly Bear, thereby demonstrating to the ultimate degree what sport hunting, properly, is all about: the elevation of primitive skills to high art. If hunting is more on the defensive today, perhaps it is because too many hunters, caught up in a mechanized, high-tech world, are losing those skills, and the will to elevate them to art. *Meet Mr. Grizzly* tells us how it was done, with hounds, with horses, with life on the frontier, when it was done right.

M. H. Salmon - Mimbres Valley - September 1987

M. H. Salmon hunts with both trailhounds and coursing hounds. He is the author of *Gazehounds & Coursing*; *Gila Descending - A Southwestern Journey*; and the novel *Home is the River*.

Cover artist Fred Barraza is a native of Central City, New Mexico. His drawings, etchings and sculpture have been exhibited on a number of occasions.

CONTENTS

ILLUSTRATIONS

PREFACE

ALL that I am about to relate occurred about thirty-five to fifty years ago, so it can hardly be said that I have rushed into print on this subject. Nor would I do so now, were it not for the importunities of friends and relatives alike, who seem to think it would be a pity not to record my grizzly bear hunting experiences in writing, especially as they are in a field of sport of which relatively little has ever been written from first-hand knowledge.

Having now acceded to their wishes, I must ask my readers to kindly allow me to arrogate to myself the privilege of relating my adventures in an informal, conversational way, and ask them to imagine themselves sitting around a campfire, listening to the yarns, perhaps I should say rodomontade, of an old grizzly bear hunter, in a series of what might be called "Camp Fireside Chats."

I would also add that I have used fictitious names for all persons about whom I may write who do not show up in a favourable light, in deference to their relatives or descendents whose feelings might be hurt if real names were used.

It is with some diffidence that I write this book, for I shall say many things that are contrary to popular beliefs. I have observed that an authority who lectures or writes upon this particular subject, generally prefaces or interludes his remarks by saying: "Contrary to popular belief . . ."

I have tried to solve the riddle of why so many popular beliefs are erroneous. The best answer that I have been able to evolve, so far, is that someone starts a rumour which is false. The next person who hears this rumour remarks: "You cannot believe all your hear," but nevertheless repeats it, and by constant repetition, it merges into: "Everybody says so." When everybody says so, it becomes an acknowledged fact and popular belief is thus born. After this, if anyone ventures to assail its truth, he is likely to be looked at and considered "queer."

M. S.

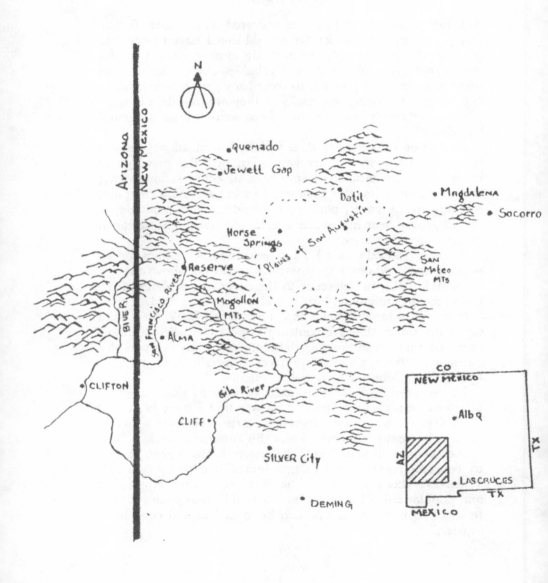

CHAPTER I

WELCOME TO THE FIRST CAMP
FIRESIDE CHAT

IN telling my story, I shall endeavour to help my readers envisage the true inwardness of bear hunting; that is, to give them the "meat" of the subject, which recalls to my mind the time I took out hunting a friend who was anxious to get a fine deer head. A buck with a magnificent head was running in a certain area of the forest, remote from the ranch. So we packed a camp outfit, and with Tom, one of my cowboys, made for the desired spot. As we expected to kill game, the only meat we took with us was bacon.

Unfortunately, it rained for two days, but on the third it cleared up, and we sallied forth to kill the Monarch of the Forest—if we could find him.

After a few hours' hunting, we had the good fortune to run on to a big herd of deer, in the midst of which was the buck we were looking for. A fallen tree lay between us and the deer, so we crept up to it on our hands and knees, and cautiously peered over the trunk.

My companion, of course, was to take the shot, and he aimed at the buck, but every time he was about to shoot, a doe would intervene, and he had to wait. Finally, a doe, who probably scented us, came to within twenty yards of us, and this was too much for Tom, who blazed away and killed her, while the rest of the herd promptly disappeared.

He turned round to look at us, and noted in my face a look of strong disapproval, while on that of my friend was a look of blank horror. Then, as it dawned on him that he had done something wrong, Tom exclaimed vehemently:

"By Gosh! Don't we want meat?"

My friend and I continued our hunt and got a good deer head, but nothing like the Monarch of the Forest we had been so near to getting.

Like Tom, my readers will want to get the "meat" of bear hunting, without any sensational frills, and that is what I shall endeavour to give them.

Once, when I was hunting with two professional hunters, the argument arose as to whether a cinnamon bear, which both hunters regarded as a separate species, would climb a tree.

One of them contended that he had treed a cinnamon bear. The other said his hounds had bayed a cinnamon bear under a tree, but he wouldn't climb it, so he had to kill him on the ground. The argument became more and more heated, until in desperation, they turned to me to hear what I might have to say on the subject—not that either of them thought I knew anything about it!

My reply was most unexpected.

"You are both right and both wrong," I said, "and furthermore, there is no such species as a *cinnamon* bear. One of the bears about which you were arguing was a species of *black* bear, and he could climb a tree. The other was a *grizzly*, which could not. There were a few moments of stunned silence. Then one of the hunters said to me abruptly:

"Where did you get that stuff?"

"Last year," I explained, "when I was in Washington, I called at the Smithsonian Institution to get reliable information on bears and was informed by a well-known authority on the subject that the species of a bear was decided, not by its colour, but by its anatomical structure. There is no such animal as a *true cinnamon* bear. At least, not on this continent."

Another still longer silence ensued, which was finally broken by the other hunter:

"Did that there professor ever hunt bear?" And my answer was: "No."

"If he ain't never hunted bear, what the hell does he know about 'em?"

This closed the argument for the time being, but the two hunters agreed to refer the question to some of their professional brethren at a later date.

Professional bear hunters would be supposed to possess a comprehensive knowledge of their subject, but this incident illustrates to what heights ignorant prejudice may rise.

To the sportsman and to the hound there is a vast difference between hunting the so-called black bear and the grizzly. The reason I say "so-called" black bear is because black is its prevailing colour.

This bear, the Ursus Americanus, or American bear, has three colours—black, brown, and cinnamon. A black she-bear usually has two cubs, sometimes a black and a brown, and sometimes a black and a cinnamon. But both these brown and cinnamon cubs invariably change back to the normal colour, black, when they shed off in their second, third, or even fourth years.

The other species of bear is the Ursus Horribilis, or grizzly, and has two colours, the normal colour being dark brown turning to black at the feet, and also cinnamon. In both cases the hair over the back has pearly or silver-grey tips. Hence, it is locally known as the "silvertip." The cinnamon grizzly also changes to its normal colour, brown, in its second, third, or fourth years. The fact that these two species are the only two in the Rocky mountain region leads to some confusion, in that when they are of the same colour one species may be taken for the other.

The principal differences between these two species are:

The black bear is smaller, rarely exceeding four hundred pounds in weight when full grown, whereas a grizzly will run up to eight hundred pounds. I speak, of course, only of the Rocky Mountain grizzly, not of the old Californian species, which greatly exceeded that weight. This difference is due to the fact that the Californian grizzly had all the fish he could eat during the summer months, while the Rocky Mountain grizzly had to content himself with scratching for a living, digging up roots or yellow-jacket nests, or ripping the bark off dead trees to get the acorns that the woodpeckers had stored there the fall before.

The head of the grizzly is longer, in proportion, than that of the black bear.

The grizzly has claws as long as a man's fingers, and blunt at the extremities, on his front feet, whereas the claws of the black bear are sharp and retractile, like a cat's. Hence, the black bear can climb a tree, and the grizzly cannot. The tracks of these bear are easily distinguished on soft ground by the fact that the grizzly's claws make small holes a couple of inches or so in front of his fore feet. The black bear's claws, being retractile, make no marks whatsoever.

Before going further, I would like to say that in 1888, I lost my left arm, on what was probably the most unfortunate happening in any "wild goose chase." While hunting wild geese in California, and riding a friend's horse of which I knew nothing, I had a loaded, double-barrelled shotgun in front of me, laid across the saddle. Suddenly the horse shied and bolted off among some bushes. I grabbed the muzzle of the gun with my left hand, and held it away from me, while I tried to pull up the horse with my right. A branch caught between the hammer and the barrel, pulling the hammer back and at the same time jerking the gun around, when it went off and blew my arm to pieces. Well, since then, it has naturally been awkward for me to handle a rifle properly, but I have managed to get along all right, though it is somewhat of a handicap in an emergency; and when shooting grizzlies at close quarters in dense brush, emergencies are not infrequent.

In hunting black bear and grizzlies, there are many points that are similar, and others that are widely divergent, and though it is the object of this book to write about grizzlies, I have to include the hunting of black bear for purposes of comparison. Also, hunting black bear is a necessary stepping-stone in training hounds to hunt the grizzly.

In the first place, the black bear ranges mostly in the foot-hills of the high mountains, while the grizzly ranges round the tops. In the Rocky Mountain region, where I lived for many years, my ranches were on both sides of the main divide, where the valleys are more or less seven thousand feet in elevation, and the mountain tops run to ten thousand feet, and more. These foothills, which are just above the valleys, are fairly good ground for horses to run over. Hence, the hunter is often able to keep within hearing of the hounds in trailing black bear, especially when the bear contributes to his own undoing by climbing a tree.

As I usually had friends and professional hunters with me, if the hounds should get out of hearing, we would scatter in

Author in 1893

The Author in 1943

different directions and if anyone should hear the hounds and get to the treed bear, he would light a fire close by, throwing on dead leaves to make a dense column of smoke. This would be readily seen by the other hunters, and when all the party had got together, the guest of honour would shoot the bear and get the hide. After the bear was skinned, the dogs would get a good meal of entrails and some meat, and the rest of the animal would be quartered and packed back to camp.

As a rule, a black bear will tree before he has been run many miles, an easy chase for hounds, and also easy on their feet, especially if the ground is covered with grass. On the other hand, running a grizzly over rocky ground for long distances may make their feet tender for a week.

Then, again, the black bear fights hounds in a different way than the grizzly. Whenever he turns on the hounds, he runs at them collectively, but the grizzly will select one particular dog that he thinks has bothered him the most, and try to catch him singly. While he must be considered a slow-moving animal, it is astonishing how fast he can run for a short distance of say thirty yards. I have frequently seen a grizzly nearly catch a dog, and when he gives up, with his head under the dog's tail, he will give a terrific snort, which will so scare the dog that he will become "grizzly-shy" from then on.

In running black bear, I have often caught up with the hounds and watched them attack. I could, of course, easily have shot the bear, but I did not wish to do so on account of the rest of the hunting party, so I would follow along until the bear found an opportunity to climb a tree.

There is a popular belief to the effect that a bear climbs a tree with his front paws on either side of the trunk, and I rather think this idea is derived from pictures in children's books depicting a bear climbing thus. This assumption, however, is due to the artist's imagination, and not to true facts. A bear can climb a tree only when the trunk is large enough to allow him to place his front paws side by side.

Being a heavy animal in proportion to his size, he can only raise his body by throwing out his claws at full tension into the bark, which enables him to climb. If the trunk of

17   B

the tree is too small for him to do this, he cannot throw his claws sideways deep enough to sustain his weight, so he slides down. Time and again I have seen a bear, when hard pressed by the hounds, spring at a small tree and go up several feet, aided by the momentum of his first jump, and then slide down again among the hounds and run to another tree, where he repeated his effort. Finally he reaches a tree big enough for him to climb, but by this time he is often so out of breath that this feat is impossible; so, realizing his situation, he will sit down on his haunches with his back to the tree, thus facing the dogs. When he regains his wind he will rush suddenly at the dogs, who will naturally start to run away, and he will then whirl round and climb the tree before they can turn and grab him, and, from the first big branch high enough to be out of reach, he will calmly survey the dogs baying him from below.

Once the black bear is treed, the chase is over as far as the hounds are concerned, but it is very different in the case of the grizzly. He will always make for the top of a mountain and run around the crest, crossing the timbered heads of the canyons, over sharp rocks and rough ground where the grass does not grow. He will continue running until he is tired out, when he will stop in a dense, quaking aspen thicket on a very steep mountainside. There he will sit down with his back to a tree and face the hounds. As he frequently will run twenty or thirty miles before stopping, it takes hounds with the greatest staying qualities to continue chasing him. It is not surprising that hounds, after running for hours over rocky ground, will get both tender-footed and thirsty, and with no hunter catching up with them, get discouraged and quit the bear, one by one, or even in twos or threes, and leave the lead dog to go it alone.

The non-arrival of the hunter is due to the fact that the bear runs over such rough and timbered ground that he cannot follow directly on horseback, but has to make detours, and while he is doing this, the hounds will get out of hearing. All the hunter can do then is to ride to the top of the mountain and listen, and spend the rest of the day rimming round the heads of the canyons in the hope of hearing the hounds bay. Generally speaking, high winds blow at these altitudes, which adds to the difficulty of sounds reaching him, so that his chances of getting into contact with the hounds again are very remote. Once in a while he will hear them, and will leave his horse and climb down to where he thinks the bear is bayed, only to find him gone. He has then to decide whether to go back to his horse, or follow the hounds on foot as long as he can stay within hearing of them. He may follow the bear a long way, and finally give it up when the dogs get out of hearing. Then he has to trudge back to his horse, which by this time may be a long distance away. To add to his discouragement he may not be able to find exactly where he left him! Assuming he finds him, and that he is sufficiently enthusiastic, he will ride along the mountain top, which is generally good going, until, with luck, he may again hear the hounds baying the bear, which has taken refuge in a dense thicket. Now comes the hunter's chance to shoot him, but this chance is minimized by the fact that he must get to within at least thirty or forty feet before he can even see the bear hiding in the brush. It is very difficult to approach him without making some kind of sound, such as breaking a dead branch, or stumbling over a loose rock. While bears have relatively poor eyesight, their senses of hearing and smell are very keen, and should they either hear or scent the approach of a man, they would plunge down the mountainside and be gone.

After that it becomes hopeless for the hunter ever to catch up with him again on that day, if it is near nightfall; for the bear, when he is once frightened, will not stop going for a long time. The hunter then realizes that he is probably twenty miles or more from camp, and he has to wend his weary way through miles of heavy timber and rocky canyons, in the dark. He finally reaches camp, provided he has a good bump of location, but he will be lucky if he gets in before midnight. Some of the hounds will have preceded him to camp, while the others will streak in during the night.

This is typical of what usually happens when hunting grizzly on the "hit or miss" principle, which I followed for some ten years, until I eventually evolved a new method of catching

19

them with reasonable certainty. It is my purpose to recount in this book the difficulties which confronted me until this objective was attained.

It took me ten years to kill five grizzlies, when hunting them in the customary way, and as nearly as I can average it, it took about six failures to achieve one success. This success, apart from perseverance, was based on pure luck, and that is why I have called this method of catching grizzlies the "hit or miss" principle.

There are very few hounds who will stay with a bear after nightfall. In fact, I knew of but one, out of numberless ordinary hounds that were called "good bear dogs," that would stay with a grizzly until after dark.

It can be realized, therefore, that hounds who can successfully catch black bear cannot be depended upon to catch a grizzly. When a hunter claims to have a good pack of "bear dogs," it does not necessarily mean that he has a pack that will catch grizzlies.

CHAPTER II

CONCERNING BEAR HUNTERS

THE term "bear hunter" is somewhat vague, as it embraces many different classes of hunters. Those in the tenderfoot class are hunters who bear hunt for the first time. Naturally, they know nothing about it, and so have to be taken care of by those who know more. This class comprises the majority of so-called bear hunters, because they seldom have more than one opportunity to hunt.

In the next class are those who can hunt from time to time, and are thus able to realize the fascination of the sport.

Then comes the trapper, who is generally called a bear hunter, but, strictly speaking, he does not *hunt* bear, but merely catches them in his traps. Very often these trappers have two or three hounds which they use to trail up animals which have escaped with their traps. They do not hunt bear on horseback, with hounds, as, because of the expense of feeding several horses, it would never pay them to do so. Actually, there is no money in trapping. All the trappers I have ever known have only made a bare living out of it, but they do it because they like the life. They usually make more out of bounties for killing coyotes, panthers, bobcats, and other predatory animals than they do by selling their hides. Also, they make a little money in the hunting seasons by taking parties out to deer hunt.

The black bear hunters who hunt with two or three hounds were generally ranchmen, who could be hired at times, though they were not professional hunters.

My definition of a black bear hunter is a man who not only kills a black bear, but has trained the hounds with which to catch them. Hunters who kill bear through the medium of hounds that have been trained by other men are not, strictly speaking, bear hunters, except in a purely amateur sense. At least, that is the way in which they are regarded by those who catch bear with dogs of their own training. These latter, while not professionals, since they do not hunt for commercial purposes, regard themselves as sort of super-amateurs.

When I first started bear hunting, I had already had considerable experience in big game hunting in the West, but I had only still-hunted, never using hounds.

In September, 1880, while I was still at Cambridge University (Trinity College), England, I came to America with two college friends on my second long vacation, and we hunted in the Medicine Bow Mountains, north of Rock Springs, Wyoming.

At Cheyenne, I met James H. Cook, who was a professional big game hunter, and he allowed us to accompany him on one of his hunts. We were successful in getting some very fine elk heads, as well as some mountain sheep and antelope. These we took back to England with us and set up in our rooms at college with considerable pride.

The first elk I killed I shot four times before he fell. As it was my first bull elk, with a fine head, I felt quite proud of myself, and when Cook was helping to skin the animal, I asked him what he thought of my shooting, expecting to get a compliment. All he replied was:

"You're a good butcher, anyway!"

This was the general term that these professional hunters used for those who took more than one shot to kill their game.

Jim was generally considered one of the best, if not *the* best, game shot in the West at that time. He very rarely took two shots to kill an animal, because, as he would tell me:

"If you can't be sure of killing with one shot, don't shoot!"

Also, at Cheyenne, I met Pete Bergesson, the gunsmith, from whom I bought my rifle and ammunition. He was a wonderful target shot, and, I was told years afterwards, won first prizes at champion rifle shooting tournaments.

It was under the able instruction of these two experts that I learned the finer points in rifle shooting which I never would have learned otherwise.

In June, 1881, I was graduated, and that fall organized a party of eight among my college friends, while Cook got together the necessary equipment, and we again hunted in the Medicine Bow Mountains in September.

In the spring of 1882 I started ranching in New Mexico, and the following fall made another hunt with my college friends. At that time we hunted on Powder River, in Wyoming, and in the Big Horn Mountains. On that hunt, we got buffalo, in addition to elk, mountain sheep, etc.

For the next few years I hunted deer from the ranch from time to time, but it wasn't until about 1889 that my foreman, Dan Gatlin, and I started bear hunting, with hounds. While this was a new form of sport for me, I could scarcely be classed as a tenderfoot hunter. After a few hunts, we began to catch on to what bear hunting really was. Between us, we got a few hounds, then hired a neighbour who had two or three hounds with which he had caught bear, and we would go on a hunt in the fall, when the cattle work was over for the season.

Dan started to work for me about 1886, and while my foreman, White, ran the outfit, I always worked with the cattle, just like my cowboys did. In this way, I worked alongside Dan, and soon realized what an excellent cowboy he was. It was, therefore, not surprising that when White left my employ a few months later, I offered Dan his job of running the outfit, and he held this job for years.

For those of my readers who are not familiar with the Rocky Mountains, in general, and where they traverse New Mexico, in particular, I feel I should digress here, and give an idea of the climate and the sort of terrain over which I bear hunted.

It was in the fall of 1882 that I bought my first ranches from early settlers, and so little was known of New Mexico in the East that I was several times asked if we didn't have monkeys and parrots here.

I was visiting in Silver City when word came in that a band of Apache Indians were on the warpath, and had killed some mining men in Clifton, just across the line in Arizona. There was a call for volunteers, so I joined a civilian expedition under the leadership of Sam Eckles, a prominent citizen of Silver City, to bring in the bodies of the slain men.

The Government sent troops to catch the Indians, and I

became acquainted with some of the Army officers in command of them, and as their guest, joined in several Indian hunts. In this way I got into western Socorro County, where I bought my first ranches.

It was not long before the country was settled by cattlemen. Later on, I bought out some of these ranchers, from time to time, until finally I had ranches scattered over an area of some eighty by thirty miles, generally known as the SU Ranches and range, SU being my cattle brand.

These ranches were situated on both sides of the main divide of the Rocky Mountains, which pass through western Socorro County, now known as Catron County. Besides the main divide, there were groups of mountain ranges in all directions, and it was in the intervening valleys that these ranches lay. Some of these valleys were several miles wide, and others were narrow. Their elevation, as stated, was around seven thousand feet, while the mountain peaks, in some instances, reached a height of nearly eleven thousand feet.

Between the valleys and the main mountains were the foothills, and these were covered, in most places, with forests of pine, cedar, piñon, juniper, and oak trees, and it was through these foothills that the black bear roamed in search of their feed of piñon nuts, juniper berries, and acorns.

At about eighty-five hundred feet elevation, the timber changes to spruce, balsam, and quaking aspen thickets, and here the grizzly makes his home.

Finally, at about ten thousand feet elevation the timber quits growing on the mountain ranges I hunted over. Strictly speaking, timberline is eleven thousand five hundred feet, but in our bear hunting parlance it meant the line at which timber quits growing. This line varies on different mountains, due probably to change of soil or other reasons. Above these lines the mountain tops are bare or, as we called them, "bald." When riding with friends at the higher elevations, they were enthusiastic at the magnificence of the scenery. This was especially so during the rainy season. Heavy rains fall during the day, but towards evening it generally clears up, leaving a mass of fleecy clouds all over the sky. As the sun sinks on the horizon, these clouds are tinged with a red glow, making a glorious sunset, while the tops of the mountains and the perpendicular cliffs, that often surround them, stand out in bold relief, while wave after wave of timbered mountain ridges and the green valleys below make up a scenic picture which is unforgettable.

Naturally, my friends liked to remain as long as possible to absorb the beauties that so enthralled them. This did not apply to Dan, who was sometimes with me on these rides, and who was not impressed. He would get restless and whisper to me, "Let's get going." From his point of view, he regarded sunrises and sunsets as just "sunups" and "sundowns." To him, "sunup" meant that you were up and dressed, ready to work, while "sundown" represented "quitting time," while as regards scenery from his practical standpoint, he told me that if my friends had to ride after cattle over that scenery, they wouldn't be so darned stuck on it!

New Mexico has been aptly called the "Sunshine State," especially in May and June, when as a rule we have cloudless, superbly blue skies. I can recall one time when a friend from England came to visit me in May, he had been telling me about a long spell of bad weather that had occurred just before he left England, and during which he had not seen the sun for days. So it was only natural that he was greatly impressed by our wonderful climate here. After a week, I was talking to one of the cowboys, Tom, who remarked:

"That there friend of yours from the Old Country is sure a fine man, but ain't he a little nutty?"

I replied: "No, what makes you think so?"

"Why," answered Tom, "when he comes out mornings and sees me he says:

" 'Good morning, Tom,' and then he looks round. 'What a fine morning!' says he."

"I don't see anything wrong with that," I remarked.

"Maybe so," said Tom, "but what in H—— does he expect?"

Tom was like the most of the rest of us, who do not properly appreciate good things that come our way, but take them as a matter of course, and it is only when a stranger brings them to our attention that we realize our good fortune, and this especially applies to our good climate of New Mexico.

Dan was jovial and good-natured, of a cheerful disposition, and always ready to see the humorous side of things, even under the most depressing circumstances; in short, he was an optimist. We got along famously—not that we agreed on everything, but we agreed amicably to disagree, and let it go at that.

When we started bear hunting, Dan had already mastered one of its most difficult problems. From having run wild cattle for years through the timber and brush on the high mountains, he had become an expert endurance rider and could judge the country to be ridden over, so as to be able to pick his way with the least loss of energy to his mount. It is generally admitted that it is inadvisable to swap horses while crossing a stream. This would imply that there would be a horse to swap to if you should so wish; but in the middle of a bear hunt there is no horse for you to change to, and if the one you are riding plays out, the only choice you have is to walk back to camp. As Dan had been astride of a horse practically since infancy, this method of locomotion didn't appeal to him in the least, which probably had not a little to do with the expert care he took of his horse.

Incidentally, Dan also had an excellent bump of locality, which always brought him back to camp even after nightfall or through a blinding snowstorm.

There were, however, two points in endurance riding on which Dan and I differed. One was in the matter of spurs. It would be as impossible to visualize a cowboy without spurs as an angel without wings; and to Dan, like other cowboys, the idea of going without them was quite unthinkable. However, from my point of view, they are an insult to a good horse. As only the best of horses are eligible for hunting grizzlies, it follows that the only kind of horse I would want to ride would be one that didn't need a spur.

Of course, when I rode ordinary horses, I was obliged to wear spurs whether I wanted to or not. They are so accustomed to spurs that they could not be ridden without them.

But top-notch horses, such as my pets, George and Roaney, need gentle repression, not stimulation. Many high-spirited horses easily become excited when they are fresh, and they know instantly when you are wearing spurs, although you may not use them, Therefore, they are apt to fret themselves into a sweat, using up much energy needlessly.

A high-spirited horse should not be excitable, but as gentle as possible. Loss of energy caused by fretting becomes noticeable only towards the second half of a long day's ride, when the horse begins to tire and plays out, which means that you cannot get him out of a walk. Under such circumstances, it is useless to spur him, because it will break his spirit, and once his spirit is broken, he is ruined for hunting grizzlies, since he will lose the prime incentive to do his best.

While our opinions differed on the matter of spurs, I have to credit Dan with the fact that he used his as little as possible, and never without good reason.

There was another serious objection to spurs in hunting grizzlies. As the bear would be bayed on a steep, rocky hillside in dense brush, he would have to be approached quietly, on foot, and for this reason the clinking of spurs on the rocks was a great handicap.

Furthermore, should an emergency force you to quicken your pace, you would be very apt to forget all about the spurs, and they would be likely to trip you up abruptly. To make matters worse, cowboy spurs are naturally attached to cowboy boots with high heels. They are all right for riding, but are not adapted to walking even on level ground, much less on steep hillsides.

When Dan and I first hunted grizzlies, we would leave our horses and approach the bear together, but we soon found out that such a method would not work, because no matter how cautious we might be, two men will make more noise than one. Also, there was always the chance, for one reason or another, of becoming separated, and if the bear should happen to come between us, neither would dare to shoot for fear of hitting the other.

My suggestion to Dan that he should take off his spurs when making such trips afoot met with an unfavourable response, and he finally decided that he wouldn't go on any more such jaunts, but that if I wanted to, it was all right with him.

Of course, since I always wore high laced boots, and didn't

use spurs, I was under no handicap, and it was relatively easy to sneak through the brush without making much noise. So, with Dan raising no objection, when it came to shooting grizzlies in rough places, I got the shot.

Notwithstanding this fact, Dan's aid was invaluable in many ways. He was far and away the best hunter I ever hunted with.

The other point on which we differed was whether we should help our horses by getting off and leading them, under certain circumstances. My maxim for endurance riding was "Put yourself in the horse's place and act accordingly."

Dan and I agreed on this view, except that he made one reservation. He didn't propose to get off his horse and lead him up steep places. Indeed, he considered any sort of work, except on horseback, as beneath the dignity of a self-respecting cowboy.

There is nothing that will knock a horse out quicker than crowding him up a steep hill. While hunting grizzlies, I had no objections to getting off my horse and leading him up steep places from time to time. It followed that he would be in far better shape, after a few hours of hard riding, than equally good horses whose riders had stayed on their backs.

It is not surprising, therefore, that the merit of my method of endurance riding, though not showing any advantage during the first half of the day, became quite apparent towards the end of it. The results were that, in our friendly rivalry, in the case of short runs, Dan would be in the lead, while on the long ones I managed to euchre him out of that lead.

During my first year of bear hunting, in the late eighties, I was not able to secure any hounds except those that had been trained to hunt only trapped animals. The hunts with Dan and the neighbour whom I've already mentioned marked my initiation into that sport.

The next year we hunted again, but by that time, Dan and I had secured a few young hounds and added them to the pack, with the view of training them and having a pack of our own. After these hounds learned to trail bear without the aid of the other more experienced hounds, we had no further need for outside help, either canine or human. By this time, we had learned the finer points of bear hunting, and had, at last, graduated into the class of full-fledged black bear hunters.

Finally, to our great joy, we succeeded in buying from an old trapper a really reliable hound who would not run deer. "Old Drive" became our lead dog. The trapper would never have parted with him, but for the fact that he had inherited a farm in Arkansas, and concluded to give up trapping to go back there and farm.

Drive was a typical southern states hound, black and tan in colour and the best silvertip hound that I ever hunted with, apart from the pure bloodhounds I had subsequently. Being quite old when we got him, and unable to run like the younger hounds, when he would finally reach the bear he would hobble along, about thirty yards behind him and bay about every ten seconds, his cracked voice sounding more like a canine croak than anything else.

Curiously enough, this was his greatest merit, as being the lead dog, he slowed down the younger dogs. As a matter of fact, speed is a detriment to a good bear dog, because, though the hounds may strike a hot trail, the bear himself may be many miles away, and the faster the hounds run, the sooner they get out of hearing. Also unlike other hounds, Drive would stay with a silvertip, even after nightfall. I assume this because he reached many more silvertips than we did, and he must have stayed with them, through the night, as he only showed up in camp the evening of the next day.

Old Drive must have been shamefully beaten as a young hound, probably for running deer, because, when we first got him, he would cringe whenever we spoke to him.

Dan and I welcomed him with delight, as he was our first reliable silvertip bear dog, and I need not say that he got the best treatment we could give him. When I called him, he would come timidly to be patted, till finally he became bold enough to rub his head against my knee.

On his first hunt with me, he made his bed in some leaves under a tree near the campfire. The night was cold, and I noticed that he shivered from time to time. So, armed with my saddle blankets, two thick Navajo rugs, each a yard square, I routed him out of his bed, laid one down on the spot he had selected, induced him to lie down on it, and then I covered him with the other blanket, all but his head.

When I had made his bed for several nights, he looked upon my doing so as a matter of course. I always let him select his own bed, and then when I approached, carrying the rugs, he would hop out, watch me put down the first blanket, then lie down on it, wagging his tail until I covered him with the other blanket. It was pathetic to see, by the light of the camp-fire, his eyes glistening with gratitude as I walked away.

The poor old fellow had, all his life, been literally "treated like a dog," and it was difficult for him to grasp the idea of being treated humanely.

What a super-hound he would have made, had he been intelligently trained, and the good qualities he possessed developed to their utmost! Instead, his excellent traits had been stunted by ignorant methods. In other words, he was a wonderful bear dog, not because of the training he had received, but in spite of it!

The big difficulty in training young hounds is to break them from running deer, for there are many more deer than there are bear. It follows that you have to cross many deer trails before you strike a bear trail, and the young hounds run off after the deer, and may not come back for hours, leaving the pack reduced to the reliable lead dog.

My experience has been that most hunters try to break their hounds from running deer by beating them, a method of which I strongly disapprove. Apart from the humane side of the question, it breaks his spirit and makes him afraid of you, which is the one thing a dog trainer should avoid. Consequently, when the young hound is tired of running deer, he comes back to the pack. If his owner beats him, the hound, who has long since forgotten all about the deer, thinks he is being beaten for returning to the pack, and the next time he runs deer, he makes for the camp.

When his master returns in the evening and sees his hound there, he gives him a still more severe beating, and this time the poor hound thinks it's because he came back to camp.

Therefore, on the next hunt, when he again runs off after deer and gives up the chase, remembering the two beatings, he concludes his best policy is to sneak back to the home of his master. After the hunt is over, and the latter reaches home and sees the dog, he is apt to take his rifle and shoot him, deeming him worthless, thus ending the life of possibly a very promising hound.

Every allowance should be made for a hound running deer, for the simple reason that it is his natural instinct. So strong is this instinct, that I have known young hounds, who have never seen a deer and run on to their trail for the first time, to take it, evincing the greatest excitement. On the other hand, no hound in my experience will take the trail of a bear naturally, and he can only be trained or persuaded to do so by the example of the older dogs. In other words, the training of a bear dog consists in preventing him from running what he wants to run in favour of running something he doesn't want to run.

To accomplish this task successfully, the best method is by prevention and persuasion, which consists of necking the young hound to a dog that will not run deer, and only turning him loose when the lead dog starts on a hot bear trail, baying loudly. The young hound will then naturally run to him, and probably stay with him until the bear is treed.

After the bear is killed, the persuading part of the programme comes in; that is, when he is given all the bear meat he can eat. Under this simple treatment, it is not surprising that the young hound soon becomes an enthusiastic bear hunter.

In order to increase my knowledge of bear hunting as quickly as possible, I would hire any professional trapper, especially if he had a good bear dog or two, to hunt with me. I learned what I could from each of them so that in time my knowledge was based on different sources of information, and was fairly comprehensive.

Professional bear trappers, like other authorities on any subject, disagreed on many points, and these disagreements helped me greatly to form my conclusions. These hunters were either voluble or reticent, according to their individual personalities, but they had one thing in common; they didn't

31

want to tell you their real opinions, for the very just reason that they didn't want to give away the knowledge they had acquired from years of experience, which was virtually their stock in trade.

To obviate this difficulty, I would hire two hunters at a time, when possible each having his own hounds. When we hunted, something would always transpire that would start a difference of opinion between them, and around the campfire at night, they would argue on either the merits of their respective hounds, or on what the bear did, or did not do.

It was quite immaterial whether we got the bear or not. The differences of opinion still existed. It is said that people tell the truth when they quarrel, and this applies equally to those who argue. So that all I had to do was to listen quietly and absorb all I could from their heated debates.

During my first years of bear hunting, I caught a good number of black bear, but no grizzlies, as they were beyond the capabilities of the hounds we had at that time.

It is true that we ran on to cattle killed by grizzlies, and would thereby occasionally get a fresh trail, which the hounds would take. But that was generally the end of the hunt, as far as we were concerned; because we put in the rest of the day trying to get in touch with the hounds, and not succeeding, except on very rare occasions.

Dogs wooling a black bear. Dan Gatlin, the author, a hunter and General Miles

The author on his favourite horse, George

CHAPTER III

GENERAL MILES HUNTS WITH ME
THE FIRST TIME

It was in October, 1893, that I had my first big hunt, in which friends who wanted to hunt bear participated. General Nelson A. Miles, at that time Chief of Staff of the United States Army, had written and asked if he could hunt with me that Fall and, incidentally, mentioned that he would like to get a grizzly. I replied that I would be delighted if he would come, and that I felt sure I could *guarantee* his getting black bear, but I could not answer for more than the fresh tracks of a grizzly. He decided to come, as he wanted to try hunting bear with hounds, which would be a new experience for him.

General Miles greatly distinguished himself in the Civil War, and later was a prominent figure among the nationally known. It was in 1885 that I first met him in Albuquerque, where he made his headquarters when he was in command of the troops, some five thousand in all, that had been sent to fight Geronimo and his band of Apache Indians. The latter took refuge in the Mogollon Mountains and adjacent areas in South-Western New Mexico. The troops were scattered mostly in small units of one to three companies of soldiers through the above-mentioned mountains, so that wherever the Indians committed depredations or killed settlers there would always be soldiers somewhere close, to take after them at short notice. In this way, I had two companies of soldiers and one company of Navajo Indian scouts stationed at my home ranch near Reserve, while other companies were camped on some of my other ranches in that area.

From time to time, the Indians would waylay and kill settlers travelling on the roads and trails through the country.

Whenever such killings took place in our vicinity, the soldiers were at once sent after them, and I would accompany these expeditions as a guest of the officers in command. In this way, I obtained considerable first-hand knowledge in Indian warfare. During the year or more that the soldiers were camped on my ranches, some of my experiences were quite humorous; on my occasional visits to Albuquerque, I related them to the General, who smilingly referred to them as my unofficial reports from the front.

I remember telling him, one time, of a freighter whom the Indians killed and then robbed his wagon. Among other things there were some wooden buckets of coloured candy, of the kind where each piece had a paper motto stuck to it. The Indians helped themselves liberally to the candy, and as we took their trail, it was marked here and there with those paper mottoes as long as the candy lasted. It reminded me of a paper chase, a game of my schooldays. As we were going along, I spied a small, pale green object on the ground, and I got off my horse and picked it up. It was a piece of scented soap which bore deeply indented tooth marks. Evidently an Indian had bitten into it and then thrown it away, probably because it lathered in his mouth. I put it into my pocket as a memento, and subsequently placed it on the mantelpiece of our ranch sitting-room. Sad to relate, some time afterwards when I was away from the ranch, a stranger, not finding soap on the wash-stand, remembered seeing some on the mantelpiece, and used it, washing off the tooth marks, thus reducing my memento to just another piece of soap.

Whenever the Indians went on the warpath, it was only natural that everyone went about fully armed, but by a curious paradox this did not add to their safety, although I did not know it at the time. Some years later I was talking to an Apache who could speak Spanish, and I asked him why the Apaches killed the settlers who had done them no harm. He made the astonishing reply that it was because they were armed. The Apaches, he said, had no money with which to buy arms and ammunition, and the only way they could get any was to take it from those who had some. Therefore, they would waylay trails and when a settler would come along armed with rifle, pistol, and cartridge belt, the only practical way to get them was by killing him. On the other hand, if he was unarmed they let him pass unharmed since, from their standpoint, he was not worth killing. Unaware of all this, I was lucky enough to avoid this danger, although fully armed, by not going along any of the established trails, but instead taking parallel courses at safe distances on either side, and while the Indians might still get me, it would not be by ambush.

The General arrived with an escort of cavalry commanded by Lieutenant Hoppin, from Fort Wingate, and a large party of friends, including Colonel Michler, Leonard Wood (later Major General), Frederic Remington, the well-known artist, and the General's young son, Sherman, now Major General.

Just before the date of the General's arrival, I established a hunting camp and put in a few days looking for a cow that had been killed by a grizzly. Being lucky enough to find one, put me in a position to insure him seeing the fresh tracks, as I had promised. It was up to him and his party to do the killing provided they could contact the bear.

I then left my camp, which was located about five miles from the dead cow, and met General Miles on his way to meet me, and guided the whole party to the camp.

The next morning at daybreak, we started out, and when we reached the dead cow, on which the grizzly had been eating during the night, the hounds took the trail in full cry. The chances looked very favourable for catching the bear, before he got to the heavy timber at the mountain top.

The dead cow was lying near a spring at the mouth of a canyon, some twenty miles long, that led up to the highest peak. As is usual in such cases, the bear had "bedded up" during the day a few miles from his kill, and the hounds jumped him within about five miles, and followed him up the canyon as he headed for the top of the mountain.

We came on as rapidly as we could, but owing to the roughness of the canyon, that wasn't very speedy, so the hounds quickly got out of earshot.

35

We continued for some ten miles up the canyon until it boxed; that is, became so rough and full of boulders that it was impossible to go further on horseback. So we were forced to climb up about five hundred feet to the top of the ridge forming one side of the canyon, and follow it several miles, before we could again drop into the bed.

We could see no tracks on the rocky ground, so we followed the canyon bed clear up to its head at the mountain-top. There we spent the rest of the day, riding around and listening for the hounds, but we never heard them.

Towards evening, we decided to return to the camp, where, to our amazement, the hide of a bear was pegged out near the campfire.

What had happened was that when we were riding on the ridge at the side of the canyon, where it boxed, we undoubtedly got a little ahead of the bear, who probably winded us, and decided to turn around and take his backtrail down the canyon. He emerged near the spring where the dead cow lay, into a narrow valley, which he had to cross to reach the mountain on the other side.

Unfortunately for him, my cowboys had just rounded up a bunch of cattle close to where he was crossing the valley. On seeing the bear, the boys quit the cattle in a hurry, and took after him. One of them roped him by the head, another by the hind foot, and another by the fore foot, and stretched him out, while the fourth cowboy cut his throat with a pocket knife.

Thus, they put an inglorious end to our noble quarry! They had skinned him and delivered his hide at our camp, where they thought we might like to have it.

Incidentally, this was only a young bear, weighing not over four hundred pounds. Had he been a big one of eight hundred pounds, it would have been a different story, for he would have snapped every rope as soon as it was thrown on him and tightened!

I was delighted to get this bear for two reasons; one being that the General had now gotten his grizzly, though not exactly in the way he wished. The other one! *That* I cannot, even now, recall without a shudder!

When I met the party the day before, they had stopped for lunch, and I had hardly been introduced all around, and started to tell the General the good news of finding the dead cow, when a man who had a farm ranch in the neighbourhood rode up.

After saying "Howdy!" he remarked:

"I suppose you're out on a deer hunt!"

"Oh, no," replied the General, "we have come to hunt bear."

"Bear," exclaimed the rancher, "I lived here for years, and I ain't never seen one yet, and don't reckon you'll see one either!" With that remark, he rode away.

Everyone regarded me with consternation, for, having come some two thousand miles for a bear hunt, to be told by a local inhabitant that there were no bears in the country, placed me in a most embarrassing position!

There was nothing to be done but take it, so I assured them, as cheerfully as I could, that I hoped, in the course of a day or two, to prove that our pessimistic friend was mistaken. This little episode cast a wet blanket on our former conviviality, and I felt that a vague feeling of distrust had been created which I was unable to dispel.

A couple of days later this same man rode up to our camp. I immediately drew him to one side, and using a popular phrase of the day, said:

"You're from Missouri, aren't you?"

"Yes," he answered, mystified.

"Well, you like to be shown, don't you?" I asked.

He nodded, not quite understanding what I meant. So I took him over and showed him the bear hide, still stretched on the ground. Pointing to it, I said severely:

"That was skinned from a bear caught here yesterday. In the future you will not be able to tell strangers that there are no bear in the country!"

Without a word, he turned and went on his way.

After resting a day, we again hunted bear, and treed a black one, which the General shot. I was anxious for him to continue to hunt, but he couldn't spare the time, so they all left, bidding me a reluctant farewell.

An article describing this hunt was written and illustrated by Frederic Remington, and appeared in *Harper's Magazine*, August, 1894. It was also incorporated in the artist's book, entitled *Pony Tracks*.

CHAPTER IV

FIVE HITS AMONG MANY MISSES

GRIZZLY NUMBER 1

Beginner's Luck

IT was the next year that I got my first grizzly. It will be remembered that he does not tree, so it was essential that some method be found to stop a grizzly before he reached the heavy timber and quaking aspen thickets around the mountain-tops.

When one's first efforts towards any undertaking are rewarded by an undue measure of success, this is called "Beginner's luck," and it was to this I attributed getting this bear.

Hounds are not fighting dogs in the strict sense, and the accepted method at the time was that fighting dogs should be added to the pack.

To carry out this idea, I secured dogs of different breeds, with which I experimented for years with that purpose in view. For reasons which will be explained later, this method proved a failure.

There was, however, one dog, other than a hound, that was of real use, and that was my fox terrier "Twist."

Of course, he couldn't fight a bear, but he did what he could, which was to bark in his face. In dense brush his help was invaluable, as he would run ahead of me, and tell me exactly where the bear was. If the bear moved, the sound of the barking would move with him, so that I could not be taken by surprise.

Among numerous failures, over a period of some ten years, I did manage to get five grizzlies under the "hit or miss" principle. While it included a great many exciting adventures, this was rather a poor showing, but in view of the many handicaps in hunting with ordinary hounds and fighting dogs that were of no help, the results might have been worse.

There were only two of us, Fred, an old hunter, and myself, and fortunately we managed to stay together during the entire hunt. When the hounds at last struck the hot trail of the bear, we followed as rapidly as we could, but when they ran out of hearing, we were forced, as usual, to climb to the top of the mountain, a matter of two hours' time. We spent the rest of the day riding around, stopping from time to time, hoping to hear the hounds. Finally, as it was getting late, we decided to go back to camp, and just as we reached the point on top of the mountain nearest the camp, we heard the hounds baying the bear some five hundred feet below us in a quaking aspen thicket.

I jumped off my horse, pulled a half-dollar out of my pocket, and offered to toss as to who should take the shot. The old hunter looked at me, and said curtly:

"Put your money back. I'll shoot from my horse!"

"But," I exclaimed, "suppose the bear doesn't leave the brush?"

"He can stay there," said the hunter. "I ain't lost no silver-tip in them quakin' aspens!"

"All right," I replied, "if that's the way you feel about it!" Then I made my way on down to the bear.

There were only three hounds remaining with the bear, and they stood about thirty yards below him, baying in turn, while he sat on his haunches looking at them. I sneaked down to about fifteen yards of him, and killed him with a shot that went through the back of the ear and into the brain. He rolled down hill and lodged against a tree. I was delighted to think that, at last, I had succeeded in obtaining the sporting blue ribbon of the Rockies by killing a grizzly!

I shouted to the old hunter to come on down, and while waiting for him, I think I must have had an attack of abnormal elation, for I found myself stroking the bear's head and making such silly remarks as:

"I wouldn't have been taking these liberties a few minutes ago!"

As the old hunter approached, he observed my strange display of posthumous good-will with a grim smile, and then, pointing to the bear, he said:

"You got him this time, but the next time he will get you!" Then, evidently highly pleased with himself at having chilled my enthusiasm by his prophetic warning, he proceeded to skin the bear, after which, packing the hide and as much meat as we could carry on our horses, we returned to camp.

In talking over the hunt with my cook the next day, he smilingly informed me that Fred had given him his version, and that our stories differed in one respect—that in regard to tossing for the shot. Fred had told him that he had given me great credit for offering to go fifty-fifty as to who should shoot the bear. He assumed, of course, that the loser would take the shot, while the winner would play safe by staying on his horse to await the outcome. He was, therefore, much surprised when I went down to the bear after he had refused to toss; but he put it down to my foolishness, and thought that one such experience would cure me.

To explain his mental attitude in the matter, it should be said that he had often acted as hunter and guide to deer hunting parties of "tenderfoot" sportsmen from the East. As some of these gentlemen were ignorant of the art of rifle-shooting and had failed to get bucks with good heads, Fred would be called upon to supply the deficiency. So in addition to receiving liberal pay for his services, he also collected a bonus. As this was the first time he had hunted with me, he took it for granted that I would look to him to kill the bear for me. While I would get the credit and the hide, he would get the bonus.

Fred being more of a trapper than a hunter, had trapped many a black bear, but only one silvertip, the latter having been caught by one leg in a heavy bear-trap. It had taken four shots to kill him, and his behaviour was such after the first shot that Fred made up his mind never to shoot at that kind of bear if he were footloose! So he could hardly be blamed for refusing to toss with me.

GRIZZLY NUMBER 2

Chasing and Catching the Rainbow

When I got my second grizzly, a large party of both invited and uninvited guests was with me. Deer hunting parties would drift through the country during October and November —the game season—and hearing of my being out on a bear hunt with my hounds, would send word to me, asking if they might be allowed to join in the hunt. Of course they were welcome.

On this hunt we caught several black bear during the first week or two. We became very well acquainted, and joking one another became the order of the day. This developed into playing practical jokes, but it was understood that jokes calculated to hurt anyone's feelings or do physical harm would be considered as "hitting below the belt."

I had been getting off a few harmless jokes on some of the party, for which they were determined to get even with me at first chance, and such an opportunity soon presented itself.

One day, during my absence, one of the men reported that he had found a rattlesnake close to camp, and thereupon, a keg, which had contained horse-shoes, was emptied, a dish-pan was borrowed from the cook, forked sticks were cut from surrounding trees, and thus armed, the whole party advanced on the bush under which the snake had been seen. He was still there, and was promptly ejected and pinned down with the forked sticks, then pushed into the keg, on top of which the dish-pan was placed and secured with a heavy rock, the whole thing being then hidden in the bushes.

The next morning, I was awakened by the cry of "Breakfast ready," so I got up and began to dress. Usually, I was one of the first ones up, but this morning, everybody seemed to be around the campfire eating breakfast, and though it struck me as strange, I thought little of it.

I reached for one of my lace-top boots, which I always wore, and started to draw it on, when to my horror, my foot touched something cold and squirmy. This was a case that called for swift action, and casting dignity to the winds, I threw myself on my back and kicked off the boot, flinging it through the air. And out of the boot flew a wriggling rattlesnake.

At the same moment, a roar of laughter came from the crowd around the campfire, and then I tumbled. It was a practical joke. I got up to retrieve my boot, saying loud enough for them all to hear:

"It seems to me that putting a live rattlesnake in a man's boot is hitting below the belt."

"Before you say that," shouted one of the jokers, "look at the snake."

I did so, and saw that the snake's head had been cut off.

Like eels, snakes wriggle for a long time after they have been killed, so when I touched it with my foot, as this one was still quivering, I thought it was alive. The joke was on me and I returned to my bed and put on my boots.

The evenings around the campfire were spent in telling stories of hunting adventures. On the occasion of this hunt, I had hired two hunters, one a great deal older than the other. The elder man was a good-natured, simple-minded soul, who listened to our tales with great interest. In one story, the word "paradox" was mentioned, and when the old hunter asked the meaning of the word, it was agreed that each one of us should give him a definition. Such time-honoured expressions as "not seeing the forest for trees" were trotted out, and when it came to my turn, I said:

"Common sense is the least common of all the senses."

This was rejected on the ground that it was only a frivolous wisecrack, so I gave them:

"If you want to deceive, one of the best ways is to tell the truth." The objection to this was that it wasn't so, but I had occasion to prove it on our next chase.

The following morning, I got word that a cow had just been killed by a silvertip near a spring about twenty miles away. So, amid great excitement, we moved and made camp a few miles from the spring.

At daylight the next day, we sallied forth in high hopes of getting this bear, for he had been eating on the cow during the night, and had left a hot trail for the hounds. As usual, they soon ran out of hearing, and we all got separated. It had been previously arranged that we should meet on the top of the mountain, which was above timber-line and quite bare, where we could see each other at a distance. So we all got together again, and spent the rest of the day listening in vain at the heads of different canyons for the hounds.

Towards late afternoon, it was decided that it was useless to continue with the hunt, and as we were about to start down the mountain, we could see the smoke from our camp-fire in the valley below some ten miles off. It gave promise of the supper that was cooking, and as everyone was very hungry, an untactful suggestion on my part was promptly overruled. I remarked that it was quite possible that the bear, after running hard all day, might go to a little spring on the side of the mountain, about four miles out of our course, for a drink. This proposition was resentfully rejected, with many unkind remarks, so I made up my mind to go to it alone, and as I left them, someone shouted out:

"You'd chase a rainbow if you thought a silvertip was tied to one end of it." And another added:

"Hope you catch your rainbow."

As I rode on, I began to suffer from a severe attack of intro-spection as I quite realized that the chances of running on to this bear were so very remote as to justify my fellow hunters in deeming me obstinate to an asinine degree. But as I had started for the spring, I resolved to cast off these depressing thoughts and go on. I reached the canyon where the spring rippled over its rocky bed for about a mile to a ledge of rock, three or four feet high, which crossed the canyon. The stream trickled over this ledge, forming a pool beneath it.

As I drew near the pool, I concluded that my cold-footed companions were right, and then something unexpected happened. A coincidence came about, so extraordinary that I must ask my readers to "believe it or not," depending on their individual predilections.

A steep bank of soft earth butted up against the ledge on the farther side of the canyon, and there, on top of this bank, sat Old Drive, looking below him with a quizzical expression.

Without thinking, I called out, "Why, hello, Drive!" and the next instant, the silvertip, who had been lying in the pool below, jumped on to the ledge, shaking himself vigorously and throwing a heavy spray of water around him in all directions. The rays of the setting sun lit up the spray, and there appeared, for a full three seconds, a perfect rainbow, in the centre of which was the bear.

He turned and jumped on to the bank, but, as it was of soft earth and very steep, he slid down, his front paws leaving deep furrows. Then he ran down the canyon, and I followed him.

I had two dogs with me, my fox terrier, Twist, and Czar, a wolf hound, kindly lent me by General Miles, who had obtained him from the kennels of the Czar of Russia.

After running a short distance down the canyon, the bear climbed the farther bank, which was not very steep. The dogs took after him, Twist, as usual, running ahead and barking in his face, while Czar, who had had experience in fighting black bear, nipped his heels.

Like a flash, the bear whirled round, and literally pounced on Czar, crushing him to the ground, and biting him through the fleshy part of the thigh.

In the meantime, I had jumped off my horse, and was aiming at the bear. I shot him in the shoulder, just at the moment he took hold of Czar. He snapped viciously at the place where the bullet had struck him, and then, catching sight of me, bolted into the canyon and came towards me.

I ran back to my horse, George, who, unlike most horses, luckily was not in the least afraid of bear. Throwing another cartridge into my rifle I awaited the grizzly's coming. George was standing still, and I was on the upper side of him, looking over the saddle. The bear ran around behind the horse, while I ran round the head, and as he passed George's head, I ran to his tail, getting ready to shoot as soon as I got a good opportunity. But instead of coming round the horse's head, as I had thought, he kept straight on, making several ineffectual attempts to catch Twist, who was still barking in his face. Then he turned, re-crossed the canyon, and started up the other side, going straight away from me. This gave me a line

45

shot on his backbone, and I fired, breaking it. He rolled over, and going up to him, I found him alive, but unable to get on to his feet, so I finished him with my six-shooter.

After the unpleasant job of gutting him, I went to the stream to wash my hands, but changed my mind, and returning to the bear, cut off a tuft of hair, showing the silver tips, which I placed in an old envelope I had in my pocket. I then mounted my horse and started for camp.

By this time, it had grown quite dark. There was no moon, and my progress was slow, as I had to travel mostly through thick timber, giving me ample time to think things over.

Here, at long last, was my opportunity to get back on the whole party for the rattlesnake joke and others they had played on me, as well as the unkind remarks they had made! One remark was to the effect that when I said anything with an air of injured innocence, I was least to be trusted, but I have to admit that the man who made this remark had good cause for saying it.

As I rode along, I began to form plans, which, if I could carry them out, would enable me to make a grand slam on the whole outfit. My plan was to tell them I had killed the bear, but in such a way that none of them would believe me, proving my repudiated paradox: "The best way to deceive is by telling the truth."

I easily located the camp, as there was a huge fire burning, and as I rode up, there were cries of:

"Did you get lost?" To which I replied:

"No, or I wouldn't be here!"

Some of the party were professional men, whom we regarded as "wise guys," and a "wise guy," as I take it, is a man who knows more than is good for him, and who is, therefore, easily fooled, provided he is approached in the right way.

The younger hunter was of a very suspicious nature, and that kind, also, is not hard to fool, because he generally suspects in the wrong place. But these tactics would not work on the older hunter, because, right or wrong, he would believe anything I told him, whether it was true or not being quite immaterial.

The cook had kept my supper hot, so I turned to him and

apologized for being so late, explaining that I had to kill the silvertip on the way in, which delayed me. At this, there was a roar of laughter, and someone shouted:

"You were always good at excuses, but this one takes the cake!" With an air of injured innocence, I held up my hand, with the dried blood on it, in the full light of the fire.

"Look at the blood on my hand," I said, "there's my proof!"

"You can't fool me," yelled the younger hunter. "That blood is from a deer you killed on your way back."

"Very well," I replied, "have it your way."

Then I went off, washed my hands, and returned to eat my supper. While I was eating, I was the target for innumerable sallies of wit at what they deemed my boastful claims as to the killing of the bear. When I had finished my supper, I said:

"Well, if you want more proof, I have it here."

I pulled the envelope out of my pocket, and removed the tuft of hair, which I passed around for inspection, and when it reached the old hunter, he remarked:

"This is silvertip hair, all right." Then he handed it to the younger hunter, who looked at it and said:

"Yes, this is silvertip hair, all right, but you cut it off that old silvertip hide you've got at the ranch."

The old hunter asked to see it again, and this time he looked at it more closely. Then he said:

"The hair on an old hide straightens out, but this hair is crinkly, so it must have come from a fresh hide."

This opinion caused a general look of surprise, and to my dismay, the crowd looked as though they might believe it. The only way to save the situation was to create a diversion, so I seized the tuft from the old hunter's hand, and looking at the others, said:

"You remember telling me that I would chase a rainbow if I thought a silvertip was tied to one end of it? Well, I caught that rainbow; that is, I was near enough to hit it with a rock, if I had wanted to. But the funny thing was that the bear was in the centre of the rainbow—not tied to one end."

This was too much for the crowd to swallow, and out of

the corner of my eye, I observed one of them tap his forehead significantly, while the others slowly nodded their heads in silent approval.

It seemed to me that this was the right moment to retire, so I bade them "Good night," and went to bed.

At breakfast next morning, one of the party remarked:

"You seem to have forgotten all about that silvertip you killed yesterday."

I replied that I had and to make good this oversight, I directed Telesfor, who had charge of the saddle horses, to put pack saddles on two of them, and be ready to go with us to fetch the bear. Then, with a bored expression, I said to the others:

"I suppose you want more proof, so I'll give it to you."

At my call, Czar, who was sleeping by my bed, came hobbling along, dragging his injured leg. He had been licking the wound all night, so that the four round holes made by the bear's canine teeth showed up plainly in his silky, white hair."

In an unguarded moment, the younger hunter exclaimed: "Why, what's the matter with him?"

"Oh, nothing much," I said. "Those four holes were made by the teeth of the deer you said I killed yesterday."

All the crowd, except the younger hunter, laughed at this.

Incidentally, a deer only has front teeth in the lower jaw, and these are flat, not round.

Deer hunting was the order of the day, as the hounds had to have a rest. The horses were all saddled, and at my suggestion, the party agreed to accompany me as far as the spot where I had left the bear. I led the way to the canyon, and pointed out the ledge on to which the bear had jumped from the pool, then from the ledge to the steep bank on the other side, where the claw marks in the soft earth proved he had slid down when he tried to climb it. Then I went to the place where the bear had jumped on to Czar, showing a lot of white hair on the ground, which had been rubbed off in his struggles to escape. Then we went on down to the bear, which the hunters began to skin, while the rest of us sat around and smoked.

Twist, fox terrier, and Grip, bull terrier

Dan skins grizzly while the author looks on.
Miss Morley's horse in the background

The old hunter, very much impressed by what he had seen, thought that I had not been fairly treated by the crowd, and feeling that he should make amends, he raised his skinning knife in the air and, looking at me, proclaimed solemnly:

"From now on, I'll believe anything you say, even if it's a damned lie!"

Then one of the crowd called out, questioningly:

"What's the big idea in trying to fool us all into thinking you hadn't killed the bear, when you had?"

Without repressing a smile, I answered:

"Because you all repudiated my paradox, that one of the best ways to deceive is by telling the truth. I've tried it out on you fellows and it seems to have worked."

There was a moment's silence, and then, being sportsmen, all the hunting party, with the exception of the younger hunter, shouted lustily:

"You win!"

And this chivalrous admission permitted me to think that the rattlesnake joke had been repaid in full.

GRIZZLY No. 3

Thrills with Chills

The killing of my third silvertip recalls to mind my most unpleasant bear hunting experience. On this hunt, the hounds, after striking the hot trail, went off at full speed, and the old formula then repeated itself—I found myself on the top of the mountain listening for them!

I rode for hours in wrong directions, but at last I heard the hounds in the quaking aspens on the steep mountain-side below, and leaving my horse, I climbed down towards the sound of their baying. There were only three hounds out of the pack of about a dozen with which we had started that morning, and they were looking in the direction of the bear, who had backed up against a tree, some twenty yards above them. I caught a glimpse of him through the trees thirty yards below me, so I pushed on through the thick brush and quaking aspen saplings, in order to get a more favourable position from which to shoot.

My rifle, a 30-40 Winchester carbine, had a leather sling attached to it, and I was carrying it strung on my shoulder with the muzzle straight up. This left my arm free to part the branches in front of me, while I kept my eye on the spot where I had seen the bear. As I was moving cautiously forward, for some reason, I looked back, and there, above me, was the bear in the alert attitude of a cat about to pounce on a mouse.

I have often heard that when a man is scared, his hair raises on his head, or that his heart jumps into his mouth, but I don't remember ever hearing of these two reactions occurring simultaneously. In this case they did. The situation was critical, and my judgment was more or less paralysed. To unsling my rifle and aim it at the bear was out of the question. He would never have given me time to do so.

Luckily, we all have the instinct of self-preservation, and by obeying its dictates, I got myself out of trouble. I walked on without changing my pace, apparently ignoring the presence of the bear, but as I went, I unslung my rifle, and twenty-five feet away, I turned and raised it to shoot. While the bear was still looking at me intently, wondering, I suppose, what to do next, I took careful aim and shot him between the eyes. He collapsed and rolled over, and though I did not do likewise, I *did* sit down on a rock, and removing my hat, wiped the perspiration off my forehead!

Thinking things over, I remembered what the old hunter had said: "You've got *him* this time, but the next time he will get *you*!" And it struck me that he came very near being right.

In a few minutes, when my mind was again functioning normally, I went to the bear, called the hounds, and gave them the welcome feed to which they were certainly entitled. Then I began to study how it was possible that the bear, which I had seen some thirty yards below me, could have run through that thick underbrush without making any sound that I could hear, and then appear suddenly above me. So I back-trailed him to the spot where I first saw him and then the answer dawned on me—something that had never struck me before—that bear who have frequented a given area for some time, make their own trails for their own convenience, literally making tunnels through dense thickets and underbrush. In order to avoid trees or big rocks, these trails are very tortuous, although they hold to their general directions, and the tunnels are sometimes as much as a quarter of a mile long.

Even if they have been recently used by a bear, they would hardly be noticeable, unless a man was on the lookout for them. If these tunnels were straight, they would resemble avenues, but as they twist and turn, they are virtually invisible, particularly if they have not been used for some time, for high grass, weeds, and flowers grow up and obliterate them. This, however, makes no difference to the bear, who knows exactly where the tunnels are.

But for my recent experience, I would never have been aware of these runways. On several previous hunts, when I didn't get the bear, but managed to get a glimpse of him gliding silently through the quaking aspen, like a ghost, I wondered how he did it. I asked this question of several hunters, who had noticed the same thing, but they also could not account for it.

This incident caused me to study bear trails, and thus I learned much about them. I found that when silvertips inhabit certain areas for some time, they make their own special trails, one going round the top of the mountain, about three or four hundred feet below the crest, while another encircles the base.

Bear trails run more or less horizontally, differing from cattle trails, which run up and down canyons, or the intervening ridges. Bear will often walk on cattle trails, and the latter on bear trails, which is somewhat confusing; but there is one easy way to distinguish between them—by fallen trees on the trail. A bear will hop over the trunk without leaving the trail, while a cow will walk round one end or the other of the fallen tree, and get back to the trail that way.

On this memorable hunt, I appreciated the value of the help of my fox terrier Twist, who unfortunately got lost from me, as he couldn't keep up. Had he been with me, he would have scented the bear ahead, and by his barking, would have let me know where he was, and the bear would never have "stolen a march" on me.

The above experience brings to mind a question that I have often heard discussed, viz: Will a dangerous wild animal attack when confronted by a man who shows no sign of fear?

It is generally considered commendable for a man to have the courage of his own convictions, but this does not apply to this case, for I have never yet run across a man who held this belief, who cared to put it to a test in actual practice. It is true that I happened accidentally to accomplish this feat for the excellent reason that I was not aware of the bear's presence until after I had passed him; and after that, as I did not quicken my pace the bear must have thought that I was still unafraid of him.

Naturally, this experience would incline me to think that there was some truth to this belief. Nevertheless, I would object to knowingly repeat what I did, for the reason that there are exceptions to most rules, and I would not care to run the risk of being one of those exceptions. However, this does not prevent one from offering a surmise as to why the bear did not attack.

When two dogs walk round each other, growling, each one seems to hesitate to attack. But if one dog should show signs of fear or start to run away, the other dog would at once jump on to him. Similarly, as long as a man showed no signs of fear, a dangerous wild animal might hesitate to attack him, and if, during that period of hesitation the man should walk out of the zone of danger without quickening his pace, he might then conclude that he could repeat such an experiment with safety. But I strongly doubt that any man ever would.

GRIZZLY NUMBER 4

Good Luck from Bad Luck

On the next successful hunt, when I got my fourth silver-tip, Dan and I were camped in the Datil Mountains, at the

White House Ranch, which was owned by Mrs. Morley. We were told by her daughter, Miss Agnes Morley, later Mrs. Newton Cleaveland, author of that most interesting book, *No Life for a Lady*, that a big grizzly was watering at her trough. She said that she would like us to kill it, if possible, and with that purpose in view, we started out early next morning.

Miss Morley was accustomed to riding in the mountains, and was very eager to go with us, so with her mother's reluctant consent, we rode off. While we were glad of her company, we felt the responsibility, as one never knows what may happen on a bear hunt. She was used to riding the range, and working her mother's cattle with the cowboys, and it was only because of this that I was somewhat reconciled to the responsibility I had assumed.

A light snow had fallen during the night, so all tracks would be fresh and easy to follow, and as the ground was good for fast riding, it would be easy to keep in hearing of the hounds.

Some thirteen miles to the west, we struck a grizzly's tracks coming east, and following these tracks, we found that they led out on to a precipice, its walls being nearly perpendicular. It was fifteen miles long, varying from about five to eight hundred feet in height, and when we reached the edge, halfway from either end, we saw the bear on the plain below. He was some distance away, but we could see him turning on the dogs from time to time. It was no use trying to shoot him, as there was little chance of hitting him, while the risk of injuring a dog would be great.

We were at a loss to know what to do. To ride to either end of the precipice would have meant a seven-mile detour, and the time that it would have taken precluded the chance of catching up with the bear before dark. The only alternative was to study how the bear got down.

Dan got off his horse and followed the tracks down a steep ravine, which seemed to be a cleft in the walls of the precipice. After a while he returned, saying that he thought we could make it, so Miss Morley and I dismounted and followed his lead. It was so steep in places that the horses literally slid

53

down on their haunches, using their front feet to maintain their balance, while we had to keep well on one side, lest they run over us.

About half-way down, it was a shock to find that we were on a projecting ledge, with about a ten-foot drop of sheer wall beneath. The ledge was fifty yards long, each end butting up against the cliff like the sides of a balcony. We were in what Dan called a "Hell of a fix!" It was absolutely impossible for the horses to climb up the way we came down, and we could not go forward, so *we* thought!

Luckily, both Dan and I had new, thirty-five foot saddle ropes, so I suggested tying these two ropes together, making a double rope which would be strong enough to support the weight of a horse. I pointed out to Dan that we could put one end of the double rope round a horse's neck, and with two turns round a small pine tree, which grew right on the brink of the ledge, then lower the horses down gradually. At first, Dan looked upon this plan with some disfavour, but finally he said:

"All right, I'll handle the rope round the tree, while you lead the horse over the cliff."

"I have no intention of *leading* the horse over," I explained. "*Backing* him over strikes me as a much better way."

Dan grudgingly admitted that this scheme might be worth trying. In this fashion, we succeeded in lowering two of the horses over the bluff, with nothing worse happening than the bark of the tree smoking from the friction of the rope. But when it came time for my horse, George, to go over, it was a different matter. He had viewed the disappearance of his two companions with obvious mistrust, and refused point-blank to allow himself to be backed over the ledge.

"What to do now?" was the question. We debated for a while, and finally decided to use a little strategy on him. Dan took the double rope off the tree, coiled it and handed it to me. We had unsaddled all the horses before attempting to lower them, but had left their bridles on. So holding the end of George's bridle and the rope around his neck, I led him back and forth about ten feet from the edge of the bluff. After doing this about three or four times, to gain his confidence,

54

I blindfolded him with my handkerchief, and continued as before until he overcame his distrust.

Then I led him near the edge, and Dan took the rope and gave it the two turns around the tree. I then turned George sharply at right angles, causing him to step off the bluff with his hind feet, and then he was lowered. But in struggling to regain his feet, he fell over, and rolled under a tree that had fallen across a small gully. Eventually he got himself wedged, with his back under the tree and his feet up-hill.

Dan slid down the rope, took it from George's neck, and threw it up to me, and after putting it around the tree, I threw the two ends down the ledge. Then Miss Morley, holding the ropes together, slid down safely. I followed suit, and when I was on the ground, all I had to do was to pull one end of the double rope, loosening it from the tree.

George had been struggling all this time, endeavouring to free himself. The tree was too heavy for us to lift at either end, so he could not be pushed through underneath, and he was too heavy for us to pull up-hill. Fortunately, we always brought a hatchet along to use in quartering any big bear we might kill, to facilitate packing. With this hatchet, and some flat, sharp rocks, we cut the loose dirt from under the horse, and at last, enough dirt was removed to enable us to push George under the trunk.

After this delay, we saddled our horses, and led them down to the plain below, and though the going was very steep, as before, we did not run into any further difficulties. We mounted our horses, and took the bear trail, which was very plain on the fresh snow.

Unfortunately, George had lamed himself in his struggles under the tree trunk, and I could not keep up, so Miss Morley and Dan rode on ahead. Miss Morley, noting that I had fallen behind, turned back, and seeing that my horse had gone lame, generously suggested that we change horses, and that she go home, which she did, thus giving me the chance to follow Dan, who was already out of sight.

I rode some fifteen miles along the foothills, until I came to the top of a ridge, and looking across a little valley to an opposite ridge, the top of which was about two hundred yards

55

off, I saw a silvertip starting to run down it. He stopped short on seeing me, and turned around to go back up again, and as he was doing so, I jumped off my horse, pulled the rifle out of the scabbard, and aimed at him. By this time, he had reached the top of the ridge, and had stopped to look back. At that moment I fired, and he kicked up his heels and disappeared over the ridge. I learned afterwards that the bullet struck him on the left flank, ranging forward to the right shoulder. This, by the way, was the only long shot I ever had at a grizzly.

I mounted again, and galloped to the point where the bear had disappeared. From there I took his trail, which showed drops of blood here and there on the snow, indicating that he had been wounded.

Twist, my fox terrier, and Princess, a great Dane, were with me, and when the silvertip stopped under some big junipers, Twist ran ahead of me towards him and started barking. Again leaving my horse, I made ready to shoot as soon as I could get a good chance. Just then, the bear ran out on to some open ground, and I shot him again, this time hitting him in the *right* flank, the bullet ranging to the left shoulder. He fell over, straightening out his legs, in his death throes.

Twist immediately began "woolling" him, encouraging Princess to take hold also, and suddenly the bear came to and jumped up, seizing Princess by the throat and shaking her like a rat. Luckily for her, she wore a three-inch leather collar, with a brass buckle which the bear had in his mouth, thus preventing him from closing his jaws, but allowing his four big teeth to penetrate the collar.

For a few seconds I was unable to shoot, for fear of hitting Princess, when the bear again fell over, this time stone dead. I did not know, at this time, whether this was the same bear we had been trailing all day, but I got proof later that it was.

It was now sundown, and as I was some thirty miles from camp, I gutted the bear as quickly as I could, and started back.

I reached the Morley Ranch at one o'clock in the morning, and as the ranch house was lighted up, I went in, and found

Mrs. Morley, her daughter, and Dan sitting up, waiting for me. Dan told me he had finally caught up with the bear, and had shot him in one hind foot, but because it was impossible for him to pursue the bear further in a rough canyon full of boulders, he reluctantly gave up the chase and returned to camp.

He asked me what I had done, and was somewhat taken aback when I told him I had killed a silvertip, and that it must have been the same one he had shot at, though I had not noticed whether the bear was wounded in the foot or not. Dan thought I was joking, and insisted that I give him my word of honour before he would believe me.

It was now two o'clock in the morning, and as we had started out the previous morning at five o'clock, we concluded we would turn in and resume our conversation at breakfast.

When we went to bring in the bear next day, Miss Morley, with her camera, accompanied us. We reached the place where I was sure I had left the bear, but I could not, at first, find him. Just then, we saw Old Drive approaching us, wagging his tail, and going in the direction from which he had come, we found the bear.

Drive was not with the silvertip the evening before, so I assumed he had been following as fast as his age would permit, for all the other hounds had returned to camp with Dan. Coming upon the dead bear, and a good meal on the ground in front of him, he naturally figured that this was a good place to camp for the night, and so he stayed on in the morning, waiting for us to come and get the bear, which he must have felt sure we would do.

Before beginning to skin him, Dan looked at his hind feet, and, sure enough, there was a bullet hole through one of them. When he had skinned him and cut him up, we found that the bullet from my second shot had gone through the heart. This proved that a shot through the heart does not instantly kill a grizzly, for though he fell over on being hit, he came to long enough to grab Princess and shake her for several seconds before death came. From this, and other experiences, I am convinced that no shot will kill a grizzly instantly, except one through the brain.

57

We loaded as much meat as we could on our horses, and started back to camp, and as it happened that the back trail of the bear was precisely in the direction we wanted to go we followed it, the tracks being plain on the snow. It was then that we realized what had happened.

After the grizzly had left Dan in the rough canyon, he had circled round to his back trail, thinking he would fool the hunter who was after him by changing his direction. But he had not figured on my coming along, and he met me only a mile or so from where he struck his back trail.

The fact that the bear did this established a very important fact. Instead of running haphazard the previous day, when trying to get away from us, he had been following a bear trail around the foot of the mountain.

And had it not been for the bad luck I had in my horse being lamed, and the delay caused by it, I never would have had the good luck of meeting the bear on his back trail when he escaped from Dan.

GRIZZLY NUMBER 5

Success Within Ten Minutes of Darkness

In October, 1896, when General Miles hunted with me for the second time, I got my last silvertip on the "hit and miss" principle, the hunt having taken place in the San Mateo Mountains, about forty miles south-west of Magdalena, New Mexico.

A few days before the General's arrival, his escort, a troop of the Seventh Cavalry from Fort Bayard, commanded by Captain Slocum, met me at the designated point from which I intended to hunt. I had been told that a grizzly had been killing cattle on the mountain at the foot of which I had established our camp, and during the few days we had to wait for the General, I rode all over the mountain to see if I could come on to the tracks of this bear. By the greatest of good luck, on the day preceding my return, I found a cow he had just killed a few miles from our camp, and thus, when the General arrived, I again had a hot trail ready for his hunt.

General Miles was accompanied by a large party, including Mrs. Miles and two other ladies, also Colonel Michler, Major Hoffman, and Captain H. T. Allen, later Major-General.

The Captain, a keen sportsman, had brought with him four fox hounds from the pack owned by the Officers' Hunt Club, of Fort Riley, Kansas. I was very glad to have these hounds to add to our pack of twelve, as I was much interested in finding out what they would do. But I regret to say, not only were they of no help, but they came very near causing us to lose that bear altogether.

We started out next morning before daybreak and headed for the dead cow, hoping that the silvertip had been eating on it in the night, thus ensuring us a hot trail. I was in great hopes that we would get to him on ground over which we could gallop, before he reached the heavy timber, round the top of the mountain, where it was difficult or virtually impossible for the horses to follow him.

The party who hunted with me that day was the biggest I ever had, for besides the General and his party, some eight in all, there were two professional hunters, whom I had hired as guides, one with the General and one with Captain Allen. In addition, Captain Slocum had given permission to many of his troopers to join the hunt, and besides there were some cowboys who came along anyhow. As Dan and I were supposed to run the hunt, we acted as free-lances, riding ahead, leading the party.

We had planned, by galloping our horses to the limit, to catch up with the bear before he got out of the open country, and by firing a shot to cripple him, enable the hunting party to catch up, thus giving each of them a chance to get in a shot to finish him.

To begin with, the plan worked out fairly well, in that the hounds got a hot trail, but although we rode rapidly, the hounds got out of earshot. Nevertheless, we continued in the direction we thought they had gone. Suddenly, Captain Allen's fox hounds appeared, running back! They had evi-

59

dently caught up with the bear, and from his looks had concluded that they had better return to camp. We stopped them, and finally encouraged them to take up the trail again. They caught up with the hounds, but then returned to us once more, and again we urged them to go back to the trail.

We had been riding up a main canyon, and had reached a point where it forked. We first caught a glimpse of the bear going up the brush-covered ridge between the forks, where he had evidently stopped to get his wind, as it was very steep. By this time, we knew he was pretty well blown, with the run he had already made, for the baying of the hounds remained in one place, so I dismounted, leaving my horse with Dan, and taking my rifle, I ran up the ridge as fast as I could. And then I caught sight of the grizzly, sitting down under a tree, with his tongue hanging out. As I was raising my rifle to shoot, he started on, and I lost my chance. Had he stopped one second more, I would have shot him through the body, crippling him, for the whole party to finish, and thus the hunt would have been a glorious success. But he didn't give me that second.

So I had to return to my horse, and, in the meanwhile, the bear had gotten a good start. We rode up the ridge as fast as we could, and near the top, here came the fox hounds from the left-hand fork. Of course, we concluded that the bear had gone that way. The ground was very rocky, so we could not see any tracks, but, at the moment, that didn't seem to matter, and we kept on crowding our horses as much as possible.

We rode up the side of the canyon for about five miles, and then dropped into the sandy bed, upon which we could not see the tracks of either bear or hounds. Then we realized, for the first time, that the fox hounds had fooled us, and that the bear must have run up the other fork.

There was nothing to be done but to return and go up the right-hand fork of the canyon. When we got there, we saw the tracks made by the horses of the whole party. We learned later that they had stopped there, while the hunters had ridden ahead up the right-hand fork, and found the bear tracks, so they all went that way. We followed up their trail, and kept passing them, one by one. The leaders of the party had halted on the edge of the heavy timber, but General Miles and Captain Allen, with their respective guides, had gone on foot into the heavy timber in the hope of hearing the hounds.

Dan and I decided that our only chance of getting the bear was to ride to the top of the mountain by forcing our way through the quaking aspens, and in doing so, we passed the General and his guide, who were trying to trail the bear. We reached the top and rode around, stopping from time to time to listen.

It was getting late, and the sun was sinking below the horizon, leaving the chances of our getting the bear virtually nil. All at once we thought we heard old Drive's cracked voice. Listening intently, we heard it again, and then again, a little louder, indicating that the bear was coming our way at a level of about three hundred feet below us.

I left my horse with Dan and climbed down the mountain in the hopes of intercepting the bear as he came by. As the brush and timber were very thick, it would be impossible to see him unless he passed within thirty feet or so. The chance of getting a shot was very remote, and if he once passed me without my seeing him, any chance of getting him would be gone.

All this time, at about ten-second intervals, I could hear the sound of Old Drive's voice coming closer. Then I had a piece of amazing luck, for in my descent I crossed a dim trail, which I followed for some fifty yards, when I came to a fallen tree. As the trail did not go around either end of the tree, it could be none other than one made by a bear. As I climbed over the trunk, I heard Drive's bark coming nearer and nearer, and I had to make a decision as to what I had better do.

Some three feet from the trail, I took up my position at a leaning tree, under which the trail passed, and on the other side was a little open space of about thirty feet in diameter.

It is at such moments that rapid fire thoughts pass through one's brain, and I couldn't help thinking how, in this instance, the bear and I had changed roles. Usually, the bear would

61

hide in dense brush, waiting for the hunter to come by; whereas, the hunter was now waiting in the brush for the bear to come by.

There were just two alternatives between which I had to choose. One, to shoot at him when I would first see him, off— say about twenty feet; the other, to wait for him to pass under the tree, and shoot him as he went by the end of my rifle. To shoot him at twenty feet, when it was too dark to see the sights on my rifle, would probably only result in wounding him, and the prospect of having to tackle a wounded grizzly in the dark was singularly uninviting. Waiting for him to come by, and shooting him at the distance of two feet, struck me as equally unattractive. This was no time for splitting hairs for I heard Drive's bark coming quite close, so I decided on the latter alternative, as I felt that I was a better shot at two feet than I would be at twenty.

As I stood waiting and peering through the bushes, suddenly I saw the dark form of the bear loom out from the brush and come shambling along, and just as he was passing the tree, he caught sight of me and started to turn his head. At that instant I fired, shooting him through both shoulders, breaking the one nearest to me. He rose up on his hind feet, his head towering above me, while his foreleg fell helpless from his shattered shoulder. Then he let out a blood-curdling roar, or "bawl," as hunters call it, and fell over backwards down-hill. He tried vainly to rise, so I stepped forward and shot him through the head with my pistol, then shouted to Dan to come down. I think I must have been excited, for while waiting for him, I called Drive to me, and patting him on the back, I said:

"Fifty-fifty, old boy! I'll have the outside of this bear, and you can have the inside!"

This may not have been a very fair division, but it was one of which Drive highly approved a short time later.

By the time Dan reached me, it had become dark, so we lighted a fire, and by its light, Dan cut the grizzly open, and I proceeded to feed Drive with the share that was coming to him!

When this task was finished, I pulled the bear's head round, so that one foreleg touched his nose, making an irregular circle, into which I thrust a lot of dead leaves. Thus I made a bed for Old Drive, who was far too tired to return to camp with us. He knew what I was doing, as I had often made a bed for him before, and he lay down on it when I motioned for him to do so. As we left to go to our horses, I looked back at the old dog in the light of the dying embers, and I thought, with wry humour, that "sport" as well as "poverty" makes strange bedfellows.

We were fully thirty miles from camp, and owing to the thick timber and rough ground, the going was slow, so we didn't make camp till about eleven, though we rode as rapidly as we could.

The General had a big fire made, so that we would be better able to locate the camp from a distance, and when we rode up, he came forward to meet us, saying:

"You're rather late, aren't you?"

"Better late than never," I replied. There was a pause, and then the General asked:

"How about the bear?"

"He's all right," I said. "I left him on the top of the mountain with his waistcoat wide open!"

General Miles looked puzzled for a moment, and then he put out his hand to shake, and congratulated me.

Dan and I had ridden anywhere from seventy to eighty miles, and as we had not had anything to eat or drink since daybreak, it was not surprising that we devoured our suppers hastily, and went to bed.

In the morning, Captain Allen, Dan and I, and two Army packers, with three pack mules, started out to bring in the bear. Remembering that Old Drive must be suffering from thirst, since he had had a long day's chase the day before, and that there was no water within miles of where the bear lay, I took along a canteen of water with me. As we approached our destination, Old Drive, who had either scented or heard us, came towards us, wiggling his body and tail with delight. After we all dismounted, I called him to me, and as he could not drink out of the canteen, I took off my felt hat, and, pressing down the crown, I poured the water into the hollow at

63

one end, while Drive drank from the other. After he had finally had enough, he did not need much urging to return to the bear and continue eating the share that so rightfully belonged to him.

Dan, aided by the packers, had skinned the bear, cut up the meat, and it had been loaded on the mules—and then, just before we left, a peculiar coincidence occurred!

As we were looking at the spot where the bear had fallen, one of the packers picked up a bullet. As a rule, a bullet will go through an animal and lodge in the hide on the other side, but this bullet had penetrated the bear with such force that it went through both shoulders, and then dropped to the ground on the other side.

The next day, we hunted again and got a black bear, but this was another great disappointment. Of course, I was most anxious for the General to kill a bear himself, and with that in view, I arranged for him and one of the hunters to ride to the top of the mountain, from where they were to listen for the hounds. Dan and I were to hunt through the foothills, in the hope of jumping a bear, who would probably run up the mountain, while the General, hearing the hounds, could head him off and shoot him as he went by.

We had hoped to strike another silvertip's trail, but instead hit a black bear's trail, which the hounds followed.

In running through some thick timber, Dan and I became separated, and I rode for some distance until I got within hearing of the hounds, and caught up with them just after they had jumped the bear from his bed. Luckily enough, the bear took up one of two long canyons which headed up at the same place, and it was there that the General was waiting.

There were many big trees in the canyon, and the bear would make for first one and then another as he passed by them, so I had to keep running between him and a tree to prevent him climbing it. Then the canyon went into a box, and I was obliged to climb out on one side for several hundred yards. Just as I was dropping into the canyon again, above the box, I heard a shot, and riding on some hundred yards, I came upon the hunter, jumping up and down and shouting excitedly:

Sleuth, a portrait of canine intelligence and dignity

Tony and Chino, Apache scouts. The author on mule under tree

"I've got him! I've got him!"

"Got what?" I asked.

"Why, the bear!" he answered, amazed at such a question.

"Why did you kill him?" I exclaimed angrily.

"I was afraid he would get away," he replied.

"Get away," I fumed, with rising ire. "Why, I've been driving this bear up the canyon for the last five miles, stopping him from climbing trees, until I could get him to the General."

It developed that General Miles, who was on the ridge between the two canyons, had heard the hounds coming, but not being sure which canyon the bear was in, had sent his sergeant down one canyon, and the hunter down the other, expecting whichever one heard the hounds coming to let him know by shouting.

But upon hearing the shot, he came down to where the bear was, not over three hundred yards. I was so annoyed with the hunter that I'm afraid I lost my temper, and told him that if I ever hired him again for a hunting party, he would only be armed with a stick.

I apologized to the General for the hunter's blunder but he good-naturedly told me not to mind, as it was his own fault for having sent the hunter down.

General Miles and his party left the next day, so that evening was the last one spent round the campfire.

To preserve the silvertip hide until it could be mounted by a taxidermist, I had it treated with salt and alum, and it was tied up in a neat bundle which I had intended throwing into the transport wagon when it left with the General's baggage. He, however, was unaware of this, and as he was keen on getting this hide, he asked me if I had disposed of it.

"No," I answered, "all requests for it are still in order."

Then the General said:

"I have come over two thousand miles from Washington, and I've spent a whole day riding and walking round the top of that mountain, hoping to get a shot at that silvertip. This should entitle me to some claim on the hide."

I fully agreed with him, but said that as I had, incidentally, *killed* the bear, I thought *I* had some sort of claim on it too. He fully agreed with me, in turn, and we went on, arguing the point, agreeing with each other, but getting nowhere. I had told the party some of my simple solution stories the night before, and remembering this, the General, with a twinkle in his eye, remarked:

"It seems to me that this is a case where one of your 'simple solutions' would come into good play."

This elicited an outburst of hilarity and as the laughter subsided, I said:

"All right, General, if you will resign all claims to this hide in favour of Mrs. Miles, I will do likewise."

This brought forth even louder laughter, and I think the General laughed the most heartily of all. Mrs. Miles graciously assented to this compromise, so the matter was settled to everyone's satisfaction.

After the General's party left, Dan and I continued to hunt, hoping to strike the tracks of another silvertip on this mountain, but we never did, though we did strike the trail of a black bear, and Dan and I again became separated.

I finally caught up with the hounds and bear, running down a canyon, the hounds being all round him, with the exception of Old Drive, who was, as always, following some thirty yards behind. Suddenly Dan dropped into the canyon just ahead of us, and this caused the bear to double back on his tracks. As he passed by Drive, who apparently was so surprised that he didn't move, he struck the dog a glancing blow with his paw, then ran a short distance, climbed a tree, and we shot him.

I returned to Old Drive, lying helpless on the ground, and found that he was injured internally. After skinning the bear, Dan gently lifted the old dog and laid him in front of me on my saddle. We rode slowly back to camp, where we made a bed for Old Drive and laid him on it, but he died that evening.

These five *successful* silvertip hunts will, I hope, present a fair idea of the difficulties in hunting these bear. I would like to point out that the success I had was overshadowed by the uncomfortable feeling that it was only obtained by the scantiest of margins. For instance, I got one through a lucky guess that the bear would be thirsty; another, because of delay due to a lame horse, combined with the fact that the bear doubled

66

back on his own tracks; and a third, because I happened on a bear trail with a scant ten minutes of daylight left in which to kill him.

Then, from the hound point of view, in two cases, there were only three hounds that had stayed with the bear, and in two more, only one—Old Drive. In the remaining case, there was no hound at all.

These five grizzlies represented the optimistic side of the picture, and were the results of untiring effort.

CHAPTER V

TWO NEAR HITS

Of the grizzlies that I did kill on the "hit or miss" principle, I got three of them by the slimmest of margins, and bearing that in mind, I think I should mention two grizzlies that I *didn't* get, by equally slim margins.

In the case of the first one, after the hounds had run him all day, I finally got within hearing of them. As usual, I was on top of the mountain, while the bear was bayed some three hundred feet below me, in the dense timber on the steep mountain side.

He moved on as I got near him, so I followed. I do not know whether he scented me or not, but every time I got near him, he moved on again. I was at an elevation of about ten thousand feet, and it was very hard on my wind to keep on following as rapidly as I could, by what one might call a running walk, and after going a couple of miles I could no longer catch my breath. This predicament, in local vernacular, is known as the "thumps." I was about to give up the chase, when for some reason, probably the same as mine, the bear stopped, backing up to a tree.

I approached him as cautiously as I could, and caught sight of him through the branches, about forty feet ahead, and moving to within a few yards, where I got an unobstructed view, I sat down, resting the muzzle of my rifle on a convenient branch in front of me. I was all ready to shoot him back of the ear, but I couldn't hold the rifle steady. I couldn't get my breath. I couldn't even breathe freely for fear he might hear me. So there I sat, unable to shoot. Time and time again I tried to aim, but each time the end of my rifle barrel waveringly described a circle, so I had to wait until my breathing could get back to normal.

I must have been fully three minutes before I felt that I was in a condition to shoot. I aimed carefully, with the rifle

68

fairly steady, but just as I was about to pull the trigger, the bear started to move. It was too late for me to stop, and the rifle went off. The bear slumped down and rolled over, apparently dead. I walked up and put my foot on him, but as his legs were still twitching, I concluded I had better finish him with my six-shooter. As I was in the act of reaching around to pull it out of its holster, he suddenly came to, and sprang into the air. Combing his forehead with his claws, and emitting that terrifying bawl which I had heard only once before, he dropped down on to his front feet and rushed at the dogs baying furiously below!

Then he plunged down the mountain side, crashed through the dense brush, and disappeared, leaving me stunned, but not altogether speechless.

As it was near sundown, and my horse was some two miles back, there was no use trying to follow, so I had to pick up my rifle and trudge back, with feelings that can better be imagined than described. I could not help saying over and over:

"Of all the ——!" I could never get further as the English language did not seem adequate to supply a suitable word to complete the sentence. The only Job's comforting consolation in which I could indulge was that the bear would "keep." He did, for three years later, I caught this same bear on this same mountain, and when his forehead was skinned, while there was no mark of a bullet entering the skin, there was a noticeable scar where the bullet went out. On scraping the skull, there was a faint but distinct furrow along the side of the forehead where the bullet must have grazed it, which accounted for his being temporarily stunned by the blow.

When I missed getting the other bear, I had been riding all day, until late afternoon, trying to find the hounds. Then, suddenly I heard them below me as I was riding above the timberline.

The bear was going through heavy timber, some two or three hundred feet below me on the side of the mountain. As I was on open ground on the upper edge of the timber, I galloped ahead in the direction of the baying of the hounds, and when I thought I had got far enough, I got off my horse, pulled my rifle out of its scabbard, and ran down through the timber to a point where I thought I could get a shot at the bear as he went by.

It was impossible for me to tell exactly where he would pass by me in the dense brush. Whether he had scented me or not, I didn't know, but he got by me without my seeing him, and then I had to go back to my horse and gallop ahead again. I left my horse a second, and a third time, on similar excursions, but failed each time to get a shot, and then it was that I approached a long ridge, running from the top of the mountain on down for miles.

Evidently, the bear was making for a gap in this ridge, just ahead of me, and I galloped on, expecting to kill him when he would come out of the timber into the open, to go through the gap.

The hillside just above the gap was very steep, and I had to ride down rapidly in order to get to the gap before the bear did. My side of the gap was fringed round with a perpendicular ledge of rock about fifteen feet high. When I reached the top of this ledge, I jumped off my horse and ran around his head to grab my rifle when, to my horror, I found that it had slipped out of the scabbard as I rode down the steep hillside, and was lying on the ground about fifty feet above me.

At the same moment, a very large grizzly came running around the base of the ledge where I was standing. As he passed, not thirty feet from me, he seemed so surprised that he stopped short and looked at me for fully two seconds, and then went forward and plunged down the other side of the gap into a canyon a thousand feet deep. Sadly, I have to relate how it was that my rifle had slipped out of the scabbard. To avoid just such an occurrence, I always had a stout, lace-leather horn string attached to the horn of my saddle. When my rifle was in its scabbard, I always wound this horn string round the stock, and then looped it back over the horn, thus preventing the rifle from slipping forward. The last time I had put my rifle back in the scabbard, I had failed to put the horn string round the stock, because of my haste to get to the gap before the bear. But, of course, I had not anticipated having to ride down such a steep hillside to the gap.

So it was that, owing to this slight omission, I missed the opportunity to kill a big grizzly without any danger to myself. In short, I lost this bear by a horn string, so to speak.

Had I known what I learned later, that there is nearly always a bear trail running through the timber and brush around a mountain at three hundred feet, more or less, below the top, I probably would have gotten this bear. Instead of riding a short distance ahead of the bear, I should have ridden quite a long distance, thus giving me plenty of time to look for signs of a bear trail. Once found, I could have stationed myself at a good vantage point from which to shoot him as he passed by on his own habitual trail. My mistake was to try to guess where the bear would pass me from the baying of the hounds, but as the latter were usually at least thirty yards from the bear, and were just as apt to be that distance either above or below him as behind him, it was hard for the hunter to guess the exact course the bear would take.

CHAPTER VI

FOR THE GLORY THAT'S IN IT

FROM such experiences, it is obvious that I had to be an enthusiastic optimist to continue hunting this kind of bear on the "hit or miss" principle. After some nine or ten years of strenuous hunting, I concluded that I would either have to quit altogether or find some more reliable method for catching grizzlies.

Many people think that an optimist is a visionary or impractical sort of person, and that a pessimist is more or less reliable and conservative. I do not, however, hold this view. Within reasonable limits, I regard an optimist as one who makes the best of a bad job, while a pessimist is one who makes the worst of a good one. Therefore, following my views in making the best of a bad job, I decided to continue trying to find a solution to the problem.

I was often asked what prompted me to be obsessed with such a desire to kill grizzlies, and I replied that it could be best explained by relating an incident which happened in my childhood.

Two old ladies had gone to a circus in which the principal feature was an act wherein a lion tamer put his head in a lion's mouth. When they left the show and were standing outside waiting for their carriage, one of the ladies remarked:

"No amount of money should induce a man to take such a risk with a wild beast."

Then the tamer, who had just come out of the tent and overheard, said in a stentorian voice:

"It's not for the money that's in it, Madam, but for the GLORY!"

I suppose I must have been infected with the same idea of glory, for there was a time when I thought that to kill a grizzly was the apex of human endeavour.

I have been credited, or perhaps I should say, discredited,

with having an iconoclastic complex. In other words, I have the habit of doing things differently from most people. I think this criticism is not altogether just, because I believe in doing things in the conventional way first, but when I find it does not work well, I venture to try to improve on it, and often wind up doing things exactly opposite to the customary way.

It should be borne in mind that the automobile was originally high-wheeled and short-coupled, but wound up low-wheeled and long-coupled; that the eye of a needle started in at the head, but wound up at the point, as in the sewing machine.

When I first started bear hunting, I was naturally in that state of ignorance of the sport which is aptly described as "blissful." I took for granted that what the hired hunters did or said was correct, but there was one fly in the ointment—they seldom agreed with one another.

As time went on, I gradually learned the many essential points of the problem that had to be solved before attaining real success, and I realized that what knowledge I had gained was probably half right and half wrong, but as obviously I could not distinguish between the two, I could not rely on any of it. So I concluded to scrap it all, and start afresh.

The underlying cause of all the trouble was that what I knew and what the hunters told me was based on guess-work. What it all amounted to was that the best hunter was the best guesser, and he might be, and usually was, mistaken.

It is a far cry from solving chess problems to catching grizzlies with reasonable certainty, but had it not been for the former, I am quite sure I would never have been successful in the latter.

When I first commenced cattle ranching in 1882, I spent the winters on the ranch, and during the long evenings, I put in my time reading. After several hours, I would tire of this, so I would get out my chess-board and play chess. Unfortunately, there was no one to play with, so I got around the difficulty by playing out the championship games, the reports of which were in my *Illustrated London News*. I would play both sides, and after about the first ten moves of each player, I would take my score-card and guess at the next move that

73

each player would make, before looking at the move he made in the print. If my guess were right, I would credit myself with that move by making a cross; if wrong, a nought, and at the end of the game, I would add up my totals. If the crosses exceeded the noughts, I considered that I had won the game.

As, however, I played both sides at the same time, I would sometimes win on one side and lose on the other, and I would call that game a draw. I am afraid my chess-playing readers will look askance at this method, but I beg them to take into consideration that it was the choice between that or nothing. In any case, it was a good way to study the game, as played by the experts.

When I ran out of the printed chess games, I would fall back on solving chess problems, sometimes solving one in less than an hour. At other times, I spent hours without success, until I reached the point where I thought my failure was due to a misprint. However, I would keep on until I finally solved it. Eventually, I came to the conclusion that no matter how hard the problem, the solution, when found, was extremely simple—just as simple as in the case of those that had been solved quickly.

The all-important point was that, in each instance, the *obvious* move, the one that at first sight appeared to be the best, was invariably wrong. Otherwise, it would not have been a problem.

The actual winning move always looked absurd at first sight, although it would be the only one that would do the trick.

Then the idea struck me. Why not apply this principle to the problems of life?

It was not long before an opportunity came for trying this out. In the spring, when I started out rounding up the cattle for calf-branding, it was necessary to hire a few extra hands. Thus, I employed two cowboys who came along asking for work for a short time, as they were broke, and wanted to earn a few dollars for expenses in going to their destination.

About ten days later, our weekly mail came in, and there was a letter for one of these two men. He and his companion went behind the cook house to read it. It so happened that the cook overheard them, and learned that they were advance agents of three horse thieves who were coming on behind. Their mission was to find out how many cow ponies could be stolen in my locality, and where they could be found, in order that they might be rounded up easily and driven off.

My cook told me all this under my promise of absolute secrecy. I had about thirty saddle horses in my pasture, and there were also a few cow ponies grazing on my range, that belonged to neighbouring cattlemen.

I was considerably worried by this news, and at a loss to know what to do. The obvious move, of course, was to apply to the law authorities, but as my ranch was one hundred and fifty miles from the county seat, Socorro, where the sheriff lived, it would take five days to get there to seek his help, even if he offered it; and it would take as long to get back. During this time, the thieves could have stolen my horses, and would have had several days' start in case of pursuit, so I had to reject this idea.

My next thought was of taking my cowboys and following the thieves after they had stolen the horses, but there were objections to this plan also, because my boys had only worked for me for a short time, and I didn't know them well. In any case, it didn't look right for me to expect them to go with me and take the chance of getting killed, merely because of the theft of my horses.

I then considered following them alone, with the hope of getting help along the way, but upon reflection it struck me that if I did that, I would probably only lose my life in addition to my horses. So that idea lost its appeal.

However, figuring out what *not* to do didn't get me anywhere, and for the next two or three days I worried trying to figure out a plan that would work, but the case seemed hopeless. To add to this, I had to hurry. Some solution had to be found quickly.

I think it was the third night, while tossing sleeplessly in bed, that I suddenly had a humorous inspiration. I turned over with a smile and went to sleep.

Next morning, I told my men to round up all my horses

and bring them into the corral, while I went to a neighbouring sheepman and borrowed a pair of sheep shears. Without
a word of explanation to the boys, I proceeded to cut all the
horses' tails off, flush with the tail-bone. When I got through,
I observed the looks of blank astonishment on their faces. At
length one of them remarked:

"What's the big idea?" Another said:

"Cutting off their tails is an English custom, I suppose!"

I said it was, and that I hoped they wouldn't mind the
joshing they would get for riding "bob-tailed" horses—they
could blame me for it.

A few days later, two of my neighbouring cattlemen, who
had made fun of my boys, appeared and asked if we had seen
some of their horses, which they couldn't find.

I replied that I had not. Then one of them said:

"I have heard that some horse thieves have just ridden
through the country, and maybe they got them." He added:

"Have you lost any?"

"No," I replied, and continued ingenuously, "You see, horse
thieves do not approve of English customs any more than some
of my neighbours do."

They were silent for a few seconds, and then one of them,
looking hard at me, said:

"Is that why you cut off your horses' tails?"

"You're a good guesser," I replied.

The cowboys all laughed, tumbling, at last, to my reason
for doing what I had done.

I heard, some time later, that the thieves had rounded up
my horses in the pasture, and when they realized that it was
impossible to steal them, owing to their easy identification,
they were very indignant. Thieves do not like to be balked
of their prey, especially by those whom they intended to rob.

One of them wanted to shoot the horses in reprisal, but his
suggestion was overruled by the fact that they were short of
ammunition.

My readers may wonder what this theory has to do with
my secret ambition of catching grizzlies with reasonable certainty. My answer is, that this example, and many similar
ones that followed, which seemed very difficult to solve, but

had equally simple solutions, encouraged me to stay with the
the grizzly bear problem.

It is not an easy matter to gauge the difficulty of a problem,
but I can only say that if length of time be accepted as the
yard-stick of measurement, while it took only a few hours to
solve a chess problem, and a few days to think out a way of
preventing my horses being stolen, it took me ten years of
persistent endeavour before achieving success with the grizzly
problem.

It was in the early part of 1896, the year that General Miles
hunted with me for the second time, that I had to make a
decision—whether I would continue bear hunting, or quit
altogether.

Dan had left my employ in order to start a cattle ranch of
his own, thus leaving me to hunt alone. I missed his help
keenly. I began to feel that I had killed enough black bear,
and so lost the desire to kill more. But this did not apply to
grizzlies. While I had killed five individually, with the aid
of the ordinary hounds of the country, I had to admit to
myself that it was a very poor showing. I felt like a golfer
would on making the rounds of the course at ten strokes to
the hole.

I had to abandon the idea of using fighting dogs, for it
had been thoroughly tried and found wanting. The same
thing applied to the use of the ordinary hounds. On top of
this, my business permitted of my taking but very little time
to bear hunt. Nevertheless, I had always had a hunch, or
perhaps it should be called an obsession, that grizzlies could
be caught with reasonable certainty, *if one could only find out the
way of doing it*!

I would be the last to belittle the value of experience,
nevertheless, it has its drawbacks and shortcomings. Viewed
as a commodity, it is very expensive. At least, I have generally
found it so; and where it is mostly found wanting is that its
help is so purely negative as to be virtually useless.

My favourite definition of experience, therefore, is a lively
sense of knowing what will happen when you do something
wrong. But experience is far too non-committal to point out
what you should do.

It reminds me of the old joke which appeared in *Punch*, and which ran:

"ADVICE TO THOSE ABOUT TO MARRY—DON'T!"

Similarly, whenever I wanted to put into practice some new idea for catching grizzlies with reasonable certainty, all I could get out of experience was the same negative advice. Then, if I had the temerity to try out a new idea and it failed, I was promptly greeted with the old refrain, "I told you so!"

Under these circumstances, it took a lot of moral courage even to attempt to do anything at all. Nowhere did I meet with encouragement. On the contrary, cheap ridicule met me at every turn although I am pleased to say that sometimes ridicule backfired, as evidenced by the following incident. I started off on a hunt with Joe, another of my men named Telesfor, and the hounds, and stopped at a local store and post office to post some letters. As it was about time for the mail stage, there were many people waiting outside the store.

After posting my letters, I walked towards my horse and the hounds standing by him, and while doing so, I overheard a man telling the crowd that he would "eat the guts of all the bear that outfit catches."

Everyone—but me—laughed at this coarse and uncalled-for remark, but, remembering I was out to hunt bear, not trouble, I swallowed my resentment, and walking up to the man, said: "I overheard what you said, and will make a note of it, and if you will come to my camp in a few days, I feel sure that I will be able to furnish you with what you want."

Then, turning on my heel, I walked off.

About a week later, I was camped in some timber about a hundred yards from a road. That morning I had killed a black bear, and had packed it in on my horse, and dumped it off in some thick brush, close by the camp, but out of sight. While Telesfor was skinning the bear, all the dogs sat around him, patiently waiting for the meal they knew was coming to them.

I was scarcely through eating my dinner when I saw two men on horseback leave the road to come up to my camp. As they approached, Joe recognized them, and excitedly told me that one of them was the man who had made the coarse remark at the post office. They got off their horses about twenty yards away, and walked up to the campfire to warm themselves. It was not until then that they realized it was my camp to which they had come.

This was not surprising, since all the dogs were out of sight in the brush with Telesfor.

Our mirth-provoking friend looked bewildered. He started to go back to his horse, but his companion, an acquaintance of Joe's, who knew nothing of the affair at the post office, stopped him, saying, "I ain't a-going till I get warm and had a cup of coffee."

Then Joe interposed by saying pleasantly to the other, "I guess you've come after them guts you said you would eat. You've come just at the right time for we killed a bear this morning. The guts will be nice and fresh, and I'll cook them for you right away."

As all this talk was incomprehensible to his companion, Joe proceeded to enlighten him, much to the embarrassment of the joker, who looked very sheepish.

To relieve the situation, as host, I interposed in my turn by saying, "That's all right, Joe, but I think he might prefer some bear steak smothered with onions, that you know how to cook so well."

"Maybe you're right," replied Joe, and with a grandiose flourish of the cooking spoon he had been holding in his hand, he added, "But why shouldn't he have both?"

I changed the conversation, and while Joe started to cook their meal, the men had coffee. It was not long, the tension being relieved, before we were at our ease and talking gaily. They told me that they had never tasted bear meat and asked me what it was like.

"It depends altogether on what the bear has been feeding on," I replied. "If he has fattened on acorns, juniper berries, and piñon nuts, his meat is like good quality pork, only richer. But if he has been eating on dead cows, I am unable to say, never having eaten that kind of bear meat."

When the two men had finished their dinner and were preparing to leave, they thanked me for their bear steaks, which they had so much enjoyed. I had Joe cut them each a big chunk of hind-quarter bear meat to take home with them, and they bade me farewell with much cordiality, and went to their horses, accompanied by Joe, who helped them tie the meat on their saddles. Then they rode off, while Joe returned to the campfire in roars of laughter.

I should mention here that in addition to his culinary accomplishments, Joe was a fiddler, and played at the local dances; and he also prided himself on shaking a hoof.

Small wonder, then, that on returning to the campfire, he should give me an exhibition of his proficiency in the latter art.

It is difficult to describe what his dance was like. It seemed to me like a cross between an Indian War Dance and the erratic gyrations of a recently decapitated chicken, with shouts of laughter as an accompaniment.

When he had stopped for breath, I said, "Why all this mirth, Joe?"

"Because," he replied, "it's the best joke I ever got off on you."

"Well, let's have it," I said.

"All right, here it is," laughed Joe. "While I was helping to tie the bear meat on his saddle, the 'Guts' man (which was the impolite term he used when alluding to him) said to me, 'I was only joking when I said I would eat them guts, but he seems to think I was serious.' "

"I told him of course you was serious," continued Joe. "I said you had invited him to come to your camp to eat them guts, and you was a-worryin' that maybe he might come before you had a batch ready for him."

"But, Joe," I remonstrated, "that wasn't true!"

"I know it wasn't," he confessed, apologetically, "but I thought you wouldn't mind."

Indulgently I replied: "Go ahead with your story," overlooking the matter as being just one of his minor peccadillos.

So he went on: " 'Haven't you ever heard that a serious-minded Englishman don't tumble to a joke?' I asked him, and he said he thought he had." Then Joe added, while his voice rose to a falsetto: "I got him to believe you was that kind of an Englishman."

Bob, old English bob-tailed sheep dog, father of the
slow-trail dogs

Grip, with a piece of bread on her nose, doing her
trick of " On Trust "

"That sure was a good joke on me," I said, laughingly, "and I have to hand it to you for making one of the best double-header jokes I ever heard."

"How's that?" asked Joe. "I don't get you."

"Because," I replied, "I think, if he believed you, you got off as good a joke on him as you did on me."

"You're right," said Joe. "I never thought of that."

And then he proceeded to give me an encore of his weird dance to celebrate his double-header.

CHAPTER VII

SLEUTH

I HAD read quite a little about bloodhounds, but otherwise knew absolutely nothing about them. One thing in my reading riveted my attention: A bloodhound would trail a man if trained to do so—an impossible feat with an ordinary hound, or fox hound, as they are often called.

For various reasons, for which I will try to account, the general belief about bloodhounds is either vague or erroneous, or both. If you should ask the man in the street what he knows about bloodhounds, he would tell you that: they are ferocious; they bay on a man's trail; they trail a man by his footsteps; and finally that they would lose the trail if he went through water.

All these four statements are the exact reverse of the truth. In the first place, by nature, a bloodhound is the most kindly-dispositioned and friendly sort of dog. As far as I have been able to learn there are two reasons to account for his alleged ferocity, the first one being that most people in England who had country estates kept thoroughbred bloodhounds as a family tradition, not for trailing but as watch dogs. Therefore, they were generally chained to their kennels, and keeping them on a chain the whole time made them morose to begin with and ferocious to end with. This, however, would apply to all dogs, irrespective of breed. The second reason is that there is some confusion brought about through the misuse of the term "bloodhound." There is a dog known as the Cuban bloodhound, which was used in the old days for trailing runaway slaves in Cuba. This dog was a most ferocious one and it is not unlikely that the old English bloodhound got his bad reputation through his spurious Cuban cousin. This is particularly unjust because, according to the American cyclopædia, the Cuban bloodhound was not a bloodhound at all, but a mastiff.

I have never been able to find out why the old English

82

bloodhound did not bay on a man's trail. The only suggestions I have ever heard are that it was either due to a lack of desire on the part of the hound, or that certain hounds would bay on this trail and others would not. As silent dogs were preferable for trailing men, it followed that such dogs would be the ones used to continue the breed. In England, during the Wars of the Roses, when leaders of the defeated side would try to escape, bloodhounds would be employed to capture them, and, naturally, it was important that these hounds should be silent as otherwise they would give the fugitives advance notice of their coming.

The other two points above mentioned are fully explained in other parts of this book. I think that these four erroneous beliefs are due to what people read in *Uncle Tom's Cabin* about the dogs Mrs. Stowe called "bloodhounds," but which were generally known by their owners as "nigger" dogs. These "nigger" dogs are not to be confused with the Southern hound, which is, I think, generally accepted as being the equivalent or counterpart of the English fox hound. The latter was descended, as were all other varieties of hounds, from the old English bloodhound. As the bloodhound was too slow to catch foxes, he was crossed with the old English white greyhound. From this cross the modern fox hound was developed. This dog is generally white, with black or lemon-coloured patches all over him, being a combination of the colours of the white greyhound and the bloodhound.

The Southern hound, however, gets his two prevailing colours from the two strains of English bloodhounds, the St. Hubert, which is black and tan, and the Talbot, whose prevailing colour is reddish-gold. Where he gets his speed I do not know, and although the colour of his coat does not indicate greyhound descent, there must be some present, as it is the fastest dog known.

I was told by many Southerners who owned and hunted with hounds, that in the old slavery days, slave owners, finding that these Southern hounds would not trail runaway slaves, imported the Cuban bloodhound. I have never been able to find anyone who could answer the question of why these Cuban bloodhounds, who were really not bloodhounds at all, should have the natural impulse to trail a man. Suffice it to say, they were imported and crossed with the Southern hounds, producing what was known as the "nigger" dog, whose ferocity and man-trailing proclivities were inherited from the Cuban bloodhound, while his baying propensities were obtained from the Southern hound.

Hitherto, all my hunting had been done with ordinary hounds, and all that one could learn from them was pure guesswork. Since the hunters disagreed about what the hounds did, there was no way of learning anything, either from the hunter or the hounds. But it occurred to me that the case would be different with a bloodhound, since, if he would trail a man, it would be an easy matter to find out the method by which he did so.

I felt that until I could answer the question: "How does a bloodhound trail?" I could not make any real progress in hunting with hounds. I, therefore, decided to get some bloodhounds, and after much inquiry, I got in touch with Colonel Roger D. Williams, of Lexington, Kentucky, who was a noted breeder of champion bloodhounds, and a great authority on dogs in general.

From him I bought a four-year-old, registered female bloodhound, Cymbeline, who had been bred to a champion, and later I bought a male puppy. Cymbeline was a St. Hubert, and the puppy was a Talbot. These two strains differ in colour as above mentioned, but are otherwise practically the same, except that the St. Hubert, so far as my experience went, is a little the heavier of the two.

With these two hounds, and the puppies that Cymbeline had, as a start, I bred a great many bloodhounds, and while I didn't register them, they were eligible for registration. Cymbeline was a great disappointment to me. She could, of course, trail a man, but she didn't want to, and I couldn't make her. The trouble was that she had been brought up in kennels, and used only for breeding purposes, so she knew absolutely nothing about man-trailing, and was too old to be worth teaching, on the principle that you cannot teach an old dog new tricks.

The puppy, though, was quite different. He was only eight

84

weeks old when I got him, and I started right off training him to do what I wanted.

I called him "Sleuth," and he proved to be rightly named, for he turned out to be a marvellous success, far greater than I had ever anticipated. He was a remarkably intelligent dog, and like most such dogs, had a highly nervous temperament. I treated him accordingly, making a great pet of him, for I realized that anything approaching rough treatment would ruin him. The severest measure I ever took with him was to scold when he was in the slightest degree disobedient.

In training Sleuth, and later, Cymbeline's puppies, I always demanded strict obedience, but obedience without fear. As to beating them, I always held that if there were no other way of making a hound obey than to beat him, I didn't want him.

The best way to teach a puppy to obey is to teach him tricks. I started in by putting a piece of bread on the puppy's nose and saying "On trust." But should he move his head before I said "Paid for," thus dropping the bread, I would grab it, and after scolding him, put it back on his nose and repeat the trick. After a few lessons, he learned to stay quiet until I said "Paid for." Then I would put his food in a plate a few feet from him and make him "pay for" it the same way. By using these methods over and over again, I taught Sleuth instant obedience, without scaring him.

As he grew older, I continued to give him lessons, all with the view of exacting instant obedience. For instance, I would say to him, "Stay there," and wherever he happened to be, he would stop.

Then I would walk off, say fifty yards, and suddenly call him. He would, of course, start off at full speed to come to me, and when about half-way, I would say "Stay there," and he would stop instantly. Of course, if he didn't, he got scolded, and I would take him back to where he was before and start the lesson all over again.

I always had a lot of jerky on hand; that is, meat that has been dried in the sun. Dogs like it because it is pure, raw meat, and it is a very clean food to handle, or put in one's pocket. Whenever a dog did quickly what he was told to do, he was rewarded with a piece of jerky, with equal promptitude.

After about a month of these primitive lessons in obedience, I started training Sleuth in man trailing. The first lessons consisted of my leaving him in the house and going off some fifty yards, and hiding behind a tree. Then I would blow a whistle which I had for my dogs, and someone would open the door and let him out.

Not seeing me, Sleuth would run around until he struck my trail, and then follow it up until he got to me. His reward was a pat on the head and a piece of jerky and, from this gratifying result, he concluded that man-hunting paid big dividends.

From that start, the lessons progressed into a higher grade. The distance increased to a hundred yards from the house, and then to five hundred yards. Then I would get on a horse and go a mile or more, until gradually distance made no difference to him. Later I used Telesfor, who cooked the food for the dogs in addition to doing the outdoor chores of the ranch, to take my place for the important lessons in man trailing.

I would shut Sleuth up in the house, and send Telesfor off to hide. At first, it was straight trailing, and I would watch from a distance of fifty or a hundred yards, to see exactly the course taken by Telesfor. After letting Sleuth out of the house, I would put him on Telesfor's trail by walking along on it, and saying "Go on."

After Sleuth had learned to go along on it until he reached Telesfor and got his jerky, I put him on the trail by holding Telesfor's handkerchief to his nose, with the object of impress-him with the fact that that was the scent I wished him to follow. He soon caught on to this, and than I would take him out by the back of the house, and circle round until he was headed for Telesfor's trail, which might be two or three hundred yards off. Then I would let him smell the hand-kerchief, and say "Go on," but as there was no scent of Telesfor anywhere near, he would start to hunt for it, putting his nose to the ground, and zigzagging until he finally struck his scent in the air, when he would quit zigzagging and run with his head up until he reached Telesfor. Incidentally, when a houng zigzags, it means that he changes his mind. If he is hunting for a trail he will go in a certain direction to find it. Not finding it he will think that the trail is somewhere else, and will change his direction as well as his mind. This constant changing of mind causes him to zigzag.

I will have to explain here that a man leaves two trails behind him, his footsteps, which are his actual trail, and his scent, which he leaves in the air.

It is human scent that the bloodhound follows, not the scent of the boots a man wears.

Scent is something that has peculiar qualities of its own. In the first place, it has no temperature, and it has the peculiar property of impregnating almost everything with which it comes in contact.

The scent which a man leaves behind him comes mostly from the clothes he is wearing, especially his underwear, that being closest to his body and catching most of the scent which emanates from it. Naturally, the longer he wears his underwear, the stronger the scent he leaves behind him. The scent that actually leaves his body is relatively very faint, but can become highly concentrated in his clothes.

This scent in the air is naturally controlled by the direction of the wind. When, however, there is no wind, the scent will probably scatter at least fifty yards on either side of the man's actual trail, so that when the bloodhound is said to strike his trail, he strikes the edge of the scent which comes from the man when walking on his actual trail. It is then that the hound changes direction and runs along the edge of the scent zone, which, of course, is parallel to the actual trail.

There is no particular reason for the hound to enter the scent zone any further than is necessary. When zigzagging, he runs along with his nose to the ground, hoping to catch the scent which is no longer in the air, but may linger in the grass. But when he strikes the man's scent in the air and runs along in it, his head and tail revert to normal positions, and he quits zigzagging, indicating that he has at last found the trail.

Although a bloodhound trails a man by the scent given out from his body and his clothes, this does not apply to his boots, because the scent of the leather is stronger than the scent of the foot, and, curiously, enough, the scent of the leather does not give the least suggestion that it has covered a human foot. To this fact I had accidental and unexpected corroboration from trappers, who told me that when setting traps for coyotes, they were very careful never to kneel or touch the ground, except with their boots; or to touch the trap and bait except with leather gloves, which leave no human scent. If they did, the coyote would scent that a man had been there, and would be suspicious of the trap. This would go to prove that a bloodhound could not scent a man through his boots alone, and unless he had previously associated the boots with the wearer, he would be unable to trail him.

While there is no yard-stick by which to measure the keenness of a hound's scent, there is, however, a way in which to get an approximate idea. When a hound approaches the trail of a man at right angles and scents his trail in the air, how does he know whether the man went to the right or to the left? Usually, he takes the right end of the trail; that is, the way the man went, the other way being called his back trail. But sometimes, due probably to the wind or some other atmospheric condition, the hound is not sure which way to go and he will run some twenty yards in each direction alternately several times, until he has fully made up his mind which is the right end of the trail to take. In my experience he is invariably right. The question therefore arises: How much difference is there in the strength of the scent twenty yards one side or the other of a given point? That difference is the measure of the keenness of a hound's scent.

Another problem that bothered me was how to find out how far away a bloodhound could scent a man under favourable conditions of wind and weather. I studied the matter for quite a while, but I couldn't figure out a practical way to test the capabilities of a bloodhound in that respect. However, luck or accident solved the problem for me.

I happened to be riding along a trail one day with my bloodhounds, when suddenly they began running around in front of my horse and exhibiting uneasiness. I couldn't understand what they wanted, and so paid little attention to their actions. After going a short distance, they quieted down, but in a few minutes I met a man riding towards me on the same trail. At the time, I attached no significance to this meeting, but a week or so later the same thing happened all over again, on another trail. This time, it struck me that the way the hounds had acted both times was due to the fact that they had winded both men. As I had been riding about four miles an hour, and about ten minutes had elapsed since the hounds showed signs of uneasiness and my meeting this second man, the distance I had travelled must have been close to two-thirds of a mile. As he must have travelled about the same distance, this meant that we were about a mile and one-third apart when the dogs had first scented him, assuming that that was the cause of their uneasiness.

A few weeks later, I got the proof I wanted. This time, I was not on a trail, but just riding through the mountains, when my dogs acted in the same strange way that they had previously. Unlike before, I said to them "Go on," and away they went. I followed them for about a mile when I met a man who was riding around as I was. This confirmed the fact that they had winded this man, and the distance at which they had done so was at least a mile and a half. How much farther they could have winded him I do not know; but, at any rate, they had proved that they could scent a man at that distance.

This might or might not appear of much importance at first sight, but my chief motive was to get an idea of how far off, under favourable circumstances, a grizzly could scent a man who was hunting him—assuming, of course, that his scenting ability was about the same as that of a bloodhound.

I think this accounts for the fact that so few men have ever run on to a grizzly by accident. Even cattlemen who rode their ranges regularly, and whose cattle were constantly killed by them, only saw their tracks. The most likely reason was that the bear scented them from a distance, and so kept out of their way. While I occasionally ran on to a black bear, I never saw a grizzly except through the medium of hounds.

Often when I have had a bear hide pegged out on the ground to dry I have seen horses and cattle that came near it snort and run away as soon as they scented it. Strangely enough, their actions suggested to me an idea that I was able to put to practical use. When out on a hunt I always took along a lot of baled hay for the saddle horses, and it was always thrown on top of our provisions and bedding on the wagon. On reaching camp these bales were thrown on one side and covered with a wagon sheet. Sometimes when we camped near a ranch the cook would leave camp temporarily to go to this ranch for the purpose of buying eggs and vegetables. On his return he would find that milk cows or other gentle cattle had pushed aside the wagon sheet and were eating on the hay, breaking some of the bales and scattering the hay everywhere. The cook complained to me about it, so I told him in future to put a bear hide on top of the wagon sheet that covered the hay. After that we had no more trouble with marauding cattle.

Bear hides, however, sometimes get one into trouble as well as out of it. I remember one time when I was rounding up steers we moved to a new site about ten miles away. Most of the boys drove the herd we had gathered while the cook loaded up the wagon and piled our rolls of bedding on top of the load, and then drove off. The team consisted of four big, gentle old mules who hardly ever went out of a slow walk. One of the cowboys had told me the previous evening that he had seen the fresh tracks of a black bear at a spring that was only a few miles out of our course. As we were close to the home ranch I rode over there and got the hounds. I took the cowboy with me and went to the spring, where we struck the hot trail of this bear. He soon climbed a tree, and after shooting him out of it, the cowboy skinned him and we took the hide and as much of the meat as we could conveniently carry on our saddles. We then went to the road and followed up the wagon which we could see in the distance. On reaching the wagon the cowboy threw the bear hide on top of the mess box, just when the cook had put the reins between his knees, preparatory to rolling a cigarette. The mules at this moment got a whiff of the bear hide and bolted, while the reins slipped to the ground. The road was quite rough at this part of it, so the rolls of bedding were bounced off, one by one. The cook, with a scared look on his face, clung helplessly to the wagon box. The cowboy and I galloped our horses ahead to stop the mules, one on each side of them. Finally I grabbed the bridle of the lead mule on my side, while the cowboy got hold of the bridle of the other lead mule and we gradually brought them to a halt, but not before we had gone a quarter of a mile. Then the cook, after regaining his reins, drove the team round to go back down the road to pick up the debris.

After the rolls of bedding had been bumped off, most of the rest of the load followed suit. There were several sacks of flour that burst open when they struck the ground, two sacks of potatoes and a keg of horse-shoes did likewise, while a miscellaneous assortment of cowboy belongings were strewn everywhere. It took us over an hour to retrieve the lot while the cook expressed, in no uncertain terms, what he thought of any man who had no more sense than to throw a bear hide on a mess wagon.

CHAPTER VIII

MAN TRAILING

As time went on, I gave Sleuth harder and harder problems in trailing. Instead of straight-away trails, I gave him trails that were anything but straight. I had two set trails that I generally used. By a set trail, I mean not the same exact trail each time, but the same in principle, but varying in detail.

One of these trails I called the "hook trail," and the other the "criss-cross circle trail." The hook trail was shaped like an interrogation mark consisting of a stem, a three-quarter circle, and a gap. The size of the hook varied every time. The length of the stem might be a quarter mile or a half mile, and the same with the diameter of the circle. Then I could vary the hook by making it either a right, or a left-hand hook.

Telesfor would leave the house from in front, after I had told him the size of the hook I wanted, and walk it out. I would take Sleuth out at the back of the house, and then circle around and head him for the stem of the hook, giving him Telesfor's handkerchief to sniff and saying "Go on!" This he would promptly do, and after reaching the trail along the stem he would run along until he came to the point where the circle started to leave the stem to form the hook, and there he would either go around the circle with his head and tail in normal positions like before, until he reached Telesfor, who had hidden himself somewhere at the end of the hook, or if he winded Telesfor direct, he would throw his head up in the air and make a bee-line for him across the gap.

The criss-cross circle trail was made by Telesfor in the following manner: He would walk straight for a certain distance, then walk in a circle; then turn and walk around the circle the other way; then across the circle backwards and forwards in all directions, and finally leave it at a point more or less opposite to where he had entered it, then walk a certain distance until he reached a place where he could hide. This set trail could, of course, be varied in size, like the other one.

It is obvious that if Sleuth tried to follow this trail by Telesfor's footsteps, when he reached the circle he would have a hopeless job on his hands, figuratively speaking. Owing to the fact that the scent came to him from every side, there was nothing for him to do but to throw his head up in the air as he did when winding. He didn't go in a straight line, but would veer from side to side as the scent reached his nose in varying strength, until eventually he would reach the point where Telesfor had left the circle, that naturally being where the scent was strongest. Just as soon as he left the circle, his head would again drop to its normal position, and he would follow the trail till he got to Telesfor in the usual way.

Sleuth solved these first two trail problems without the least hesitation. I invented new trails that I supposed would be much harder, but they seemed all alike to Sleuth, for he solved them all with the same degree of ease. What appeared difficult to me did not appear so to him.

As time went on, I gradually learned how Sleuth did his trailing. To him, this man-trailing work became a matter of routine, and at times he showed that he was bored with it. For instance, I had Telesfor do several trails on the same day, for the benefit of visitors who wished to observe the various types of trails. Sleuth did not seem to mind the first one, but when it came to the third and fourth, and I held the handkerchief towards him to smell, he would turn his head away to show he didn't need it, and then look at me as if to say: "I have found this man for you several times. Why do you keep on losing him?"

In all these trials, it would naturally be supposed that Sleuth was my pupil, but as a matter of fact it was quite the reverse, for it was he who was teaching me how a man was trailed by a hound. All I did was to explain to him who I wanted him to trail, and he did the rest.

It was not long before I began to realize that what I had learned by reading about bloodhounds was altogether different

93

from what the bloodhounds taught me. I was due for many surprises, the greatest one of all, perhaps, being that the bloodhound does not trail a man by his actual footsteps, but by his scent in the air.

To show that this was typical of the general belief, can best be illustrated by the following. It happened that one of my "candid" friends invited me and another friend of his to go to a picture show and supper afterwards. One of the scenes in the play depicted man trailing with bloodhounds. My fellow guest, who was interested in hounds, having heard that I had bloodhounds, very naturally asked me, at supper, what I thought of the scene, in which two magnificent bloodhounds appeared necked together, while a man held them in leash as they trailed, supposedly, the footsteps of a man.

Apparently the hero, or villain, I forget which, had just got away, and bloodhounds had been requisitioned to trail him up and catch him.

Having been asked for my views, I was by no means indisposed to give them, so I observed that if you had to trail a man with two hounds, the latter would co-operate far better if they were loose, and could act independently, than necked together, where each one would obstruct the free movements of the other; while to cap the climax, the man who held the leash would only obstruct them both. Of course, I continued, this delayed-action method of trailing was all in favour of the fugitive, who was given more time in which to escape.

At this juncture, my candid friend kept frowning at me, so I took the hint and lapsed into silence, while he picked up the conversation and changed it into another channel.

Shortly after this, his friend left us, and then it was that the "biter got bit."

"Didn't I know," he asked, "that the movie producers would never have released the picture if they had not been thoroughly satisfied with it? And couldn't I sense how deeply it impressed the audience and how thrilled they were with the performance? Who was I, that I should try to upset their enjoyment by throwing a monkey wrench into the machinery of their mutual satisfaction, merely to show off my *beastly* superior knowledge of bloodhounds?"

Under this avalanche of denunciation, and seeing his point, I promised not to offend any more.

From this experience, I learned to keep my criticisms to myself.

As there are exceptions to most rules, I will have to qualify this statement to a certain extent.

If a bloodhound follows the trail of a man, he will soon begin to realize that the scent which he is trailing in the air is accompanied by the scent of boot tracks on the ground. Then if, in exposed places, the scent is blown entirely away, he is forced to trail the man by his boot-tracks as a clue, until he reaches some place sheltered from the wind, where he will again pick up the scent in the air.

When I first announced to my friends this discovery that a hound doesn't trail a man by his footsteps, it seemed to cause them a great deal of amusement, as it didn't occur to them that there was any other method by which a hound would trail a man. But I stuck to my statement, notwithstanding the unsolicited advice of some of my candid friends, who told me that no matter whether I was right or wrong, I had better keep my knowledge to myself, as no one would believe me and I would only be setting myself up as a target for public ridicule. I had already told several people about it, so it was too late for me to take their advice, even had I wanted to. So I suggested to them that they come to the ranch, and I would furnish proof that I was right. Accordingly, a day was set, and five of them appeared.

We sat down to discuss how the test should be conducted. They suggested that three of them be appointed judges, while one of the two others assumed the role of the man to be trailed. The fifth man was to remain in the house and watch me and Sleuth, who was to do the trailing.

The idea was that the man to be trailed should walk a certain distance, say half a mile, any way he wished. The three judges on horseback should, from a distance of about one hundred yards, see exactly how he had walked over the ground in making his trail. They were then to come back to the house to get me and Sleuth, and I was to turn Sleuth loose on the trail by the handkerchief method. The three judges

95

would decide whether he trailed the man by his footsteps or not. I listened gravely to this proposition, but assured them that it would never work.

I added: "The only practical way to prove that a hound doesn't trail a man by his footsteps is for there to be no footsteps."

This caused them to regard me with amazement, and one of them asked if I meant for the man to fly.

I replied: "No, he could go on a horse."

This idea had not occurred to them.

"But," objected one, "he might trail the horse."

"Well," I said, "if you think that, let's have two horses and two men, and have the hound trail one of the two men."

Then I suggested that two men on horseback go together, one of them, of course, being the man to be trailed. The other three men were to be the judges, two of them to watch the trail made by the men on horseback, while the third stayed in the house with me and Sleuth.

The judges were to take the handkerchiefs of the two men on horseback, and the one belonging to the man to be trailed was to be handed to me for Sleuth to sniff.

Then I drew on a sheet of paper a criss-cross circle trail for the two men to follow, they having the option of making it any size they wished. I suggested, also, that when they got to the circle, they should separate and ride round it in opposite directions, then change horses, without touching the ground, leave the circle, go an optional distance, say half a mile, and separate again, one going to the right, the other to the left, each hiding in timber or brush.

Two of the judges should observe exactly how they went, so as to see how Sleuth would trail them, later on. This they did, then came back to the house to fetch the other judge, myself, and Sleuth.

I left the ranch by the back way, as usual, and circled round to a point some three hundred yards from the trail where the men started. I gave Sleuth the handkerchief to sniff, and told him "Go on." We were all on horseback, so that we could follow quickly.

Listening to instructions. Inveed, St. Hubert
bloodhound (*left*), and Sleuth, Talbot bloodhound

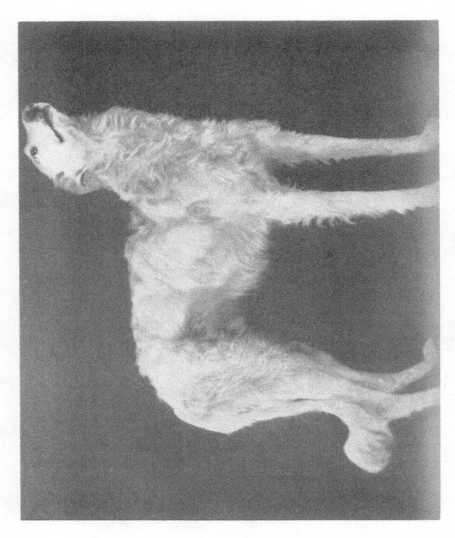

Cossack, the leader of my Russian wolfhound pack

As soon as Sleuth struck the trail of the two men on horseback, he followed it, as usual, in a fast walk. As he passed through the circle, he went straight to the place where the men had left it, and followed the trail to where they had separated. Here he took the trail of the man who had turned to the left, until he came to the place where he was hidden, which in this instance, was about a quarter of a mile from the point where the two men had separated.

The judges admitted that the handkerchief they had given me for Sleuth to sniff was the one that belonged to the man Sleuth had just found.

Then I said to them:

"Give me the other handkerchief. Sleuth knows that there are two men, and has first found the one whose handkerchief I gave him to smell. Now, I will give him the other handkerchief, and you will see that he will go straight to where the men separated and take the other man's trail." And this is exactly what Sleuth proceeded to do!

The judges then conceded that my contention was correct —a hound does not trail a man by his footsteps.

This concession was also granted by other people, with the exception of some of the kind who still contend the earth is flat, as otherwise the water in the Suez Canal would run out at both ends.

No one could say that the trial had not been perfectly fair, because the judges had conducted it in every detail, except that I had handed Sleuth the handkerchief to sniff and told him to "Go on."

In order to get strangers to act in the place of Telesfor, whom I did not wish to use for trailing all the time, I offered an award of five dollars to anyone who could make a trail that my hounds could not follow.

One day, two men appeared, each of whom had a method by which he thought he could get that five dollars. Of course, each one believed that the hound trailed a man by his footsteps, and that if in some way or other he could change the scent that the footsteps were supposed to give out, the hound would not be able to trail him.

One man's plan was to soak gunny sacks in coal oil and tie

them around his feet. The other thought that by putting pepper in the footsteps the hound would sniff the pepper up into his nose, thus putting it out of commission.

I told the man with the gunny sack idea that we would try out his plan. I furnished him with the gunny sacks and the coal oil, and he tied them around his feet. But I told the man with the pepper idea that I didn't happen to have enough pepper on hand to furnish him with the supply he would need to be effective; and in any case, it would only be pepper wasted, for the hound would never go near the peppered footsteps.

I then shut Sleuth up in the house and told the man with the gunny sacks to make a bee-line to a tree about a quarter of a mile off that was up on a hillside. I gave him twenty minutes to get there, while I asked the other man to stay with me and act as a sort of umpire. The ground between us and the tree was all open, without even any brush on it, and I told the gunny sack man that, after he had hidden behind the tree, he could look back on his trail and see for himself how Sleuth followed it.

It was a still day, so the scent of the man spread out on either side of his actual trail. I knew that Sleuth, as soon as he got to the edge of the scent, would go along on that edge until he got to the man he was trailing, so the latter could see for himself that the hound had never gone near his footsteps. But even if he did, according to his theory, Sleuth could not scent them because of the coal oil. By having the trail absolutely straight, it would make it easier for him to judge how close the hound went to his bee-line trail.

After the twenty minutes were over, I took Sleuth out of the house. Soon after getting a sniff of the man's handkerchief, he struck the edge of the scent and ran straight to the tree where the man was hiding. We followed on horseback and soon arrived at the tree. I then asked the man if he had watched Sleuth, and he replied that he had. When I asked if he had ever seen Sleuth go nearer than about fifty yards of his actual bee-line trail, he had to admit that he hadn't, and as Sleuth found him, he didn't win his five dollars. On the way back to the house, I managed to convince the man with

98

the pepper idea that he would have no better luck than his companion.

A few days after this, another man appeared who said that *he* could fool a bloodhound. He said, however, that my five dollar offer was not enough because he intended to run down the creek a mile or two, and that would injure a ten-dollar pair of boots he was wearing, but that he would bet me ten dollars. I told him I didn't bet, but in order not to disappoint him, instead of making an award of five dollars, I would make an exception in his case, so it would be a bet of ten dollars between us. His idea, of course, was that a hound trailed a man by his footsteps, and that as their scent would be obliterated by the water, the hound could no longer trail him. He had brought a friend with him who acted as umpire. He walked to the creek, which was about a quarter of a mile away, and then down the creek itself for two miles, leaving it on the opposite side and walking up on to a hill, where he hid in some bushes. I gave him an hour in which to do all this, and then his friend and I took Sleuth out of the house, where he had been shut up, gave him the man's handkerchief to sniff, and told him to "Go on" in my usual way.

The creek, by the way, was about twelve feet wide, and about eight inches deep. The weather was cold and the edges of the water were lined with ice. Sleuth followed the scent the man had left in the air, running along the edge of the creek for about two miles, until he reached the place where the man had left the creek and walked up on the hill. He stopped for a moment, looked around, and spying a big rock that stood out in the middle of the stream about thirty yards below where he was, he ran down to where he could jump on to the rock from the bank, then to the other bank from the rock, thus crossing the creek without getting his feet wet, and then went up on the hill to where the man was hidden.

We crossed the creek and waited for the man to come down off the hill. I asked him if he had watched Sleuth trail him, and he said that he had, adding that he never would have believed that walking in water made no difference to a hound trailing if he hadn't seen it for himself. When I asked him on what basis he had formed his opinion, he replied that he had always heard it that way, and for that reason had implicitly believed it.

He then drew me to one side and explained that he didn't have the ten dollars that he had bet, but would send it to me as soon as he could. I told him that was all right and that he needn't send the money, as I didn't want it. But I did ask him why he had made the bet when he didn't have the money to pay if he lost. His reply was so naive as to be truly delightful: "I was so sure of winning that I didn't think it necessary to have it."

I told him that if he wanted to do something by way of paying the bet, he could tell everybody that a man cannot escape from a bloodhound by running in water. He replied that he "Sure would." He certainly kept his promise, for about two weeks later he appeared with another doubting Thomas.

Sleuth went through the same procedure as before, finding the man, who then left his hiding-place, meeting us half-way, for we had been following on foot. As we turned and started back, he pulled a five-dollar bill out of his pocket and, giving it to his friend, remarked:

"I guess you won this bet, all right."

I said nothing at the time, but when we arrived at the ranch, and the new convert had left us to mount his horse, I asked him how it was that he came to make such a bet, when he knew that he was betting on a certainty.

He replied aggressively: "I told him that, but he said that made no difference, so we made the bet. I felt, as he was so cock-sure of winning, that when he lost, it would *learn* the damn fool in the future not to bet on something he didn't know anything about."

I listened gravely to all this, and said nothing, but I could not help murmuring to myself: "Great Scot!"

At first, this man trailing seemed to be complicated and difficult, but by constant repetition, it became simple and commonplace, while Sleuth regarded it all as mere routine work.

It was not surprising that, eventually, no matter what the man who was trailed tried to do to fool Sleuth, I had absolute confidence in his ability to find him without difficulty. The standing offer of five dollars was never won by anyone. Naturally, my confidence became such that, while one "cannot fool all the people all the time," I got to believe that Sleuth could not be fooled by "any of the people any of the time."

It was at this stage of belief that I got a great jolt! I had a visitor at the ranch who had done much hunting with hounds, and was considered a very good sight trailer. It so happened that a neighbouring ranchman came to visit, and stopped the night, leaving early the next morning after breakfast. My visitor and I had intended going with him, but I was prevented from doing so because some business cropped up that I could not postpone. I, therefore, told the ranchman that I would follow him in the afternoon, and stop at his ranch that night, and I also told him that he would be providing us with a trail, which would enable my visitor to see how Sleuth man-trailed.

In the afternoon, my friend and I started off, and I put Sleuth on the ranchman's trail. He went ahead at his usual gait of four miles an hour, while we followed him on our horses. The distance we had to go was about fifteen miles, and the trail passed through a gap in a high mountain range which lay between our ranches. On the further side of the gap was a little spring on the mountainside, round which the ground was very rocky, and where I had put in a trough at which stock was watered. The spring was piped into the trough, and from the trough the water spilled over in among the rocks.

It was a hot day, and when we got to the spring, we watered our horses, while Sleuth lay down in one of the pools and drank. When our horses had got through we went on down the trail to where the rocky ground quit, and the tracks of the ranchman's horse again showed up plainly. As we were going along, my companion remarked:

"What's the matter with your dog? Why is he staying behind?"

I looked back, and there was Sleuth, sitting on the rocks by the spring, looking at me inquiringly.

"Let's go back," I said, "and see what's up. I don't understand why Sleuth is acting as he is."

As we approached Sleuth, he turned and went up the hill, and while I didn't understand his actions, I decided to follow him. He went ahead for about three miles along the side of the mountain, over ground which was so rocky all the way that you could not see either horse or cattle tracks.

Finally, we came to a ridge leading to the valley below, and we followed a trail on this ridge until it crossed soft ground, on which were fresh horse tracks.

I said to my companion: "He might have come down here."

He replied: "Why, didn't you see his horse's tracks on the trail going down from the spring?"

I answered: "Nevertheless, Sleuth coming this way makes me think that perhaps these might be his horse's tracks, after all."

To this my friend replied irritably: "I think you're mistaken, and anyway the tracks on this trail here are more than one horse could make."

I looked at the tracks closely, and was obliged to agree with him, whereupon I relapsed into silence. We followed on down the ridge, which was very narrow, until it broadened out on soft ground, and there, sure enough, were the tracks of two horses going side by side. I had to admit that he had the best of the argument.

Sleuth walked ahead of us in his usual nonchalant way, as we rode on down the ridge, but I was feeling very depressed, as it was the first time that Sleuth had ever failed me, and I couldn't understand it.

My friend, noticing that I looked unhappy, said: "I wouldn't worry over it. Your dog will do better next time."

This cold comforting assurance did not appeal to me, and I said, dispiritedly: "There's no *next time* for me. If that dog fails me once, how am I ever to know when he won't fail me again?"

I was very disconsolate as we rode on down the ridge. When we struck the county road in the valley below, there were tracks of wagons and horses going both ways, so the tracks of the two horses we had been following lost their identity.

Sleuth, however, turned to the left, which was the direction of the ranch to which we were going. When we arrived, our host was standing on the porch and greeted us:

"You are rather late. I have had supper waiting for you for some time."

We sat down to supper, but I had no appetite. Sleuth sat near me with a puzzled look on his face. He had always been accustomed, after trailing for me and finding his man, to get a pat on the back, and be told he'd been a good dog. As I had not done so this time, he realized that there was something wrong, but was at a loss to know what it could be.

After a few minutes, my host said to me: "Well, how did you come out on the trailing?"

There was an embarrassing pause, and then I said: "It didn't come out. Instead of following your trail here from the trough, Sleuth pulled out above the spring through the hills, and then came down a ridge to the road. We followed him, as I wanted to find out why he left your trail, but I cannot make out, even now, why he acted as he did."

With a grin on his face, my host put his hand across the table and said: "Shake! Your dog was right. That *was* the way I came. You see," he explained, "when I got to the trough and my horse was drinking, a neighbour of mine came down the hill above the trough and told me he had just seen one of my saddle horses, that had somehow got out of my pasture, on the side of the mountain about a mile away, and described where he was so that I couldn't fail to find him. He then went on down the trail that I should have gone on otherwise, while I went up the hill in the direction of my horse. I soon found him and led him to the ridge down which you came afterwards."

I told him we had seen his tracks on the ridge, but assumed it could not be his as there were two horses. We supposed, of course, that there were two men, especially when we saw the horse tracks side by side.

He replied: "I am not surprised that you thought there were two men. The reason was that my horse would trot up beside me whenever the trail was wide enough for him to do so."

I cannot say how relieved I was to find that Sleuth had been right, after all. I had been much upset, and while my appetite returned, and I began eating, I had not quite returned to normal.

My host suddenly said: "I thought you never ate corn on the cob!"

I replied: "I don't."

"Well," he said, "what are you eating now?"

Then it was that I realized that I had an ear of corn in my hand and had eaten on it unconsciously.

After supper was over, I called Sleuth to me. I wanted to apologize for having doubted him. He, however, mistook my meaning, and thought I was forgiving him for something he had done wrong, so he started apologizing to me, as much as to say:

"I don't know what I did wrong, but whatever it was, I am sorry for it."

I have had considerable experience with dogs, and I must admit that I don't know how to apologize to one so that he will understand, but I promised Sleuth that I never again would doubt him, no matter what the evidence against him might be, until he was absolutely proved wrong.

From then on, I had real confidence in him, and by that, I mean the kind that comes from "confidence that's shaken, but finds itself mistaken," and vows never again to repeat that error.

And that went for all the other hounds, too.

There were several times, later on, when it appeared hard for me to keep that promise, but I kept it, and I never had cause for regret, because the hound, in the final analysis, always turned out to be right.

The above experience, though temporarily unpleasant, turned out to be invaluable to me, in the sense that it suggested many new aspects of sight and scent trailing that I had never hitherto taken into consideration.

In the first place, it showed how much more reliable scent trailing by a hound is, than sight trailing by a man. One conclusion I reached was that scent never fools a hound, whereas sight often fools a man. There is an old saying that "seeing is believing," and I think that accounts for many erroneous beliefs.

The fact is that we don't realize how unreliable our sense of sight is, compared with what it might be. In this instance, it happened that the shoes of the horses of the two men were of the same size; namely, Number 1's, and they were also in the same condition of wear. Had one set of shoes been new, the horse-tracks would have been more clear cut and this difference would have been obviously apparent. But as they were not, my sight-trailing friend was deceived. I did not, however, tell him that he might do better "next time" as that would not have been sportsmanlike. While in this instance his mistake was of no consequence, it would have been different if the ranchman had been a fugitive from justice and my friend had been called upon to trail him up. The result would have been that the other man would have been trailed to his home and arrested as the criminal. Had he then been tried, convicted and sentenced for the offence, and subsequently have been proved innocent, circumstantial evidence would have been blamed for the error.

I have often heard people say that they would never convict anyone on such evidence alone, and while this is a very laudable sentiment, they fail to add that there have been many cases where innocent persons have been falsely convicted of crimes on the evidence of human witnesses. This leads one to the conclusion that there is no evidence of any kind that is absolutely reliable in all cases.

On the other hand, if no criminal is to be tried and convicted because of the possibility of a mistake being made, then the transgressor could justifiably congratulate himself on coming into his own.

Personally I think there is no better evidence than circumstantial evidence, for the reason that it is both unbiased and genuine; whereas evidence by human witnesses may be perjured, prejudiced, or just honestly mistaken. I base this opinion on the many cases I have known where the verdict of the jury was unjust, though not intentionally so, due entirely to the unreliability of the testimony given them.

There is, however, one serious drawback to the reliability

105

of circumstantial evidence, and that is that it has to be interpreted through human aid, and if it should turn out wrong such evidence is made the scapegoat for the error, but the chance of its being misinterpreted is overlooked. It is not surprising, therefore, that it cannot function properly under such a handicap.

Sight trailing, even at its best, is too slow for trailing up a running wild animal where speed is the prime requisite for getting him, as he is likely to run a long distance without stopping.

In still-hunting, that is, hunting without hounds, to be a good sight-trailer is of the greatest importance to the hunter in helping him to be successful in getting his quarry. But it should be added that it is just as important for the hunter to be a fairly good shot, for it is of little use for the hunter to be successful in trailing up an animal, only to miss him when he gets within reasonable shooting distance. This may sound somewhat of a platitude, but paradoxically enough, it was entirely due to this combination of expert trailing and rotten shooting that I had the good fortune to learn about sight trailing from two past masters in that art, namely, two Apache Indian Government Scouts.

It was in November, 1886, shortly after Geronimo and his renegade Apache band had surrendered in Sonora, Mexico, to the United States troops, that Leonard Wood, then U.S. Assistant Surgeon (later Major General), was sent on a special mission by the War Department to Sonora. He invited me to join him as his guest, an invitation I was very pleased to accept.

The outfit consisted of two packers, one cook, two Apache Indian Scouts, enlisted under the names of Tony and Chino, a Mexican interpreter named Montoya who could speak both Apache and English, Wood and myself, eight in all.

We had about twenty big mules, eight of which we rode, and the others were used for pack animals, together with a bell-horse for the pack mules to follow. We started from Nogales, Mexico, and went 500 miles south to Sahuaripa, along the western slopes of the Sierra Madre mountains by one trail, and returned by another that was more or less parallel to it, the whole round trip taking four months. We usually left camp shortly after sunrise and made camp about three o'clock in the afternoon, thus leaving plenty of time before dark to hunt deer to supply fresh meat for the camp. The two Indians and I did most of the hunting.

On the first hunt, when the Indians started to go, I made signs that I wished to go with them, but they shook their heads so I went off in another direction. I knew they had the reputation of being wonderful sight-trailers as well as good deer hunters, judging by the number of deer they succeeded in killing. My main object for going with them, however, was to study their methods of hunting, and more especially their ability in trailing up deer. I therefore asked Montoya to beg them to let me go with them, and offered to pay them for the privilege. At first they refused, point-blank, but finally they grudgingly agreed to let me go with them, provided I would walk not less than ten yards behind them and stop whenever they motioned me to do so and crouch to the ground until they beckoned me to come on again.

I was very glad to agree to this arrangement and the next time we hunted, I followed behind them. After going a mile or so, they struck fresh signs of where some deer had passed. The ground was thickly covered with grass, so I could not see any deer tracks, but this did not seem to bother the Indians, for they trailed along at the same pace that they had been going before. From time to time they would glance back to see that I was keeping my proper distance. On one such occasion I pointed to the ground and shook my head to show that I could not see any deer tracks. Then one of them came back and pointed to the ground. Again I shook my head, meaning that I could not see anything in particular, and then, with a tired look in his eyes, he bent down and touched a blade of grass. As I still showed no signs of understanding he carefully plucked it from its root and showed me that it was unnaturally bent, signifying that a deer must have stepped on it. Then, thinking that I needed further proof, he walked along until we came to a piece of bare ground where the deer tracks showed up plainly. I smiled my thanks and we went on as before, when suddenly we came in sight of the deer about a hundred yards away. They motioned me to crouch down, and one of them plucked a tuft of grass which he threw into the air to determine the direction of the wind, and then they went off.

A full hour passed, when I heard a couple of shots, and, going to them, found that they had killed a deer. As the deer was shot in two places, they must have shot at the same deer. Apparently, what they had done was to sneak through the brush to where they could watch the deer without being seen, and decide which way they were travelling, and then circle round to a spot they judged the deer would pass, then, lying hidden, shoot at them when they got within twenty feet. They were very careful, of course, not to go to any place from which the deer might wind them.

After skinning and cutting up the deer, we divided the meat into three loads of about twenty pounds each, and started back to camp as it was getting late. As we were going along, a deer we must have scared ran past in front of us about fifty yards off, and stopped to look at us. The two Indians dropped their loads of meat and blazed away at the deer, missing him clean. They both looked back at me, and they did not fail to observe a certain tired look in my eyes, and after saying a few words to each other we went on.

To account for their missing so easy a shot, I could only surmise that they merely pointed their rifles at the deer, and while they did look along the barrels, I don't think they used the sights. I was, therefore, forced to conclude that the only reason for their success in getting deer was due to their ability in trailing them and getting within a few feet before shooting.

On our next hunt, as we were returning to camp, we scared up a fine, white-tailed buck who was browsing under a tree. He ran some hundred yards, and then stopped and looked at us. The Indians were much excited, but as it was too late in the day for them to stalk him they motioned me to shoot. The buck was standing broadside to me, and after taking careful aim, I fired. As the bullet struck him, his body seemed suddenly to shrink, his ears flapped and his tail wiggled. Then he ran at full speed for about fifty yards, sprang into the air, and after turning a graceful somersault, fell flat on his back.

The Indians grinned approvingly at me while I pointed to my heart, meaning that was where he was hit. This was confirmed later when they cut him open and took out his heart. Incidentally, I have shot many deer through the heart and they have invariably acted in this way, while on the other hand, I have never known a deer to do this when shot elsewhere. This greatly enhanced the respect the Indians had for me as a hunter, and from then on they treated me as a hunting equal, although our methods of hunting were so entirely different.

In comparing the two methods, I came to the conclusion that where deer were scarce, their method was the better of the two. But where deer were plentiful, it was entirely too slow for getting best results.

After I had hunted with the Indians for about a month I felt that I had learnt as much about sight-trailing from them as I was ever likely to learn, so I decided that we would get more deer if we hunted separately. I therefore reverted to hunting alone. As there were many deer in most of the places we hunted over, the result was that I succeeded in getting many times more deer than they did, and this was most humiliating to them, as from their standpoint a hunter who could not trail was no hunter. Their poor shooting, however, was a great handicap, for if they saw a deer, say at fifty yards distance, they were afraid to shoot for fear of missing and also of scaring away other deer that might be close by. So they would be obliged to stalk him in order to get a close shot within a few feet.

This might take a long time, during which I would be likely to run on to several deer in turn, most of which I would get if they gave me a standing shot within two hundred yards. I must, however, add that I am speaking of sixty years ago when very few Indians had rifles, and those few had a very crude notion of how to shoot them. Of course, to-day it is very different, for there are many Indians now who are fairly good shots.

However, I learnt a great deal about trailing by sight from these two Indians which was of great use to me later when hunting by scent with bloodhounds.

The most important thing I learnt was that I would never make a good sight trailer, so I did not waste any time in trying to improve on what I felt I could never do. But that did not prevent my being able to judge the sight trailing abilities of others. After all, you do not necessarily have to be a jockey in order to be a fair judge of a race-horse. Also, it is an easy matter to judge sight trailing ability, for, just as a typist can show his proficiency by the speed at which he can write, so a sight-trailer can show his efficiency by the speed at which he can trail. This, by the way, is a supreme test that there is no getting around.

A thorough knowledge of sight trailing is of great help in trailing by scent with hounds, provided you can distinguish between when it is a benefit and when a detriment. I can regretfully recall the numberless hours that were wasted when bear-hunters I hired insisted on trailing up bear tracks that were plain to the eye, but which the hounds could not trail because there was no scent in them. Another seemingly curious fact that thrust itself on my attention when studying the art of sight trailing was that illiteracy was the prime factor to be considered. In other words, the greater the illiteracy the greater the sight trailing ability. This, I think, can be best accounted for in the following way:

The eyes of an educated man are trained to read, while the eyes of a totally illiterate man are trained from infancy to read the ground. If you show a written sentence to the former, he reads it at a glance, absorbs its meaning, and thinks no more of it, unless there should be a mistake in the spelling, in which case he would instantly detect the error. On the other hand, if you showed an ordinary piece of ground to an illiterate Indian, he would also think nothing of it unless there was something unusual about it, such as a pebble recently moved out of place or a blade of grass in an unnatural position. Such trifles would at once arrest his eyes, and he would quickly grasp their meaning.

From the foregoing comparison in the training of eyes, I drew some consolation in the thought that my lack of ability in sight-trailing could best be attributed, partly if not wholly, to my not being illiterate.

I would like to add one more proof that a hound does not trail a man by his footsteps, an incident that happened by accident about a year later.

I have always been fond of paradoxes; in fact, a neat paradox has the same appeal to me as a humorous story, and the experience I am now about to relate I have always regarded as one of the gems in my collection.

I had a visitor at the ranch who was very anxious to see my bloodhounds work. He had had considerable experience with fox hounds, but admitted that he knew nothing about bloodhounds. Nevertheless, he was inclined to be sceptical about the claims I had made as to the efficiency of these hounds in that line.

I had already explained to him in detail how bloodhounds man trail, so at the first opportunity I told Telesfor to go to a certain place about two miles away, gave him an hour's start to get there, and told him to stay until we came.

It so happened that we were delayed for three hours, and after I had given Sleuth the handkerchief to sniff, my friend and I mounted our horses and followed him. He zigzagged in the usual way, until he struck Telesfor's scent, then he raised his head to the normal position, as I had previously told my friend he would do, and followed it along at his normal pace.

The trail led across an open prairie, finally dropping into a little valley, about fifty yards wide, in which a bunch of cattle was lying down.

Suddenly Sleuth began to zigzag until he found Telesfor's footsteps, and these he followed, with his nose to the ground, until he climbed up the rise on the other side of the valley. Then his head reverted to normal, and he ran along as before, until he got to Telesfor.

As soon as he started to zigzag, my friend asked me: "From what you've told me, he's lost the trail, hasn't he?"

"Yes, he must have," I replied, though I couldn't understand how such a thing could happen.

When Sleuth struck Telesfor's footsteps, my friend said to me frigidly: "I thought you told me that your hound didn't trail a man by his footsteps."

"Yes, I did," I said, "but there must be some reason for this exception that I don't understand at the moment."

After reaching Telesfor, I told him to stay where he was until I came back, as Sleuth had done something I had never known him to do before, and I wanted to find out what was the cause of it.

Riding back towards the ranch, we finally got to the little valley where we had left the cattle lying down.

During our three hours' delay before starting, the cattle must have come down the valley, and lain down on the very ground over which Telesfor had passed. As it was a hot day, the strong scent of the cattle had been accentuated, literally smothering out the scent left by Telesfor.

However, when I voiced these obvious deductions, my friend said sceptically: "Your explanation is most ingenious, but to my mind, not convincing."

This remark annoyed me not a little, and I retorted: "You need convincing, do you? Well, I can give you positive proof that I am correct, if you want it."

He raised his eyebrows, and said: "I think that would be impossible!"

"Oh, no, it isn't," I replied gaily. "I'll tell you how I can prove it. You stay hidden near here while I take Sleuth back to the ranch and get another hound, Rufus, and put him on the trail to see if he doesn't trail Telesfor in the same way as Sleuth did."

Many times before, when Sleuth's actions had puzzled me on man-trailing trails, I would put another bloodhound on the same trail to see if what he did agreed with or varied from what Sleuth had done. Invariably, it agreed, unless the wind had changed between the two trials, or some other atmospheric disturbance had occurred. I felt sure, therefore, that on this trail, Rufus would act exactly as Sleuth had done, and he did not disappoint me in this instance.

On the way home from this double-check trial, my companion was thoughtfully silent. Upon my suggestion to get a third hound for further proof, he shook his head and said it wouldn't be necessary.

Incidentally, it struck me as most curious that, without my

The hide of an 800 pound grizzly. The author with
Princess and Czar nearest the skin

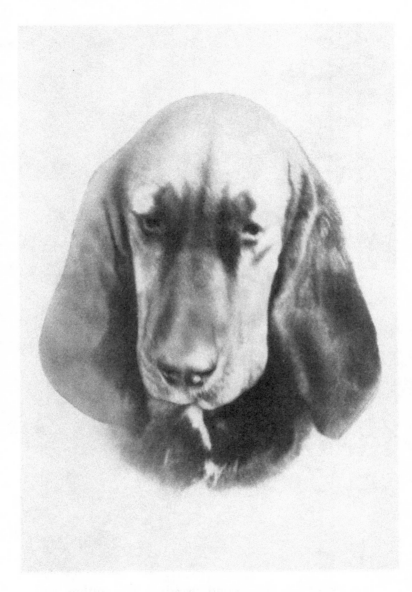

Psyche, a typical St. Hubert bloodhound

connivance in any way, I should be unexpectedly furnished with a practical illustration of how a bloodhound does *not* trail a man by his footsteps, yet proving it by his doing that very thing, and this is where the neatness of my paradox comes in.

Obviously, if a hound trailed a man by his footsteps, both hounds would have trailed Telesfor's footsteps *all* the way through, *from the start*, until they got to him, instead of doing as I have described.

This new impediment to hounds trailing by scent, namely, smothered scent, opened up a new line of study. Hitherto I had only taken into account the disappearance of scent in the air to two causes, either by being blown away by the wind, or by evaporation; that is, by air heated by the sun, rising up into space and taking the scent along with it.

But here was a third cause, either a strong scent smothering out a relatively weak one that the hounds might have been trailing, or else by a multiplicity of weak scents combining with it, causing it to lose its identity and thus confusing the hounds, who would then be said to have lost the trail.

I had often noticed on long trails that the hounds, when trailing by scent in the air, suddenly and unaccountably lost that scent, as evidenced by their putting their noses to the ground and zigzagging until they again caught that scent in the air, and then trailing it as before. It is somewhat analogous to static interference to reception on the radio, and when the static stops, the reception continues as clearly as it did previously.

As long as the scent the hounds are trailing remains predominant, the hounds can ignore these other scents, but on a long trail and after the lapse of several hours, it is not surprising that there would be places where this scent would be either obliterated by a strong one, or lose its individuality through being mixed up with a lot of minor scents, such as the smell of pines, flowers, or even certain weeds, while the stronger scents would be those of cattle, horses or sheep that might have been grazing for short distances along the trail. All these possibilities impressed on me the difficulties with which hounds have to contend when trailing by scent in the air, and it is quite astonishing how well they manage to trail under such handicaps.

But to revert to our subject.

About four months after I had started my man-trailing experiments with Sleuth, we got to a point where we thoroughly understood each other and while I was immensely pleased at the mutual success we had made, I was rather appalled at the idea of having to put in as much time in training other bloodhounds as I had done with Sleuth.

I had a fine litter of pups from Cymbeline, and they were now old enough for their man trailing to commence. Then it occurred to me that instead of training them myself, why not let Sleuth train them? Especially, as he could do so far better and more quickly than I could by the simple expedient of letting them copy his example.

I started by necking a young hound to Sleuth when he would be trailing Telesfor, and thus he would be dragged along until they got to Telesfor and their reward of "jerky."

The next time this young hound was put with Sleuth to trail, remembering what had happened before, he would run with Sleuth willingly, partly trailing on his own account, and partly running along with Sleuth.

The third time, as he would generally get wise to what was wanted of him, I would un-neck him, and he would not only run with Sleuth, but would run ahead of him and get his "jerky" before Sleuth did.

I did this with each puppy bloodhound, in turn, and it was not long before I had a whole pack of eager man trailers, their enthusiasm kept up to the mark by the certain prospect of getting the "jerky."

By this time, Sleuth was about nine months old, and the younger bloodhounds about four, so after having trained them individually with Sleuth, I began to train them collectively, as a pack. This was in the early fall of 1897. I was unable to bear hunt that fall, as these bloodhounds were too young, and the two or three ordinary hounds I had left, after Dan had taken his, were not sufficiently reliable to justify hunting with them alone.

I had a great deal of work to do at this time, and could

not afford to spare as much time in training the bloodhounds to trail bear as I wished. A solution of the difficulty finally occurred to me. I took Telesfor with me, and we selected eight big trees, which we marked by cutting a number in the bark, each of them being not less than two hundred yards away from the other, the total area comprising about eighty acres.

The idea was that Telesfor, after supplying himself with a small flour sack containing "jerky," was to go to one of the numbered trees, and from there walk in a bee-line to another tree that was numbered, both of which I had previously selected, and nail the "jerky" sack high enough up to be out of reach of the dogs. Then Telesfor could go back to the ranch, and his part of the job would be finished. In this way, I would have a man trail on tap between the two trees, any time I wished to use it.

Consequently, every morning, whenever Telesfor could spare half an hour from his regular work, he would make one of the trails described above. Then, at any time during the rest of the day that it was convenient for me, I could take the hounds to the first, or "start" tree, and put them on the bee-line trail. I would follow along until we came to the "jerky" tree, and then give them their reward.

After the first few days of trailing Telesfor by this new method, the dogs caught on to what I wanted of them, and from then on eagerly carried out my wishes.

I then started to have them trail Telesfor the day after he had made the trail, and after a few days of this, I changed to two-day-old trails. The hounds had no difficulty in trailing, regardless of the age of the trail, up to forty-eight hours, unless there was a change in atmospheric conditions during that time, such as high wind, rain, or snow. I did not try any three-day-old trails, as they would be of no practical use in hunting bear, because long before that time, the bear would be too far away to justify trailing him up.

After a week or two of trials on these bee-line trails, it began to dawn on me that here was a simple solution to a most difficult problem, one that I had been studying for a long time without ever getting anywhere. That was how to set a trail that could be studied at any given time after it was made. Such a trail, either through age or bad weather, often would become so difficult for the hounds to follow that they would give up trying, and I called this the "quitting point." It was this stage of trailing that I especially wanted to study as a reliable basis on which to form correct conclusions; that is, to learn how hounds acted on a cold trail, then on a colder trail, that they could scent in places, and finally, one so cold that they could not trail it at all.

It was in the study of these last three phases of cold trailing that the bee-line method exactly fitted into this trailing picture. It had two distinct advantages from which to draw conclusions. One was that I knew positively, in hours, how old the trail was; and the other, its exact location; that is, that it was on a bee-line between the two selected trees.

This not only afforded me an opportunity to study how a hound acted while he was still just able to trail, but also helped me to judge the merits of each particular hound in comparison with the others.

Another great advantage was that while this bee-line trail could be totally wiped out by heavy snow or rain, thus rendering it difficult, or even impossible for the hounds to follow, this did not, in the least, affect my knowledge of where the trail actually was, or rather, had been.

Consequently, when from any cause the hounds were unable to continue following it, they would stop for me to catch up with them, and I would bridge the gap between where they stopped and the next point where they could pick up the trail again. These gaps were in places that were so exposed to wind and weather that the scent would be totally obliterated. In the sheltered places, enough scent would linger on the grass or bushes to enable the hounds to again pick up the trail until they reached the next gap, when I would again have to come to their assistance, not only giving them fresh encouragement thereby, but heightening their respect for my powers of trailing. In this way, they learned to come back to me when they lost a trail, so that I could help them. This might happen several times before I reached the "jerky" tree. The bag of "jerky" was of great assistance to me in keeping up the morale of the hounds when they reached the "quitting point," and had become discouraged.

One of the most sheltered places where scent would still linger was in the bottom layers of a bed of leaves. The air containing the scent would pass over these leaves, and some of it would sink down between the interstices of the leaves until it got to the bottom, where it would stay. Wind and weather would, of course, dissipate all scent that was in the upper layers or on the surface.

All hounds seem to know this by instinct, so when all else fails, and they spy a bed of leaves, they will run to it, thrust their noses deep down, and if they strike the scent of a wild animal at the bottom, they will bark. But if it be a blood-hound man trailing, he will give a convulsive start. If any other hounds are close to him, they will notice this and run to the same bed of leaves and do just as the first hound had done.

For a trial experiment, to see what the hounds would do under the circumstances, I would select a day, say just after a snowstorm, when all trails were covered with snow and all scent absorbed by it, rendering it impossible for the hounds to trail. I would go to the start of my bee-line trail and follow along it, calling my dogs to me, and telling them to "Go on," and though I had just found a trail for them to follow. As there would be no scent whatever, they would look at me helplessly, as though asking for further instructions, but all they would get would be another "Go on."

There being nothing else left for them to do, they simply ran just ahead of me until finally we would come to the "jerky" tree, where they would get their reward the same as if they had earned it by their own trailing, instead of mine. By this method, no matter how cold the trail might be, or even if they couldn't trail it at all, they did not get discouraged.

In this way, I learned how a hound would both look and act when he found that he was unable to trail. This bit of information was quite important to know, for it prevented me urging a hound to follow a trail that was beyond his capabilities, when hunting bear.

There is a great deal of difference between sight and scent

trailing. One very important point, which I think is seldom realized, is that dogs and human beings view the same things in a totally different way. I have made many experiments along this line, and the opinions I am now about to express are the conclusions I reached on the basis of those experiments.

A person viewing a painting will realize the subject of the picture, as well as its painting; but a dog looking at the same picture will see only the paint. Similarly, if you show the footprint of a bear, made on a smooth piece of ground, to a man, he will immediately identify it as such, and he will also note the direction in which the toes are pointed. But if you show that same footprint to a hound, assuming that there is no scent in it, the hound only regards it as an ordinary piece of ground, without any special significance. There may, however, be an exception to this. In the case of a human footprint, the heel of the boot makes a deep impression in soft ground, and the hound will put his nose in it, thinking that there might be a little scent remaining, because it would be better protected at the bottom than it would be at the surface.

This he does by instinct, but to him, it has no reference to the fact that this depression in the ground is part of a human footprint.

There is an old saying, warning one against jumping to conclusions from false premises; but there is also an antithesis to this which is more than equally true: don't draw false conclusions from correct premises.

Therefore, if a hound puts his nose into the impression made by the heel of a boot, it would be natural to infer that he was doing it because it was a human footprint which he was trailing, and not because it was merely a depression in the ground.

In other words, the fact that the hound put his nose into the footprint was a correct premise, but the conclusion that by so doing he was trying to trail a man by it would be false, since it was a mere coincidence.

For these reasons, it seemed to me incongruous that a man who hunts by sight should take it upon himself to instruct a hound who hunts by scent. But this was precisely what was done by most of the hunters I hired.

For instance, we would strike a very distinct bear track on soft ground, and the hunter would, at once, call his dog to him and urge him to take the trail. But if there was no scent left in the track, naturally the hound would regard it as just another piece of ground.

On the other hand, if there had been any scent in the track, the hound, if he were running loose, would have struck this trail long before the hunter would, and would have followed it without any need of being shown the track by the hunter.

I remember one hunter, in particular, with whom I hunted a good deal. He was a good trailer, and when the hounds could no longer trail by scent, he would endeavour to help them by sight.

I would argue with him that this was useless, for if the hounds couldn't trail by scent, we had better quit that trail and hunt up another.

However, one day he got the better of me—temporarily. We had been following some cold bear tracks that finally led into heavy timber. The hounds, who had been following along with us, suddenly ran ahead, baying furiously, like they would on a hot trail.

We had been leading our horses, so we got on to them and followed the hounds, and after running some two or three miles, the bear was treed.

Well, we shot him out of the tree and the hunter started to skin him. He was very jubilant over the fact that he had stayed with those bear tracks that we had followed all day, notwithstanding my constant requests that we quit them, and hunt up other ones. I took it all quietly, but he kept on rubbing it in until finally I got a little annoyed, and said blandly:

"Are you under the impression that this bear you are skinning is the bear we've been trailing all day?"

"Why, of course!" he said, amazed at such a question.

I pointed: "Look at his hind foot. It's hardly seven inches long. The hind foot of the bear we've been trailing all day was about ten inches long!"

The silence that followed was as dead as the bear!

From the foregoing, it can be realized what an important part mere chance or luck often plays in deciding which conclusions are correct where opinions differ. Had the feet of the two bear been of the same size, the hunter could have reasonably claimed to have been right. From this instance it can be realized how easily false conclusions can be drawn from seemingly correct premises, and this applies not only to bear hunting, but also to our every-day experiences.

Among numerous examples of the latter, I recall one where the other fellow made this mistake, and another where I did. In those days, it took three days by buggy, and five days by wagon to go to our town, Magdalena, which was a hundred miles away. Several of my neighbours would leave standing requests whenever I went to town to bring back a bottle or two of whisky for them. They apologized to me for the trouble it would give me, but explained that whenever they asked others to do this for them, they willingly accepted the commission, but when they returned from town and reached the point of delivery, all the eagerly expectant one would get would be empty bottles, and apologies based on the fact that to have whisky in your possession for from three to five days was far too great a temptation for any human being to resist. This plausible excuse being highly unsatisfactory, a sort of indignation meeting was held to decide what should be done about it.

As some of them were aware that I didn't drink whisky, it was suggested that I be asked to bring whisky out from town for them. This was done, and I replied that I would be glad to accommodate them, little realizing the drawbacks that would accrue to me from such a "good neighbour" policy.

There was an old prospector that I also had to help out. As he camped out all the time, and had to pack his whisky on his burros, bottles were too apt to get broken, so he had to get his whisky in a gallon keg. He told me that hitherto, whenever he got his small keg of whisky, the keg was full, all right enough, but half of the contents would be water. He said that he didn't mind that so much, but, he added plaintively, what he did object to was that it would be filled up with *dirty* water.

The next time I went to town in my buckboard, I was requested to bring back at least a dozen bottles of whisky, as well as the prospector's keg. As the body of a buckboard is all open, anyone can see what goods you have packed in it, so there was no way of hiding the whisky. Taking this into consideration, after packing in all the goods I needed for the ranch, the last thing I did before leaving town was to get the whisky and put it on top of the load, where I could keep my eye on it.

After a few trips to town, it became generally known that every time I left I took out more liquor with me than anyone else. I explained the reason to some, but others who observed the loading of the whisky didn't ask for an explanation. However, that did not prevent them from telling everyone that as I left town with more whisky than anyone else, it followed that I must also drink more than anyone else. Thus exemplifying how false conclusions can be drawn from correct premises.

The other instance wherein I was the one who was guilty of drawing false conclusions happened in this way. I was walking down the street of a small town in winter when I was suddenly hailed by a man standing on top of a stepladder, painting a sign for a Chinese laundry. I recognized him as a man I had often employed as a cook for my mess wagon on round-ups, and as there was no work of that kind in winter, he had to hunt up odd jobs in the small towns to make his living.

"Why, hello, Phil," I exclaimed. "How are you, and what are you doing here?"

"Broke, as usual," he replied, and then, pointing with pride at the sign he had just finished painting in large letters, namely, "Laundrey," he asked:

"What do you think of my work?"

"Perfectly fine," I answered. "But . . ." and I hesitated.

"But what?"

"Well," I said, "I think you are a better painter than you are speller."

"Oh, you mean that extra 'e' in 'laundry' but you are away off on that. I know how to spell the word," he continued with an injured air, "but you see, I have to make all I can out of the jobs I get. On this job I am getting paid so much a letter so that is why I put in the 'e'." Then he added, with a significant wink, "The damned Chink don't know the difference, anyhow!"

CHAPTER IX

TRAILING IN SNOW

So far I have not touched on the subject of scent trailing on the snow. To trail a man or an animal on fresh snow by sight is the one brilliant exception to the rule that trailing by scent beats trailing by sight. A mere child can trail footsteps in the snow, but to a hound these footprints signify nothing beyond the fact that they are depressions in the snow. I had never, hitherto, given thought to the fact that there was any difference between hounds trailing in snow and trailing in a normal way. In the course of time, however, this difference was brought to my attention in purely accidental ways. One day, when I didn't have any hounds with me, I happened to be riding down a long mountain ridge running east and west to the valley below. The trail led down the crest of the ridge except in certain places where there were piles of rocks for a hundred yards or more. The trail skirted these bad places on the north or south side as the case might be. On the north side of this ridge there was timber and brush, but on the south side it was bare. It so happened that there had been a snowstorm the previous day, and as I was going down the ridge I struck the fresh footprints of a bear, that followed the trail down the ridge for some two miles or more. I didn't think anything of it at the time, but a week later I happened to go down this same ridge with some of my hounds. It had been warm weather and all the snow had melted off the crest of the trail and the south side of the ridge, but there was still snow on the north side where it had been shaded by the timber and brush. Although it had thawed, the bear tracks in the melting snow could still be seen distinctly.

As I followed the trail down the ridge, every time I came to one of the places where the trail left the ridge and went through the timber on the north side, my hounds, following closely behind me, would suddenly burst out into full cry and follow the bear tracks on the snow until they came out on the ridge where there was no snow. Then they would run around in circles wondering what had become of the bear trail, and finally come back and follow me until they reached the next similar place. While I didn't pay any particular attention, still I thought it strange that the scent of the bear's footprints should be so strong as to make it a hot trail after a week had elapsed, as evidenced by the excited way in which the hounds ran it.

Some time after this, I took my hounds out for a run and, incidentally, to catch a bobcat, if we should happen to run on to the trail of one. It had snowed the previous night, and the snow was still in a feathery condition. I was riding up a mesa that lay between two canyons that were about a half a mile apart, and along the side of one of the canyons, I suddenly struck the fresh tracks of a bobcat in the snow, which was about four inches deep. These tracks led across the mesa to the other canyon.

I followed them on horseback, and told my hounds to "Go on," thinking they would take the trail of such fresh tracks. But, to my surprise, they paid no attention to the tracks, and only wondered what it was that I wanted them to do. So I gave it up and continued up the mesa.

This was about ten o'clock in the morning, and the temperature was still below freezing. It was a bright, sunny day, and by noon the snow that lay in the direct rays of the sun began to thaw.

When I came back down the mesa, it was about two o'clock in the afternoon, only this time it was at the side of the other canyon, when I again struck the same bobcat tracks that I had crossed at ten in the morning. This time, however, the hounds took the trail at full cry, and in less than a mile they treed the bobcat.

After these two experiences of hounds trailing and not trailing in the snow, I naturally became puzzled. I then remembered that in the past, at different times, some hunters had told me that they had had good luck with their hounds trailing in snow. Others again said they had no luck at all, while still others told me they had good luck one time, but not the next. But none of them could account for these differences.

It was only natural that I should now give this subject serious attention. As in matters of trailing by scent I always thought that my bloodhounds were the best authorities I could consult, I decided to put the problem up to them in such a way that I would be able to understand their explanation.

It was not long before we had another snow at night, so, in the morning, I had Sleuth and three other bloodhounds shut up in a room while I walked out over the snow for about seventy yards and climbed a tree that was easy to climb, because of its many branches. I then whistled, and the dogs were let out of the house and started off in the direction of the whistle. From their actions, they showed that they couldn't trail me at all. They crossed my footprints in the snow several times without paying the least attention to them. They finally passed me, zigzagging in different directions, utterly unable to locate me. After they were off about a hundred yards, I whistled, and they came tearing back in my direction, and two of them actually passed under the tree without ever scenting me.

But a third hound, who was passing my tree, about thirty yards away, suddenly stopped, wagged his tail, and came straight towards me, and looking up into the tree, saw me. It was evident that a gust of wind carried my scent to him on its way to the snow, where it would have been absorbed.

Somehow, the reason for the differing opinions expressed by hunters had never struck me as strange until after my dogs, by their differing actions, brought it to my attention. It was then that the solution of this seemingly complex problem dawned on me, and it was so simple that I was deeply humiliated at not having thought of it before.

The answer was that after a fresh fall of snow, when the snow is still in a feathery state and the temperature below freezing, all scent left by footsteps or in the air seems to instantly permeate the snow, and stay there until the snow thaws, when it is again given out. As long as the snow remains frozen, that scent is held, regardless of the length of time that

125

elapses. But when the thaw does come, the scent emerges at full strength, and when scented by a hound, will then be regarded by the hunter as a hot trail, though it might be a week or more old.

Incidentally, the term "hot trail" is a misnomer. To maintain that it is correct would then be endorsing the paradox that a thing can be kept hot by freezing.

I well remember that when I first announced the discovery of this palpable solution to this problem, it was met by some with that frigid scepticism that is so dear to the heart of the supercilious.

This attitude seemed to me rather foolish, since the proof of it could be so easily demonstrated. Take, for instance, a packet of frozen fish. As long as it remains frozen, there is not the slightest odour to it. But let it thaw, and the scent of the fish is as strong as it was before it was frozen. This goes to prove that as long as it remains frozen, scent loses nothing of its original strength, no matter how long the frozen period might be.

CHAPTER X

FIGHTING DOGS

BECAUSE grizzlies do not climb trees, the idea of fighting dogs first came into being as the only method by which they could be brought to bay. Since no one could ever suggest a better alternative, I was forced to give them a fair trial, which I did for a good many years, finally becoming convinced that it was a hopeless proposition.

I tried one breed after another, but each, in turn, failed to do what was required. Then I tried cross-bred dogs, but with no better success.

The dog that came nearest to what I wanted was a cross between a sheep dog and an ordinary hound. This dog had enough hound in him to make him want to run with the pack, and enough sheep dog in him to fight the bear. I had a few dogs of this kind that worked well with black bear, but not with the grizzly.

Apart from nipping the heels of a grizzly, I have never known any dog that would actually fight him, except a bull terrier. However, it took me some time to find all this out. Irrespective of the breed of the dog, the great objection to this fighting dog method was the fact that the fighting dogs will not run with the hounds, but merely follow the hunter. On the rare occasions when I have caught up with a grizzly on fairly open ground, the fighting dogs were more of a detriment than a help in that they would keep the bear moving continuously, and thus prevent my getting a shot at him, without the risk of hitting a dog.

Most of the grizzlies that I have killed have been killed after they have been run down. But this would not often happen until he had run twenty to forty miles, and then he would stop in a dense thicket. The hounds would bay him from probably thirty to forty yards away, so I couldn't tell exactly where he would be. In order to get a shot, I would have to sneak through the heavy brush without his seeing me until I got within twenty or thirty feet. The approach was made more dangerous by the fact that he might scent me from a distance, and thus be ready for my coming. To counter-balance this I had Twist; but unfortunately there were times, after a long run of many miles, when the little fox terrier couldn't keep up with me. These were occasions when I realized what his absence meant.

I was told that the Russian wolf hounds were very fierce fighting dogs, and since they were powerful and agile, I thought they would be the very dogs to stop a grizzly. They could nip his heels to good effect. This was away back in 1895, when there were practically no wolf hounds in the United States. General Miles, however, kindly loaned me Czar—whom I have mentioned before—for a couple of years. Also, the late Mr. George J. Gould had imported a pair of wolf hounds, and he gave me a female pup out of a litter he had from them. With these two for a start, I bred a whole pack. They were of no use for running grizzlies, because, like the other breeds, they stayed with me instead of running with the hounds. However, I thought I might use them in another direction, that of running antelope on the San Augustine Plains, which lay adjacent to my ranches.

I had been given a greyhound, and I put him in with the pack of wolf hounds, and went on my first antelope hunt by myself, in order to try them out. I started out on the plains with the pack, finally sighting a big buck antelope, which the dogs took after. I galloped several miles, but the antelope ran as fast as the wolf hounds. Only the greyhound caught up, heading him, and forcing him to change his direction. The greyhound, however, had never run anything but jackrabbits, so when he faced the antelope he didn't know what to do. While he was thinking, the antelope turned and went off in another direction. The greyhound then ran after him, and again headed him, and he did this several times.

In the meantime, the wolf hounds and I were trying to catch up. Then suddenly something happened.

My horse put his foot in a prairie-dog hole, and went heels-

Four of my Russian wolfhound pack

Author with Rudolph (*left*), and Sleuth

over-head, luckily throwing me far enough away so that he didn't strike me with his hind feet when he fell.

I was badly shaken up, but not hurt. After a few minutes, I returned to my horse, who had got back on his feet. I crawled up on him, but I was in no condition to continue the chase, so I concluded to call it a day and returned to my camp. The dogs had given up, too, and they came trailing on behind. This was the first and last antelope hunt I ever went on; that is, with hounds.

However, this experience did give me some information on a question I have often heard discussed, namely, the speed of animals. It is generally conceded that the race-horse and the greyhound are the two fastest animals, but it has not been decided satisfactorily which is the faster of the two.

While the running of this antelope could not decide this question, it did offer some new data on which to help draw conclusions.

A friend of mine, while driving his automobile, happened to run on to a bunch of antelope at the mouth of a long canyon up which the road was good. The antelope bolted up the canyon, and he followed up behind, but was careful not to crowd them too closely, as otherwise they might have scattered.

On looking at his speedometer he found that whenever he exceeded forty miles an hour he gained on the antelope, but that whenever he went less than that speed they gained on him. So it can safely be assumed that that is the greatest speed an antelope can run.

In running this buck antelope, my greyhound headed him several times, showing that he could easily outrun him, which would mean that he could run more than forty miles an hour, though not how much faster.

Now the fastest race-horse runs approximately forty miles an hour, but how much faster could he run if he didn't carry the weight of a man on his back? And while this leaves the relative speed of the two still an open question, nevertheless, it does show that they can both run faster than an antelope, who is generally conceded to be the third competitor in the field of fastest animal speed.

As far as running wolves with wolf hounds was concerned,

the trouble was that there were very few lobo, or timber wolves in the country.

Then I tried running coyotes, but it was seldom that they could be seen in the daytime. On a few occasions when I could find one, it wasn't long before it disappeared from view in the brush. A wolf hound can only run what he sees, so as soon as his quarry gets out of sight he gives up.

Also, I tried running jackrabbits with them with some success, although even there, the wolf hounds were not much good, because they cut their feet to pieces on the rough, rocky ground that they usually had to run over.

Anyway, running jackrabbits was not a sport that I could get enthusiastic over, so I gave that up.

I cannot vouch for the authenticity of the following story told to me by a man who had been in Russia and was considered an authority. He said that in that country, wolf hounds were taken out on leash in groups of three, and when they sighted a wolf, they were turned loose. After getting to him, one wolf hound would grab him by one ear, another would grab him by the other ear, and the two of them would hold him while the third hound proceeded to tear out his entrails.

Of course, the ground that the wolf ran over must have been free from brush of any kind; otherwise, the wolf would have got out of sight, and they never would have caught him.

The wolves we had here were timber wolves, and didn't run on the open prairie, so that style of wolf hunting was impossible. Besides, I feel sure that the timber wolf is much bigger and stronger than the Russian prairie wolf. I think if a wolf hound caught a timber wolf by the ear, the latter would turn and kill him before another wolf hound could catch hold of his other ear. In addition, even if the wolf hounds had him by each ear, I don't think they could hold him.

I had a great number of different breeds of dogs. Besides the wolf hounds, I had a great Dane, an English bob-tailed sheep dog, an English mastiff, a greyhound, two Scotch deer hounds, Scotch collies, and a various assortment of terriers, including Scotch, Irish, fox, and bull terriers.

In addition to these, I had some nondescript mongrels, supposed to be good fighters, that were loaned me by neighbours, to try out. People wondered why it was that I had such an extraordinary accumulation of dogs, so I'll have to explain how it came about.

In the course of years, I had a great many friends who had hunted with me at different times, coming from various parts of the United States and England. Knowing that I wanted to get some kind of fighting dog that would meet my requirements, different ones would send me a dog that they thought would suit me, as a memento of their hunt. But, as time went on, I was forced to call a halt on their generosity. I had to tell the subsequent guests who hunted with me that if they ever had the urge to send me a memento of their hunt, to please send a Christmas card but NOT a dog.

But before I called this halt, a friend of mine from New York, who had hunted with me, wrote that if I wanted a great Dane, he could get one from a friend of his who wanted to dispose of his dog to anyone whom he thought would take good care of it. This dog was a female named "Princess," who had taken prizes for dogs of her class at different shows. She weighed one hundred and forty pounds, and was a fine specimen of her breed. My friend went on to explain the reason the owner wanted to get rid of her. On one occasion when his wife's sister, whom Princess did not know, came to visit, his wife met her at the door, and they naturally embraced one another. The next moment Princess, under the impression that her mistress was being attacked, knocked the sister down and stood over her. Well, of course, she screamed, and sustained a severe shock before the dog was hauled off. After this episode, the owner was undecided whether he would keep Princess any longer.

A short time afterwards, this man became very ill, and had to be nursed night and day. His wife took care of him in the daytime, but a professional nurse took her place at night.

The nurse had to wake him, from time to time, to give medicine, so she tapped him gently and leaned over him. Princess, who was in the room, thought her master was being attacked, so she promptly knocked the nurse down, and stood over her, like she had done in the other case.

Luckily, the man's wife was sleeping in the adjoining room

with the door open between, and hearing the nurse's screams, she rushed in and pulled the dog off.

After this, the owner decided that he would *have* to get rid of Princess. He offered to give her to some of his friends, but knowing what she had done, they politely but firmly declined his offer. Finally, he offered this dog to my friend, who replied that he didn't want her for himself, but that he had a friend in New Mexico who hunted bear, and that he was quite sure that he would like to have a great Dane to try out as a fighting dog for bears.

Princess was promptly sent to me. She was very sullen the first few days after she arrived at the ranch, I suppose because of the change of surroundings and being among strangers. But she finally made friends with me, and followed me everywhere.

It was my custom, at the time, to bathe in an irrigation dam near the ranch, and when I bathed, I always took my dogs with me. Of course, I took Princess, too. I dived into the water, and as I came to the surface, I suddenly felt myself grabbed by the shoulder. For a moment, I couldn't think what it was. Then I realized that it must be Princess who had jumped in to "save" me.

I struggled to get loose, but that didn't work, because she only closed her jaws tighter. I was, therefore, obliged to be taken obediently to shore.

The next day when I went to bathe, I tied her up to a tree with a stout chain. After I went into the water, she made such frantic efforts to get loose that I immediately returned to the bank, as I was afraid she would break the chain and rescue me again. After this, I kept her chained at the ranch, so that I could bathe in peace.

Shortly after, I went off on a trip, and was gone for a week. When I returned to the ranch, I got off my horse and started to the house. Princess came bounding out to meet me, and before I could catch my balance, struck me on the chest with her fore paws, knocked me down, and the next moment was standing over me!

Several of my cowboys happened to be standing around and I caught sight of one of them just about to pull his six-shooter.

"Don't shoot," I yelled, "she's only licking my face."

In the future, when Princess rushed out to meet me, I always braced myself sideways, and as she started to jump on me, stepped to one side, and let her go on by. After repeating this performance a few times, she learned to greet me in the ordinary canine way, running up to me expectantly for the pat of approval which she knew she would get.

While Princess was of no actual help to me in bear hunting, I found a way in which she proved of the greatest use. She always ran behind my horse, so close that if I stopped suddenly she would run into his hocks. In training my young bloodhounds I always had them necked, either to each other, or to some other dog, to prevent their running off after deer. So I put an extra ring on Princess' collar, and was thus enabled to neck two hounds to her, one on each side. Whenever one of the young hounds did anything wrong, such as starting to run after jackrabbits, he was immediately scolded and necked to Princess as a punishment, and kept necked until I decided to let him loose.

There were many times when hunting black bear that I would get up to the bear and ride along behind him until he treed, but Princess never ran to the dogs that were barking around the bear. She always stayed by my horse. Not until the bear was dead would she join with the other dogs in "woolling" him, which was a term we used for a dog biting a dead or dying bear, but this did not apply to grizzlies. One experience with a seemingly dead grizzly was enough for Princess! She never forgot the time she was shaken like a rat.

Now as to dogs of other breeds, the Scotch deer hounds acted like the wolf hounds, and were of no use as fighting dogs.

The bull terrier would actually fight a grizzly, and bite him anywhere he could get a hold on him. But, like the rest of the fighting dogs, they didn't run with the hounds; the only time they had a chance to fight a bear was when I was approaching to shoot him.

The most serious drawback to fighting dogs, however, was that they created a constant disturbance among my pack of hounds. Hounds are not quarrelsome, but get along together very well. But I found that these fighting dogs always started a quarrel, either with the hounds, or with each other.

This was vividly brought home to me on one of my early black bear hunts. I had caught up with the hounds just as the bear treed, and my fighting dogs joined the hounds at the tree, which was on a steep hillside and leaned over at an angle. One of the hounds, in his excitement, ran up the tree trunk about six feet, then fell down, and was promptly grabbed by the fighting dogs.

A free-for-all fight started, with about a dozen dogs participating. I jumped off my horse, and ran up to them, but one man alone can hardly part two dogs fighting, and is absolutely helpless with a bunch of dogs.

I looked up at the bear, who was viewing this performance at the foot of the tree with a quizzical expression, and then a simple solution to the problem flashed through my mind.

It struck me that with the involuntary co-operation of the bear I could stop the fight in a couple of seconds. So I simply shot him through the body, so as to cripple, but not kill, him, and he fell on to the ground, just above the pack, ready to scrap.

The dogs at once forgot their quarrels, and jumped on the bear, who, though badly wounded, could put up a pretty good fight, which I was able to stop by putting a bullet through his head with my six-shooter. When things quieted down, the casualties were: one dead bear, one dead hound, and three crippled hounds. Sizing up the situation, I came to the conclusion that this fighting dog theory needed drastic revision!

In training my dogs, I never beat nor whipped them, except for fighting. When one dog jumped on another, I gave the aggressor a cut with the whip I always carried, but seldom used. This did not apply to hounds, for they were not quarrelsome. But the other dogs would fight when they were being fed, so I had to stay with them at feeding time to keep order. Whenever a fight started between two dogs, I had to stop them, but this only postponed the fight for the time being.

Two dogs, in particular, quarrelled continually, and as they were evenly matched, neither would give in, and it was difficult to know what to do under the circumstances.

At last, I hit on a plan that worked well in most cases, and at any rate, in this instance. I had a couple of strap muzzles made, and the next time these dogs started to fight, I stopped them and put on the muzzles, and let them continue their scrap.

The first round of the fight which ensued was fast and furious, lasting until both dogs were out of wind. Then they stopped, and while pausing to get their second wind, only growled at each other.

When the second round started, their fighting was only half-hearted, and they both seemed to be very much discouraged at the negligible results of their efforts. Then they stopped and glared at each other, growling, not understanding what had happened.

But when it came to the third round, their fury had abated, and instead of fighting, they marched off in opposite directions, each one looking back to see whether he was being followed.

So the bout ended in a draw and, after that, these two dogs always avoided each other.

This muzzle method of fighting between dogs may be regarded by some as a case of cruelty to animals, but if dogs must fight, they had much better fight that way than with their bare teeth. Men fighting with boxing gloves often injure one another seriously, and yet that form of fighting seldom excites adverse comment.

While on the subject of curious fights, I think it only fitting to add one at which I was a helpless spectator. It was a fight between a badger and my great Dane, Princess, in which the former won the first round, while the latter won the second and final one.

I was riding along one day, my dogs running loose, when I heard some of them barking at something in the ground. I rode to the spot and found that they were barking at a badger, whose head was at the mouth of a hole. He was hissing at them in the usual way a badger does, but none of the dogs ventured to take hold of him.

On dismounting, I walked up to the hole with Princess at my heels. As this was the first badger she had ever seen, Princess' curiosity was aroused, and unsuspectingly she thrust her head forward, apparently to make a closer inspection.

Suddenly the badger grabbed her by the nose and braced himself in the hole to prevent being pulled out. With a howl of pain, Princess tried to pull back, but as the badger's teeth were firmly anchored in the softer parts of her nose, she abandoned that policy after the first pull. Instead, she pushed her head forward in an effort to grab hold of the badger himself, but she only succeeded in pushing him deeper down into the hole, thus making her own position that much worse.

Then occurred the most extraordinary footwork on the part of a seemingly headless body that I ever saw. It circled round that hole, first one way and then the other, then stopped, while half-stifled, heart-rending howls emerged from the hole!

After a momentary lull, the circular dance continued. I had hitherto flattered myself that in an emergency I was always capable of doing something; not necessarily the right thing by any means, but at any rate, something. But here I was, standing helplessly by the hole, entirely at a loss to know what to do!

It is true that I had a drawn six-shooter in my hand, but what good was that—when the badger was hidden in his pistol-proof shelter, so to speak.

All the dogs were ready to help, but their barking was mere empty talk, as far as helping Princess was concerned! The latter could do nothing but flop around like a hooked fish, although she was many times the weight of the badger!

At long last, the tension was broken by Princess literally breaking loose from the badger's hold—not because the latter had loosened his grip, but because his sharp teeth had cut through the soft flesh of her nose, leaving it in a most horrible condition. This rough treatment had, however, one effect; and that was to fill Princess with frenzied rage.

The head of the badger again appeared at the mouth of the hole, and instantly Princess grabbed his whole head in her mouth, and then, bracing herself with her front feet on either side of the hole, pulled back with her full might.

The tables were now turned, for while Princess could not bite the badger on the first round, in the second the badger couldn't bite Princess, his whole head being in her mouth, and his jaws clamped shut by her jaws. This time Princess could pull back without hurting her nose, but the badger had braced

136

himself so well in the hole that she could not pull him out, at first.

After several ineffectual attempts, she sat back on her haunches, and using her front feet as leverage, she pulled back, swaying from side to side.

Suddenly the badger lost his grip, causing Princess to fall over backwards, letting go of the badger, while the latter was sent flying through the air. Princess then scrambled to her feet, just in time to nose the badger over on to his back as he was bolting back to his hole, and grabbed him by the throat, a hold which she never relaxed until he was dead.

She was then ably assisted by the bull terriers, who seized hold of any other parts of the badger that were available for them to grab.

After the fight was over, Princess began to feel very sorry for herself. Dogs heal their wounds by licking them, but this treatment was denied her, as her tongue was not long enough to reach her nose, although she kept on trying to do so. She would not let me help her in any way, for whenever I tried to put salve on her nose, she would run away. After a while she would come back, and sit and look at me from a safe distance; that is, far enough off so that if I attempted to grab her by her collar, she would have a good start to get away. There was, therefore, nothing to be done about curing her nose, except to let Nature take her course. And that Nature did, but she took her own time about it!

In the meantime, the nose swelled up to an extraordinary size, which, combined with her cropped ears, gave her a grotesque appearance, reminding one of a gargoyle.

From time to time after this, the dogs caught other badgers, but just as soon as Princess discovered what they were fighting, she showed no further interest in the fight. The fact was that she had become "badger-shy."

As to my cross-bred dogs, I was under the unhappy delusion that a cross between Czar, the wolf hound, and Princess, the great Dane, would produce dogs of great fighting ability, and so I got a litter of four pups. I watched them grow with great interest, as this combination for a real fighting dog seemed ideal. A dog with the agility of the wolf hound and the rugged strength of the great Dane, would be a combination hard to beat for a fighting dog, and this proved to be only too true.

To my dismay, I discovered that I had created a canine Frankenstein.

While these dogs were puppies, they didn't do much harm, but when they got to be eight or ten months old, they began to demonstrate their aggressive tendencies on innocent victims. As long as an animal walked, he was perfectly safe, but should he quicken his pace, these "Devil Dogs," as I called them, would take out after him. If it were a horse or a cow, the unfortunate animal would be pulled to the ground, and if it were a dog, he would be killed.

Finally, I became convinced that I could do nothing with them. Taken singly, these dogs could be controlled to a great extent, though as a pack, they were quite unmanageable. So I gave them away to my neighbours, and they proved successful as watch dogs, and in fighting off marauding coyotes.

CHAPTER XI

SLOW-TRAIL OR LIAISON DOGS

WHEN I found that fighting dogs were of no practical use to contact the hunter with the bear, the idea occurred to me, "Why not train a dog to trail the pack when the latter gets out of hearing?" There was no question but that the idea was excellent, but the problem was, how to carry it out.

A long procession of ideas coursed through my mind, but all had to be rejected for one reason or another, so it was difficult to make any headway. Naturally, I started to train one hound, but I could not make that work.

In trying this out, I necked a bloodhound to Princess, who ran behind my horse. Then I would ride after the pack when they were trailing, and when they got out of hearing, I would unneck the hound, and let him take the trail of the pack. This he did only too well, for he also soon ran out of my hearing and joined the pack, but this did not help me. I couldn't blame him for it, and there was no feasible way of punishing him so that he would understand why he was being punished.

I then tried several hounds, in turn, with the same unsatisfactory result. After a few months, I had to give it up. I realized it was hopeless to expect to have any success with a full-blooded hound, so I thought I would breed a cross-bred dog, half bloodhound and half English bob-tailed sheep dog, the idea being that there would be enough sheep dog in him to make him want to stay with me.

While mentally debating the advisability of trying such a cross, I told some of my candid friends about my failure in getting a bloodhound to trail the pack, and yet stay with me. One of them who was addicted to wise-cracking, suggested, facetiously, that if I could not succeed with just one dog, why not try two? There was a general laugh at my expense, but I answered: "Thanks for the suggestion. I believe I'll try it."

At that time, I was training my young bloodhounds not to run deer, and to accomplish this purpose, I necked them together in pairs, as in that way, you have far greater control over them. If a pair should start to run off on a deer trail, you could head them off on horseback and stop them. Whereas, if you tried to head one dog, by himself, he would simply run under your horse, and be gone.

When I first started to neck the young hounds together, they gave me considerable trouble, because they would run side by side, and when running through brush, they would get entangled, so I would have to get off my horse and free them. This running side by side didn't make any difference on open ground, but to get through brush, it was necessary for one of them to take the lead, while the other followed him, throwing his head over the lead dog's back, and forming a sort of wedge, which enabled them to go ahead as if they were just one dog. To determine which should be the lead dog was up to each pair of necked hounds. At first, they would quarrel over this, but before long, one or the other of them would become boss, and take the lead, and with that question once settled, there was no further risk of their getting entangled in the brush.

It was, therefore, only natural that the same pairs of dogs should be selected every time they were necked, to avoid the boss question having to be settled all over again.

Due to the same dogs being necked together every time, it followed that they became special friends, and they would continue to run together when not necked, so that whenever you saw one of a pair of dogs without seeing the other, you could, nevertheless, be quite sure that he was somewhere right close.

The idea then struck me, why not turn the friendship of one dog for another to practical use?

It was this very idea that my wise-cracking friend had unintentionally suggested to me. So after I got a cross-bred litter of puppies, I selected two of them to be my slow-trail dogs. I not only necked them when I would be taking the hounds out for a run, but I left them necked all the time. In this way, they became great friends, and continued to be inseparable, even when not necked. When they grew old enough, I took them out with the pack on its regular run, and this was often on long summer evenings, after I had got back from my work.

And thus, I began the training of my slow-trail dogs, or as they should be called, "liaison dogs."

After I had thoroughly trained my bloodhounds to trail domestic animals, as well as men, I thought it was time to switch over and trail wild animals, of which, in this case, lynx, or bobcats as they are generally called, were the most available. There were a great many in the surrounding country, one reason being that I had several herds of sheep running near the ranch, which these bobcats would follow, to steal young lambs whenever they got a chance. I frequently ran on to the legs and heads of lambs, the remnants which they left behind them.

Among the few hounds I had when Dan left me, was one called a coon dog, which had been sent me from Arkansas. This dog was very good at trailing bobcats, so I took him along with my pack for a "start" dog for the first few times.

I well remember the first bobcat that we caught. I ran on to the remains of his meal on the ground. The coon dog and Sleuth were just ahead of my horse, while the rest of the pack was behind me. As soon as the coon dog reached what was left of the lamb, he scented the bobcat's trail, and started off in full cry. At the same time, I shouted to Sleuth to "Go on," which he promptly did, following the coon dog and barking, this being the first time he had ever bayed on an animal's trail. Hitherto he had only trailed domestic animals, on whose trail he did not bay. But this was a wild animal. It seems strange that a bloodhound should make a distinction between domestic and wild animals by baying on the trail of the latter and not of the former, but that is what they do.

I then got off my horse and unnecked each pair of hounds, who bolted after Sleuth as soon as they were turned loose, and, after about a mile, the bobcat was treed.

As time went on, the hounds caught a great many bobcats, and in this way got a lot of training in trailing wild animals.

As soon as my slow-trail dogs, whom I had named Panther and Wolf, got to be about eight months old, I began my experiments in slow-trailing with them. They had always been accustomed to being necked together, but the first time I wanted to try them out on a bobcat trail, I necked them to Princess, one on each side.

When the hounds started on a trail, I unnecked Panther, and he started off after the pack, but when he had got about a hundred yards, he stopped. It was the first time in his life that he had ever been separated from Wolf, and he was at a loss to know what to do. Finally, he decided to come back to Wolf, to get him to join in trailing the pack. As Wolf was necked to Princess he couldn't do this, so at my urging, Panther started off after the pack again. He continued with this alternate "to and fro" stunt until he reached the tree where the bobcat was being bayed.

Needless to say, I was intensely gratified at this first try-out of the slow-trail dogs. The next time we ran a bobcat I turned Wolf loose, leaving Panther with Princess, and he acted the same as Panther had. From then on, I used this method, until I felt confident that I could turn them both loose, and depend on their staying with me, and not running to the pack.

I would like to emphasize here that I trained these slow-trail dogs to run a pack of hounds, but that had nothing to do with the kind of animal the pack was trailing, whether it was a panther, bobcat, or bear. Consequently, when I felt that the slow-trail dogs were trained to run a pack that was trailing a bobcat, they were also trained to run a pack that was trailing a bear, which was my sole aim in the first place.

It is only fair to say that the credit for the change of catching grizzlies from the "hit or miss" principle to that of reasonable certainty should be given to these slow-trail dogs. While Sleuth and his fellow bloodhounds carried out their parts with the greatest efficiency, nevertheless, they didn't solve the problem of keeping me in contact with the hounds, when the latter got out of hearing.

Roughly speaking, I figured that under the former method, the chances of catching a grizzly with ordinary hounds was 15 per cent for, and 85 per cent against, success, while with the aid of the slow-trail dogs, the percentage was exactly reversed.

The 15 per cent representing failure was due to darkness coming on before reaching the bear, and at other times, a sudden heavy rain or a big snow storm made it impossible to continue the chase. I have used the term, "reasonable certainty," for the 85 per cent chance of success.

CHAPTER XII

BRONCO-BUSTING

THE EASY VERSUS THE HARD WAY

IN hunting grizzlies it is important to have a good horse. By
a good horse, I mean one that embraces the two extremes of
being high-spirited on the one hand, and being gentle as a
dog, as the expression is, on the other.

I had two horses, George and Roaney, and one mule, Gyp,
that met these two requirements in the highest degree. To
keep them always in tip-top condition, I only rode them on
the hunts which I figured would be the hardest, using other
horses for all ordinary rides. These two horses and my mule
I regarded as my pets, and they were treated accordingly.

The word "pet" is commonly used in an invidious sense;
that is, it implies that undue favour is shown. In the case of
horses, a man will not ride his pet horse when an extra tough
job of riding comes along, but will use his other horses instead.
My way of doing was just the opposite. Making pets was
always a hobby of mine, it mattered not whether it were
horses, dogs, cats, calves, or even geese.

Regarding George, Roaney, and Gyp, it goes without
saying that such animals would have to be broken in with
the greatest of care in order to insure fulfilment of the two
requirements mentioned above. Frankly, I am strongly opposed to the customary Western method of breaking horses;
that is, by hiring a so-called "bronco-buster" to break them
for you. From my perhaps prejudiced standpoint, I always
thought that all a bronco-buster ever did in breaking a
high-spirited horse was to break the only thing he shouldn't
have broken, and that was his spirit. While for the rest, by
his rough treatment, he simply ruined the horse by develop-

144

On trust

Isn't the time nearly up?

ing in him bad habits which he never would have acquired otherwise.

By bad habits, I mean the following: when tied up, for him to suddenly run on the rope and break it, and then run off so that you might be put to a lot of trouble in catching him again. When a horse once does that, and knows that he can break the rope, he is very apt to do it again and again, whenever he sees an opportunity. To my mind such a horse is worthless for practical use. The same thing applies when he is tied up with a bridle. He may jerk his head loose, and run away like he did when he was tied with a rope.

Other horses, again, will never stand still for you to put your foot in the stirrup and mount them. They will either twist around towards you, and when you have one foot in the stirrup, will tread on the other foot before you have time to lift it from the ground; or they will twist away from you, and come pretty near knocking you down, and you are lucky if they don't whirl around and kick you, in addition.

Such horses as these are hypothetically supposed to be broken, from the standpoint of the bronco-buster who is supposed to have broken them.

The regular charge, in those days, for breaking horses was ten dollars a head, and the bronco-buster was supposed to ride the horse until he quit pitching when you mounted. At that point, he would consider his part of the job finished, and the rest of the breaking was assigned to the cowboy who was given this horse to ride.

I had a great many horses at one time, probably as many as two hundred saddle horses for working the cattle, and as many mares, running on the open range, who supplied me every year with enough three-year-old colts to take the place of saddle horses which had either been crippled or had died, or were too old for further use. Consequently, I had some thirty or forty colts to break every spring, and for that purpose I had to hire a bronco-buster. Owing to this annual, compulsory job of breaking young colts, I learned a great deal about horses. Broke cow ponies were at a premium at the time of which I am speaking, and there were practically none for sale. So cattle men were forced to break all their own colts bred from the mares they might happen to have. It was customary for colts to be broken in the spring, and it was difficult to hire bronco-busters at that time, since there was such a demand for them.

It so happened, one spring, that the bronco-buster my cattle foreman had hired at that time, got thrown a day or two after he started to break my annual bunch of colts—some thirty head. He was pretty badly hurt, and it was thought that he couldn't possibly ride again for at least a month. I talked the matter over with my foreman, but we could reach no decision. He was clever enough to get out of his part of the difficulty by saying that it was *his* job to run the outfit, and it was *my* business to supply the horses. He had no suggestions to make, and the problem was left entirely up to me.

At last an idea occurred to me, and after thinking it well over, I could not see why it wouldn't work, so I went to my foreman and told him about it. He was very non-committal and while he could not positively tell me that it wouldn't succeed, he assured me it was so contrary to the customs of the country that if I tried it, I would only be laughed at. I didn't altogether like his answer, but I replied that all I cared about was that the plan should meet with success. As to being laughed at, I regarded that as immaterial.

Included in the equipment that I bought with a farm were a threshing machine and an eight horse-power to run it. In those days, about the middle eighties, horse-powers were used where power was needed. It was not till later that farm portable steam engines came into use.

This eight horse-power of mine had four sweeps, and to the end of each of these a team of horses was attached, and thus, you had your eight horse-power machine ready for work.

Each team was tied by a rope to the sweep ahead of it, in order to keep the two horses in place, the horses, of course, walking around in a circle.

My plan was to use gentle, old farm horses to work on the outer ends of the sweeps, while the broncos, which I expected to break, would be put on the inside nearest the centre of the machine. In this way, each bronco would be surrounded, on the outside by a farm horse, in front and behind by sweeps, while the driver hemmed him in on the fourth side.

The first time I started up the horses, I only put in one bronco. I used an inch tie rope, tying one end round the sweep, and the other round the horse's neck. This rope was too stout for him to break, and its length was so adjusted as to prevent his rearing more than a few inches from the ground, thus stopping him from bucking. A harness was also put on him, the traces fastened to a singletree, which was attached to a doubletree, and that, in turn, was attached to the sweep. Then, when all was ready, the driver of the horse-power shouted, "Get up," and the old, broken horses started walking around in a continuous circle.

I watched to see what he would do, which wasn't much, for the simple reason that he couldn't buck, because one end of the inch rope was attached to the sweep in front of him. The other end, being round his neck, held his head down. If he pulled back, he was dragged forward by the same rope, and by the combined power of all the other horses pulling on the ends of their respective sweeps.

On the other hand, if he tried to run away, he would merely be pulling the horse-power around all by himself, thus relieving the other horses of their share of the work.

As a rule, it took but a few minutes for the horse to realize his helplessness, and then he would go along quietly like the old farm horses did, especially as there was nothing to scare him.

After half an hour, I put in the second bronco, who acted just about the same as the first one, and when he had quieted down I put in the third and then the fourth. In less than two hours I had four broncos being broken at the same time. The horse-power method broke four horses in less time than a bronco-buster could break one. Considering the number of broncos I had to break, this made quite a difference, not only in the matter of time, but of expense.

Just as horses differ from one another, so the time it took to break them differed in proportion to whether they were naturally gentle or high-spirited, the latter taking the longest time to break. It took less than a month to break the thirty broncos. I found that, on an average, it took three days to break one, the naturally gentle horses taking only two days, while the high-spirited ones would take four or five.

On the second day a gentler horse would have a saddle put on him. While at first he would be restive and appear not to like it, he soon got used to it, and regarded the saddle as sort of extra harness equipment. After he seemed to be thoroughly accustomed to it, the driver would get into the saddle, and tell the horses to "Get up," and the horse-power would again revolve.

All the broncos acted pretty much alike when the rider got on their saddles for the first time. They would jump around a bit, that being all they could do, and finally they seemed to accept the situation, the same as they did when the saddles were put on their backs. When quitting time came, the rider would stay on the horse while someone else unhooked the traces and untied his rope, and then the bronco would be ridden up to the barn where the horses were fed at night.

Not one of these thirty broncos ever tried to pitch when thus ridden from the horse-power. As they had never been roughly handled, they weren't the least frightened of a man when he went around them; nor would they attempt to kick when someone walked behind them.

This bad habit of kicking could be cured by a simple method. After the bronco was first put into the horse-power and had quieted down, I took a piece of inch rope of suitable length and made a knot in one end, about four inches in diameter. The other end I tied on to the crupper of the harness on one side, its length being adjusted so that the knot was on the same level as his fetlock. A similar rope was hung from the other side of the crupper, so that there would be a knot touching each fetlock of the horse's hind legs. As soon as the horse-power was started up, and the horse began walking, he would lash out at these knots dangling round his fetlocks, first with one hoof and then the other. But the knots would come back and hit his fetlocks every time.

Some broncos would quit kicking after a few kicks, and become resigned, while others would kick viciously and continuously for half an hour or so but give up the unequal

148

contest at last. Judging from my subsequent experience, this was a sure cure for kicking horses.

In the thirty days it took me to break my broncos, I think I learned more about horses than I would have in thirty years, under ordinary conditions. I found that about half of the thirty broncos didn't need breaking at all. They needed intelligent handling. They never offered to pitch, and their restiveness was entirely due to timidity.

These horses, although excellent in their way, were not the best in the bunch. The best ones were those that were the most high-spirited, and therefore, the hardest to break. This did not necessarily mean that they were vicious, but in my experience I found that the majority of so-called "vicious" horses were made so by the mistreatment they received while being broken. The most high-spirited of horses can become the most gentle by kind treatment, the only difference in breaking them being the length of time. In my opinion, conventional methods are not applicable to the breaking of such horses. It is asking too much to expect to break them to the saddle all in one stage, instead of three, as I did with the horse-power method.

In the case of a small pony weighing about seven hundred pounds, and a heavy man weighing two hundred pounds, the resistance offered doesn't amount to much; but when it comes to a nine-hundred-pound bronco, it is a very different matter, the advantage being now on the side of the horse. He may break away, or pitch his rider off, both of which things he will regard as a victory. In order to break this horse, his rider must remount him, stay on his back and beat him into submission, a procedure not calculated to establish cordial relations between the two! From this time on, the horse naturally regards man as his enemy. There is also too great a risk of injury to the rider.

In the horse-power no man is apt to be injured, while the horse, being secured in the machine, cannot hurt himself, nor acquire any bad habits. Any rough treatment he gets is his own doing.

This method became the talk of the country, and excited the interest of all the cattle men, causing a great deal of comment, most of which was anything but flattering. Some of them would tune in on the grapevine circuit of gossip, and then come and tell me what they had heard. Needless to say, there was nothing lost in the telling.

In one particular case, some facetious remarks were made about the horse-power by a neighbouring ranchman, for whom, in the past, I had done many small favours. Two years before, this ranchman had hired a bronco-buster to break some young horses, among them a very fine sorrel. After he had been saddled, this horse cut up so badly that the bronco-buster concluded to turn him loose, and work on the other horses first, and when he got through with them, he conveniently forgot all about the sorrel.

The next year, the sorrel was rounded up and brought in with the others. When it came his turn to be ridden, the bronco-buster, the same one who had been hired the year before, recognized the horse, and this time refused even to saddle him. Rather than have the sorrel turned loose for another year, the owner offered the bronco-buster twenty dollars—twice the usual price—to break him; and when this offer was declined, he made a standing offer of twenty dollars to anyone else who would break him.

This sorrel, now five years old, always ran with a bunch of my mares and colts, and he was brought in with them to the corral. I told my men to catch him at the first chance and bring him to the horse-power, and I would see what I could do in the way of breaking him.

It took three men to rope him, drag him to the horse-power, and harness him. When the machine started up, he did considerable jumping around, alternately pulling back and trying to run away. After a few minutes of strenuous but fruitless effort, he quieted down. Then he broke out into another spell of trying to get loose; but no matter what he did, he was forced to keep going until quitting time. He was given this treatment for three eight-hour days, at the end of which he subsided and walked along, just as the other horses did.

On the fourth day I put a saddle on him, and also the two knotted kicking ropes, as I called them. Though he didn't seem to mind the saddle, he objected vigorously to the rope knots hitting his fetlocks. He kicked at them, first one, and then the other; and as that didn't seem to help, he kicked them simultaneously, which made matters even worse for him. After about an hour, he was convinced that his best policy was to pay no attention to the knotted ropes, and from then on, you couldn't get a kick out of him.

For four days he remained in his place in the horse-power, where he was fed and watered. He was not taken up to the barn to be fed, like the other horses were, for the reason that the less he was manhandled during his first days of being broken, the better.

In addition to hay, I fed him oats from a pail. At first he didn't know what they were, but after sniffing a few times, he tasted them, and it wasn't long before all the oats were gone. After that, when given his choice, he always ate the oats first.

It is said that the way to a man's heart is through his stomach, which seems to apply also to horses. The first day, the sorrel snorted every time I came near him, but after the third day, which was the first day I gave him oats, the snorting gradually changed to a whinny; and on the fourth day, he seemed to welcome my arrival with his feed, and allowed me to pat him on the neck, and from then on, I realized that he did not have a single vicious trait. On the contrary, he was most friendly, though he was still unduly scared of a human being.

He knew me so well by the fifth day that he was not frightened when I got into the saddle, and when the horse-power started up, and he began to walk with me on his back, he didn't seem to know quite what to do. But as nothing alarming happened, he offered no objection to my presence, and before long he regarded the whole thing as a matter of course.

I rode him for some four hours that day, and in the evening, when we quit work, I had one of the cowboys unhook the traces and untie the neck rope, and he followed the other horses up to the barn, forgetting that I was still on his back. After this, I kept him in the stable for three or four days, riding him a little every day, and he behaved as any other gentle horse would.

I then decided to deliver the horse to his owner, who knew nothing of my experiments with him, so taking another horse with me to come back on, I rode to his ranch, some six miles distant. When I reached there, and approached the ranch house, I saw him standing on the porch, and as I drew closer, I observed a look of surprise on his face.

His first words were: "I've got a dead mate for that horse you're riding!"

"I'm sorry that I can't agree with you," I replied, "but I don't think you have. Suppose you come down and look at this horse from the side."

He stepped down from the porch, and when he caught sight of his own brand on the sorrel's hip, he exclaimed: "Why, that *is* my horse."

"Of course it is," I answered. "That's why I wanted you to look at his brand."

For a moment he was speechless. Then he blurted out: "Is he gentle?"

"Certainly," I said, "or I wouldn't be riding him. You remember you made a standing offer of twenty dollars to anyone who would break this horse. So I took the liberty of catching him and working my horse-power racket on him. You can see the result."

I turned his horse over to him and got on my own horse. As I prepared to leave, he stopped me, saying: "Hold on a minute, until I can write a check for the twenty dollars I owe you."

"Never mind," I replied, "I am already well paid in the fact that I have broken a horse that no bronco-buster cared to tackle." And I added amiably: "If you feel you'd like to do me a favour in return, just give a good word for my horse-power method."

With that, I left, and I can still see his puzzled expression in my mind's eye. Of course, he hadn't the least idea that I had heard of the derisive remarks he had made.

It was something like a week later that I chanced to meet him, riding the sorrel. He was enthusiastic in his praises. But a few days later, when I again met him, he was riding another horse.

So I inquired: "What's the matter with the sorrel? Have you quit riding him?"

"Yes," he replied diffidently, "I have. I've sold him for sixty dollars," twice the average price at that time.

"Why," I exclaimed, "I thought you said you were going to keep him for your pet horse."

"I was," he explained apologetically, "but you see, everyone joshed me about riding a horse-power broke horse. I just couldn't stand it, and then a stranger came along and stopped the night with me, and he liked the looks of him so much that he offered me sixty dollars for him, and with that money I bought this horse, and now I can ride around in peace."

After I got through breaking the thirty broncos, I turned them over to my foreman to distribute among my cowboys. They were accepted by all without comment, and, as I heard no complaint, I took it for granted that they met with their approval.

The bronco-buster, who had been hurt soon after taking the contract to break these horses, had now recovered. He had stayed with me all during the month, and had watched the breaking of the horses with the greatest interest.

"Tell me candidly," I asked, "what do you think of this method of breaking horses? I will be very grateful for any practical suggestions for improvement."

"I ain't got no suggestions to offer," he replied. "That horse-power racket of yours worked fine."

As he had lost a whole month's work through being injured working for me, I thought it was up to me to help him if I could.

"Look here," I said, "I'll loan you this horse-power and the four gentle, old horses, and you can drive around the country and break broncos for all the different cattlemen who have horses to break in this section of the country. You could make a good deal more money at it because you can break four broncos at a time in the horse-power. Besides that, you would not be taking any more chances of getting hurt."

He looked at me for a moment with an expression of gratitude. "I sure thank you for your offer, but I can't accept it, though I would like to. You see," he went on, pathetically, "your position is different from mine. You can tell anybody who don't like your way of doing to go to hell, but I can't. I have to work for a living, and I have to please the people I work for. But if I went to any cattleman's ranch with that outfit to break his horses, he'd run me off with a shotgun."

This man never treated a horse rougher than he could help. It was for this reason that I had selected him to break my horses. I liked him very much personally, and I regret to say that some three years later I heard he was thrown from a bronco and died from his injuries.

The next year I abandoned the use of the horse-power. Although my foreman admitted its efficiency in breaking horses, my outfit had become the laughing-stock of the surrounding country, and he, being my foreman, thought some of the ridicule reflected upon him, and this injured his pride.

I thoroughly appreciated his point of view, and as he was an excellent foreman, I concluded the matter was not worth a dispute. So I told him to hire a bronco-buster and carry on according to the custom of the country.

Though this incident was closed, my bronco-busting troubles were not ended, for I was unable to avoid having trouble with the next bronco-buster he hired.

A friend in the East wrote me that his young son was eager to spend part of his school vacation at a cattle ranch, so, at my invitation, the boy was to come west to visit me. My young guest was to arrive in Magdalena at a time when I was too busy to meet him, so I arranged with the hotel keeper to look out for him and send him to me at the first opportunity.

Bronco-busting was in full swing at the time he was brought out to my ranch, but I was away for the day, and was not on hand to welcome him. Upon my return the next day, I found that my guest had arrived, and I was told that he was in his room lying down. When I inquired the reason, one of the boys replied, with a grin, that the boy had been given a horse to ride, which he mounted unsuspectingly only to be promptly pitched off, and while he was not injured seriously, he was badly bruised.

Feeling quite concerned about the boy, I went in to see him, and when he told me his version of the story, I learned that the new bronco-buster was the one who had got the joke off on him.

I was relieved to know that it was not one of my own cowboys, though I felt sure that not one of them would have been guilty of treating a guest of mine in such a way. Naturally, I was angry, but I was careful not to show my annoyance and said nothing about the matter that day.

The next morning, accompanied by young friend, who was just able to limp along, I went down to the corral to see a bunch of my mares, with their unbroken colts, that had been brought in earlier in the morning. There I found quite a gathering of men in the corral, and several more perched on the fence.

The bronco-buster was ready to ride, and most of the spectators were neighbours who had come to see the broncos pitch.

Among the broncos was one called "Railroad," because he was "long and narrow." He was a long-legged, five-year-old, black horse, with a Roman nose. He weighed about nine hundred pounds, and was, therefore, much bigger than the average three-year-old colt, who weighed around seven hundred and fifty pounds.

Two years before he had been saddled, but he was so vicious that the bronco-buster refused to ride him, and he was turned loose.

The following year, which was the year I used the horse-power, he couldn't be found. Had he been, he certainly would have been put in the horse-power.

This year, however, he showed up among the mares and colts brought to the corral that very morning, and it was not long before I caught sight of him.

With the group of men looking on curiously, I approached the bronco-buster, who by this time was aware of my presence, and said casually: "Yesterday you showed the boys how a tenderfoot from the East couldn't ride a bronc, so," pointing to my young friend, "I've brought him up here now to have a professional Western bronco-buster show him how *he* can stay on a pitching bronc. There's a black horse over there

155

that we call Railroad, and I would like for you to ride him."

The boys had told him that Railroad was considered the meanest bronco in the country, and my proposal evidently startled him. He looked at me steadily for a moment or two, then sneered:

"So you'd ask a man to ride a horse you'd be afraid to ride yourself, would you? No, I guess *I* won't ride him."

The interested onlookers sensed that I had been adroitly put on the spot, and there was an involuntary titter which I didn't fail to hear.

Without replying, I turned on my heel, and called to three of my cowboys to rope Railroad.

One of the boys questioned me in a low voice: "What's the big idea? You don't propose to ride him, do you?"

"I've got to," I replied, dejectedly, "there's no other way out."

Between the three of them they caught Railroad and threw him to the ground, while I asked another cowboy to bring my saddle and bridle, and after he had brought it, we blindfolded the horse, and he scrambled to his feet. Then he was saddled, the bridle was put on, and the reins looped over the saddle-horn. One of the boys held him by the bridle-bit, waiting for me to mount, and when I was in the saddle, he let go and pulled off the blindfold.

From then on I don't know what happened, except that I held on to the horn of the saddle for dear life.

Suddenly Railroad came to a standstill, and I seized this opportunity to get off his back, leaving him to pitch with the empty saddle in a manner which was most discouraging to any later aspirant to bronco-busting honours.

For the time being I was dazed and one of the boys grabbed me to prevent my falling. When I could speak, the first question I asked was, "How long did he pitch?" And someone replied, "Oh, about ten seconds or so." But it seemed more like ten minutes to me.

In a moment or two, after I felt I had returned to normal, I walked over to the bronco-buster.

"It's your turn to ride Railroad now," I said, and I was gratified to hear a second titter from the crowd.

The bronco-buster was silent, for a moment, then he started away, muttering:

"I guess we'd better go and settle up."

So we settled up.

He left shortly thereafter, so horse-breaking activities had to stop until a bronco-buster could be found to take his place. My foreman was anything but pleased at this delay, but my advice to him was that if he wished to avoid delays in the future, he had better stipulate with the next man he hired that his duties did not include playing jokes on tenderfoot visitors.

This unsatisfactory experience with Railroad further convinced me that the horse-power was the better method of handling such a bronco. I ventured this suggestion to my foreman, but he was adamant and wouldn't budge. However, I couldn't help thinking that if he had to break the broncos himself, instead of having a bronco-buster, paid by me, to do it, he might have been more inclined to agree with my view. There was no point in arguing with him. He might have quit, and I would have found it difficult to replace him at short notice. Furthermore, changing foremen would not have solved my problem, as a new man would have, most likely, objected just as strenuously to the use of the horse-power.

There was a sad sequel to the story of my brief but close acquaintance with Railroad. Some weeks later, after my bronco-busting experience, while riding over the range with some of my cowboys, we observed a dead animal in the distance. As we rode closer, we wondered and, sure enough, it *was* Railroad! With a neat little bullet hole between his eyes!

Meditatively I remarked: "I wonder who could have done *that*?" And my companions grinned knowingly.

"Maybe," drawled one, "it was some fellow who thought you might ask him to ride that bronc."

I never kept a horse for my own use that I had to watch, for as long as you can get a perfectly gentle horse, why bother with one that isn't? It seems impossible to break horses of some habits. Other habits, again, are broken more easily than one would think.

157

I always had a weakness for trying to break horses of bad habits; not only my own horses, but those of my friends, and occasionally I was surprised at my own success. I recall one time a friend had a horse that invariably tried to run away just as soon as you urged him to canter.

"If that horse were yours," asked my neighbour, "what would you do about it?"

"I don't exactly know," I answered, "but I think there is a plan that might work, if you would let me try it."

"Go ahead, by all means," he said. So I mounted the horse and borrowed his quirt. I do not believe in whipping horses, but circumstances alter cases.

I started off quietly, and then broke into a canter, and when the horse started to run away, I offered no objection but let him run as hard as he could. When he had run about five miles, he decided he had had enough. He slowed up, and I turned him round and headed for home.

Up to this time, he had set the pace, but now I thought it was my turn. So as he slackened his pace, I whipped him, and I kept on whipping him at intervals until I got back. My waiting friend had been anxious about my delay, so I had to explain how far his horse had run away before getting tired of running. I told him that I didn't think he would be inclined to run away again in a hurry, but to let me know. As a matter of fact, this horse never repeated his bad habit.

Some time later, I had a humorous experience with a balky horse. I had a good buggy team, and one of them died. In looking around for a mate for the other, I found that a neighbour of mine had just the horse I wanted. I had heard that the horse balked, but I concluded to go and have a look at him, anyhow, with the view of buying.

On arriving at his ranch, I asked the owner if he would sell the horse, and mentioned that I had heard he balked.

"Yes," he said, "he does, but I will sell him, and sell him cheap."

"Will you sell him for half price," I asked, "that is, half what he would be worth if he didn't balk?"

He agreed, so we traded, the price being forty dollars instead of eighty. I regarded the deal as a sort of even bet. If I cured the horse of balking, I won forty dollars; and if I didn't, I lost that amount.

As I was leaving with the horse, his late owner gave me some advice.

"Beating him for balking," he said, "didn't work, for I've beaten him a-plenty." This statement was confirmed by the way the horse had backed away from me when I first approached him.

Then he continued: "There's one way to get a move on him when he balks, and that is, put some newspapers under his hind legs and set fire to them. Then get back in the seat of the buggy and wait for him to get going."

I thanked him for his suggestion, which did not exactly meet with my approval, though I had no doubt it would be successful.

On returning to the ranch, I put the horse in the stable and fed him myself for the next few days, so that he should become acquainted with me and make friends.

He seemed to like the few bits of lump sugar which I added when feeding him grain, and when he got to know what it was, I would feed him the sugar out of my hand. I found this to be a good remedy for curing his habit of backing away when he was approached.

After having him about a week, I had occasion to visit a friend, whose ranch was about fifteen miles away. The road between our ranches was good and level, but the Frisco River, which ran about half-way between, had to be crossed. I hitched up the team to my buggy and started off, and I didn't forget to take along a bundle of newspapers, as I had been advised—"just in case." Not that I wished to use them in the manner that had been suggested to me, but if there were no other alternative to being left stranded miles away from the ranch than by burning newspapers under a balky horse's hind legs, I figured that of the choice of two evils, I would prefer for him to suffer—not myself.

Though it was a cold day in mid-winter, the sun was shining brightly, and I was perfectly comfortable in my warm overcoat, with a heavy lap-robe over my knees. Everything went well until we reached the river. I would say that there are two kinds of balking—physical and mental. A work horse will balk because he thinks the load is heavier than he can draw, while a buggy horse, with only a light load to pull, balks out of pure cussedness. The remedies for curing these two kinds of balking would, naturally, be essentially different, though the customary method is generally the same; namely, beating.

The Frisco River was about fifty yards wide, and the water was about two feet deep and very cold, as there was ice along the edges of the banks. The horses went into the water without hesitation until they reached the middle of the river, and then —the horse balked.

There he stood with his ears back and his body sort of squirming around, as if anticipating a beating.

For the moment, I was at a loss to know what to do. I was certainly not going to leave my comfortable seat, which was high and dry, to go into two feet of icy water to beat the horse, even if I wanted to! But something had to be done.

Then it occurred to me that, under the circumstances, it was best to do nothing. Being comfortably seated was better than standing in the water, and if my balky friend wanted it that way, he was only getting the worst end of the deal.

This policy of doing nothing seemed to indicate that I would have a long wait ahead of me, so rather than be idle, I concluded to fill in the time by reading the newspapers, which, for obvious reasons, could not now be used for the purpose for which they were intended.

So I proceeded to read, while the team stood perfectly still. Some ten minutes passed when the balky horse became restless. He lifted up one foot, then the other, showing that he was not altogether pleased with the cold water. Or perhaps he felt offended because no attention had been paid to him. At any rate, he started to walk on, and with the other horse cheerfully co-operating, the other side of the river was soon reached. Then on we trotted to my friend's ranch, making the trip in good time.

On our homeward journey, when we reached the river, the team went right on in, but I became uneasy as we approached the middle. My fears were groundless, as the balky horse not only kept right on going, but he pulled more than his share

The Jewett Gap Bear

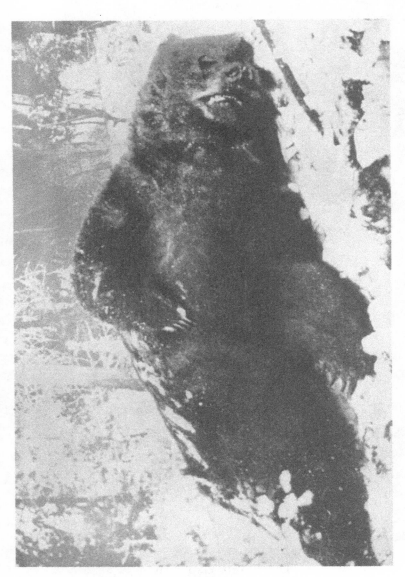

The end of the trail
Presented to the Wyndham Club

of the load, evidently realizing that standing in ice-cold water had its disadvantages.

Believe it or not, that horse never balked again. And so I congratulated myself on having won a forty-dollar bet.

For years I did a great deal of logging in connection with my sawmills, and there is no class of work that is more conducive to making a team balk than snaking logs.

Work horses often balk because they become discouraged when trying to pull a heavy log. While the log may not be any heavier than the load to which the team has been accustomed, sometimes when the driver says "Get up," one of the team gets into his collar before the other, and finding he cannot pull the log alone, he refuses to pull. The same result follows when the other horse starts to pull. Then the driver is apt to use his whip, and the team begins to see-saw; that is, instead of pulling together, each horse pulls in turn. Then both horses will balk, and if the driver continues using his whip, it only makes matters worse.

Eventually, the driver gives up, saying he cannot log with a balky team, and asks for another to take its place. As it wasn't always possible for me to provide a fresh team, I was forced to try to find some way to put an end to such an occurrence.

The problem seemed to resolve itself into the question of whether either horse could be induced into thinking he was pulling the log, when he wasn't.

At first, the idea sounded impractical, but like many other "queer" ideas, it wasn't as absurd as it might seem. So I proceeded to carry it out by buying a heavy coiled spring, which I hooked into the chain used in hauling the log.

When all was ready, and the team was told to "Get up," the horse starting first would pull out the spring, and he would imagine he was pulling the log. Before he got wise to the deception, the other horse would also be pulling, and with their combined efforts, the log would start to move. After that, the team, if driven with reasonable judgment, would quit balking.

Gyp, my mule, contracted a bad habit in her later years, which I think I should mention.

It was necessary for me to take long trips of a couple of hundred miles or so from time to time, and I generally rode Gyp, as her pace was a running walk which was very easy on the rider.

As she grew older, I thought it would be easier for both of us to use a two-wheel cart, so I bought one, and not only did it work out satisfactorily, but it had the added advantage that in the little body back of the seat I could carry provisions, a cooking outfit, and grain for Gyp, so that we could always stop anywhere and get a meal.

About three months after I had purchased the cart, I had occasion to go to a town a hundred miles away. A friend of mine, wishing to go to the same place, asked me if I would take him, so when the day came that I had to make the trip, I picked him up, and we started off.

Gyp, I would say, was not only a wonderful saddle mule, but she was also a good buggy animal. She pulled that little cart at a gait of seven miles an hour for long distances without tiring in the least. Several times before, I had made this trip; and as we went trotting along, my companion congratulated me on what a fine mule Gyp was, so gentle, and yet so high-spirited.

This, of course, pleased me, and I told him of how I had bought her as a three-year-old colt, and that she was naturally gentle, so that I broke her to harness and saddle in one day. I added that she was the one exception to the rule that high-spirited animals are hardest to break. I had hitched her to a wagon in the morning, and put a saddle on her in the afternoon but she never gave the least trouble in any way.

Then I went on extolling her virtues, without tapping wood!

We were trotting along at about seven miles an hour, when suddenly Gyp stopped dead! But we didn't—we were cata-pulted over the dash-board! I hit the mule on one hip, and my companion hit her on the other, and then we rolled down over the side-shafts on to the ground. As I weighed only one hundred and fifty pounds, the fall didn't hurt me, but my companion weighed two hundred or more, and for him it was a different matter.

I ran round in front of Gyp to help him up, while she turned her head around and looked at us with mild curiosity, wondering what we were up to.

My friend was not hurt badly, but shaken up, and as soon as he could give expression to his feelings, he spluttered, "I thought you said that mule of yours didn't have any bad habits." For the moment I was stumped. Then suddenly it struck me why Gyp had stopped so abruptly. We were passing a tree where, some two months before, Gyp and I had stopped for lunch. I had forgotten all about the tree, but Gyp hadn't. So that's how I explained it.

My friend, however, wasn't convinced, possibly due to the fact that he was still suffering from his bruises; and he seemed to regard what I said as one of those ingenious explanations my candid friends said I always had on tap whenever I was cornered. But luckily, in this case I had mute testimony to the truth of my assertion, for there on the ground under the tree were the empty tin cans which had contained my lunch of sardines and pork and beans.

In the pursuit of knowledge about horses, I learned a great deal from a negro named Henry, who worked for a neighbouring cattle outfit as their horse wrangler.

When we had our annual general round-up, he and one or two others took it in turn to wrangle the horses for the whole round-up; that is, all the saddle horses of the different outfits were thrown together in one bunch and handled collectively.

The first time I met Henry was when I was turning my mount of seven horses into the general round-up bunch, and as they walked past him, he eyed them closely.

While Henry was credited with being an A1 horse wrangler, he laboured under certain handicaps that did not apply to his professional brethren, who were white. For instance, some said he couldn't count over five, while others denied this and maintained that he could count up to ten. But whether that were true or not, it made no difference to Henry, as he did not need the aid of arithmetic in his business.

There were some two hundred saddle horses in the general round-up, and about daylight the wranglers brought in as many as they could find while the cowboys ate their breakfast, after which each one would take his rope and go up to the corral and catch the particular horse that he intended to ride that day. As a rule, the wranglers brought in about one-third of the whole lot, say about seventy horses.

If you asked one of the wranglers, a white man, how many horses had been brought in, he could tell you approximately, but if you asked him whether the particular horse you wanted was in the bunch, he would say: "I ain't sure," or "I didn't notice him."

But when Henry was asked the same questions, he would counter, by saying:

"I don't know how many horses we brought in, but what horse did you want?"

When a certain horse was indicated, he would instantly reply: "Yes" or "No," as the case might be, and invariably he was right.

Henry and I became good friends, and he would hunt me up in camp to ask me what horse I wanted to ride next day; and if it was in the bunch brought in that morning, he would saddle him for me. And I returned the favour by giving him tobacco from time to time.

Henry's knowledge of horses was gained by observation, and I was much impressed by one demonstration.

In my mount were two bay horses with black manes and tails. They were so exactly alike that I found it very difficult to tell them apart. And even when I thought I did, I was often wrong.

One day, both horses were in the corral at the same time, and so, in confidence, I told Henry of my difficulty. He lent a sympathetic ear, but looked much surprised, so I asked, "Can you tell the difference between them, Henry?"

"Oh, sure," he replied.

"But," I continued, "they look exactly alike."

"They sure do," said Henry, "but it's easy to tell them apart because one takes a longer step than the other."

Henry's answer amazed me, but I took his word for it at the time. Shortly afterwards, I had a chance to prove whether he was right or wrong. I led one horse for a hundred steps, which I carefully counted, and in taking the other horse over the same ground, I found that he took ninety steps. In other words, I figured the difference between their strides was three inches, or about 10 per cent. And this Henry had taken in at a glance when he first saw the two horses together.

"Henry," I said, "the method by which you distinguish between these horses is an excellent one, but I think I have a still better way."

"Oh, you have," said Henry, looking somewhat amused, "what is it?"

"By cutting the forelock of one," I said. "After that, I'll sure know which is which."

And Henry's reply to that was: "That *is* a good idea—if you think it is necessary."

Henry and I had many discussions about horses at odd times, and I think I learned more about them from him than I ever did from anyone else. At any rate, after a talk with him I always had the uncomfortable feeling that I didn't know as much about horses as I thought I did; whereas, with any other equine authority, I was conceited enough not to have that feeling.

I would like to remain on good terms with the bronco-buster himself. His profession is a hard one, and considering the risks he takes, he is not over-paid at the customary rates.

To my mind, he comes into his own at the rodeos taking place so frequently around the country, displaying his rough-riding abilities before large crowds and winning prizes and other rewards for his services.

By a curious quirk, the people who visit these shows are under the impression that the bronco-buster who rides the pitching horse is supposed to show the manner in which they are broken, but this is the reverse of the truth.

In the first place, there is considerable expense attached to securing a bunch of pitching horses suitable for the rodeo. As their value is determined in proportion to the viciousness with which they pitch, the one thing the bronco-buster must *not* do is to break them, and thus destroy their rodeo value. Though, as a *bronco-buster*, he is presumed to *break horses*, in this instance, he is called upon to play a double role. That is, to show the public how he can ride a horse and break it, on the one hand; and show the financial promoters of the rodeo how he can ride a bronco and not break it on the other.

A bronco-buster is supposed to ride a pitching horse until it stops pitching, and providing he is still on the horse, he gets off at this stage. If he were to continue to ride him, the chances are that the horse, finding he couldn't throw his rider, would soon quit trying to pitch, and then he would no longer be a rodeo horse.

If the rider gets off the horse as soon as he stops pitching, which is the custom, the horse is under the impression that he has got rid of him. Whether the rider got off willingly or unwillingly is a matter of indifference to the horse. He thinks he has won a victory over his would-be rider, so he is quite ready to pitch when he is next ridden. For this reason, many pitching horses continue to be useful for rodeo purposes for a long time.

All those in favour of the bronco-busting method of breaking horses are welcome to their opinions as far as I am concerned, but remembering my experience with Railroad, I know whereof I speak when I say, for my part, I prefer the easy way of breaking outlaw horses or mules.

In this connection, I am reminded of a story I heard in my youth, which may be new to some of my younger readers.

Two Irishmen had confessed their misdoings to a priest, and each was given the same penance, that of walking a certain distance with peas in his shoes.

When they had reached the end of their walk, and their penance was completed, one man's face was the picture of misery, while the other was all smiles.

At this juncture, a friend met them. Noting the miserable expression on one man's face, he asked the other what was the matter with him, and received this reply:

"He did his penance the hard way, and I did mine the easy one."

"How do you mean?" inquired the friend. "Didn't you put peas in your shoes, the same as he did?"

"Sure, and I did," replied the joyous one, "but I boiled mine first."

Before leaving the subject of horses, I think I should mention some of my unpleasant riding experiences. While hunting bear it is a very curious fact that while I rode thousands of miles over high mountains where the ground was both rough and steep, I never had a serious mishap. On the other hand, I had many mishaps when riding after wild cattle on the range or when galloping over level country. I can only account for it by saying that in the former case it was due to good luck and caution, and in the latter to bad luck and over-confidence. There were many who said that I was a very reckless rider when bear hunting, but in view of the above record, I do not think that such a criticism was justified; and besides, I did not want, through my own fault, to be the one to stop myself from bear hunting by getting crippled.

However, there was a half truth in my riding recklessly in that it appeared to be so when it wasn't. To explain this, I must say that in hunting black bear there are two phases of the hunt, the first one being when the hounds first strike the trail and run it until they jump the bear out of his bed. That distance sometimes may be as much as fifteen miles, during which time the hounds are running their fastest while I was trying my best to keep within hearing of them. As I would be riding along the foothills of a mountain, I would have to cross canyon after canyon, and while most of these are easy to cross, there are others that have steep banks down which it would look unsafe to ride. So I would be forced to make a detour either up or down the canyon bank until I could find a crossing. Owing to this delay, I was apt to get out of hearing of the hounds, and then never hear them again, thus losing that bear. Occasionally, when the steep bank was only eight or ten feet high I would ride down it, and found that it was not so bad as I had imagined it would be. By a steep bank, I mean one where the horse cannot remain on his four legs, but has to sit down on his haunches and use his front feet both as a brake and to prevent him from losing his balance. As long as he goes straight down the bank, he is all right, but if his body should swerve to either side, his front feet could no longer act as a brake nor help him keep his balance, so he would roll over sideways down hill.

Realizing the importance of riding down a steep place, thus avoiding the delay in making a detour, I got to studying the problem with the view of solving it, if it were possible. There was just one way to find out and that was to practice riding down steep banks. There were many of these near the ranch, running from five to twenty feet high. I started, of course, with the low ones. To begin with, my horse would go down with nervous hesitation, but after repeated trials down the same bank, he got so that he thought nothing of it. Incidentally, it is just as much a mistake to over-estimate a difficulty as it is to under-estimate it. The old saying, "The unknown is always great" holds good in this case. From low steep banks I gradually practised going down higher and higher ones, until I got to about twenty feet, which I concluded was about the limit of safety.

Of course, one must have a good, reliable horse before attempting such an experiment. After all, it was mostly a matter of confidence, which can only be obtained through constant practice. Once the horse has learned to have confidence in himself, and you have confidence in yourself, and you each have confidence in the other, with such a combination, aided by a lot of practice, you can do with safety what otherwise would be dangerous. It is much like high diving, which is all right if you know how, and all wrong if you don't. The result was that when I was trying to keep within hearing of the hounds and I struck one of these steep banks, I would go along it until I got to a place where I felt I could go down with safety. Then down I would go, much to the surprise, not to say consternation, of my hunting companions, many of whom were good riders, but who had never before had occasion to consider such a problem. It was only natural that they would consider me foolhardy not knowing that both my horse and myself had long practised such a "stunt." They thought I only did it to show off to them a new form of glamour-riding, whereas, from my standpoint, it was only putting my hard-earned knowledge to practical use. The dictionary defines "foolhardy" as being "bold without judgment," but there does not seem to be a corresponding word in the English language that exactly applied to my steep bank stunt, which I ventured to think was boldness with judgment.

In hunting grizzlies it was of even more importance, because, apart from keeping in hearing of the hounds, it was often a race against time. Usually it would be near sundown when I got close to the bear I had been chasing all day, and any delay might prevent me from ever getting him before it became too dark to shoot. I can recall several instances when I would have failed to get the bear had I balked at riding down steep places that were really safe to go down, although they would look very dangerous to most riders.

In ordinary riding, however, such as riding on the range, I had many mishaps. On four occasions, when I was galloping over flat country, my horse went heels over head with me, each time throwing me far enough away not to strike me with his hind feet. Although I was badly shaken up, I was not seriously injured.

People often use the expression "I felt like sinking into the ground," and I always regarded that as a figure of speech, but I never thought that I would ever accomplish this feat in reality. I was riding back to the ranch one night over level ground when it was pitch dark, and suddenly I sank into the ground about ten feet, and it was several seconds before I could understand what had happened. During the rainy season there are heavy floods which overflow level flats and start making shallow gullies, which later develop into arroyos of from two or three feet deep by as many wide, up to twenty feet deep and fifty yards wide. As they cut through soft soil they leave perpendicular walls, and as these flats are usually covered with bushes and high weeds, they cannot be seen until one gets quite close. At night a horse generally stops when he gets to one but, on this occasion, my horse didn't, or else the ground was pushed forward into the arroyo by our combined weights. All four legs of the horse sank into the soft dirt up to his body so he could not pull any of them out. After scrambling off him I took the saddle rope and, putting a loop round his neck and adding the rope to the bridle rein,

I pulled on his head, and, aided by his struggles, he floundered out. I then led him down the arroyo till I got to a place where I could get out on the other side. This mishap, though disconcerting, was not serious, but it might have been, had the drop been twenty feet instead of ten.

Casting bread on the waters sometimes returns in a curious fashion. I did a small favour to a man who, in his appreciation, determined to repay it. He was an expert tanner of hides, as well as plaiting rawhide saddle ropes, which are called reatas. I had a lot of cowhides at the ranch, and he selected one, out of which he plaited me a very fine saddle rope, thirty-five feet long, with a plaited loop to go over the horn, and another one for the slip knot for the rope to slide through when lassoing. When it was finished it was neatly coiled in coils a foot in diameter. I tied the rope to my saddle with the horn loop attached to the horn. A short time later, on a round-up, we were holding a bunch of cattle in a main canyon near the mouth of a side canyon, waiting for some more cattle to be driven in to add to our bunch. Soon some driven cattle came running, but the leaders instead of coming towards us, bolted up the side canyon. One of the boys and myself took after them, but they got into the canyon before we could head them off. As the canyon was narrow with steep sides, we could not pass them and turn them back. After following them some two hundred yards, they ran up some parallel cattle trails that went up the hillside. I rode on an upper trail, where there were no cattle, so as to head them and turn them back into the canyon, and told the cowboy to ride ahead and turn them down the canyon when they dropped back into it from the hillside. Suddenly, one side of the narrow trail up which I was riding gave way, and my horse fell sideways down the hill. Luckily, I was thrown far enough away from him not to be struck by him as he fell. As I realized that he would roll over me, and as there was no time for me to get out of his way, all I could do was to roll down the hill faster than he did. I therefore accelerated my pace, but below me there was a nine-foot perpendicular bluff between me and the sandy bed of the canyon. I shot over the bluff and was knocked unconscious for a few seconds, and when I came to, I was surprised at seeing my horse hanging in space with his heels about five feet above me.

At first I thought I was in a nightmare but to my dismay it soon crystallized into reality. I naturally tried to get out from under but I could not move. At this moment, the cowboy who had seen the accident came galloping down and, getting off his horse, seized and dragged me away.

After I had sufficiently recovered, I sent him down to the herd to get help from some of the cowboys, while the unfortunate horse was left still hanging in the air. What had happened was this. On the hillside were some oak saplings thick enough to make fence posts, which had been chopped down by a ranchman, who left short stumps about six inches high, and it was on one of these that the end coil of the reata had miraculously caught when the horse fell. How he rolled down without getting entangled in the rope, I do not know. The horse rolled over the bluff, and was stopped by the rope when the horn to which it was attached reached the edge of the bluff, and it was thus that he was left hanging in the air. There was no way of releasing him, except by cutting the rope at the horn, and he fell limp on the very spot where I had been lying. It was then that the bread I had cast on the waters returned, for when the strain on the rawhide rope came, it stretched enough to absorb the shock; but had I had an ordinary rope, it would have snapped and I would have been squashed.

My most unpleasant experience happened one day when riding in the mountains on my mule, Gyp. I was going slowly down the narrow bed of a canyon that had fairly steep sides. There were some Spanish bayonets, or daggers, as they are often called, growing here and there. The long leaves of this plant end with a sharp thorn, and Gyp's legs had been pricked several times.

A big rock had rolled into the canyon ahead of me, and one of these bayonets was growing along side of it, leaving insufficient room between it and the bank for Gyp to pass. So instead of doing so, she shot up the side of the bank, crashing through the branches of a big juniper. I tried to pull her up while holding the reins in my clenched hand, palm upward. My fist went between two stout branches, while the reins were jerked out of my hand, and Gyp went on, leaving me hanging in the air.

If anyone wants to find out what pain is like, he has only to put his forearm between two bars, one over the upturned wrist and the other three inches back under the forearm, and then raise his feet from the ground. I tried frantically to turn my wrist to get loose, but the branches just gave enough to prevent me. The pain was so great that I was about to faint, and realizing what would have happened had I done so, I made one last desperate effort, and this time, succeeded in turning my wrist, the upper branch cutting it to the bone, after which I fell limply to the ground.

King Lear, despite his adversities, found "good in everything," and similarly I found humour in my various mishaps. This time I could not help smiling to think that it was I who was left hanging in the air instead of my horse, and also that the worst mishap I ever had was when I was riding slowly.

CHAPTER XIII

PETE, THE OUTLAW

My horse-breaking experiences were many and varied, but there was none quite so exceptional as the one thrust upon me in the shape of an outlaw mule.

A neighbouring rancher, who bred horses, sold out and bought another ranch in Arizona, to which he intended to take all his horses. He had on his range adjacent to mine some two hundred mares and colts, in bunches of thirty or forty each, and running with one of these bunches was a jack-burrow. In time, several mules appeared, most of them small, but there were two weighing about a thousand pounds each when they were four years old.

One was gentle, but the other was generally known as the "Outlaw Mule." With his ears back and his mouth open, and braying loudly, he would make for anyone who appeared in the corral on foot, and no one ever stopped long enough to find out what he would have done had he reached him.

People said he ought to be shot, but as "everybody's business is nobody's business," he continued to survive.

When my neighbour left for Arizona, he contracted with a cowboy to round up all his mares and colts, to be delivered at his new ranch, at so much per head. As feed would be needed for the saddle horse he was using in the round-up, this cowboy contractor approached me, asking if I would trust him for a ton of hay, for which he offered to give me a mule in payment.

Good baled alfalfa hay was selling for $17 a ton—if you could sell it—and I had a surplus of hay on hand, so I didn't hesitate to accept his proposal.

The mares were all rounded up in a couple of weeks, and his contract stipulated that the colts be branded before delivery. Then the question arose as to what should be done about the outlaw mule.

None of the men relished the idea of being attacked by the mule when branding colts, such a prospect being too disconcerting to that latent air of self-confidence which cowboys are supposed to display under all circumstances. For a man to drop his branding iron, when threatened with attack, and bolt to the side of the corral and climb it, may be a good safety-first policy to pursue, but for anyone who aspires to be a *he*-man, such an exhibition is sadly lacking in dignity. To avoid all possibility of any such humiliating spectacle occurring, it was decided to shoot the mule.

Then, one of the men was struck with a brilliant idea. Why not kill two birds with one stone? Why not pay for the ton of hay with that ornery mule? He had no sooner expressed that enticing proposition than it was unanimously approved. Shortly after this, one of my men told me, with a grin, that a mule had been left in my corral, payment, he supposed, for some hay I had sold.

"That's all right," I replied, "but what are you smiling about?"

"Because it's the outlaw mule they've put over on you," he answered.

"I understand," I said, "they've handed me a lemon, but go and get the other boys, and we'll all go up to the corral and look him over."

The large circular corral was seven feet high, and built of thick, heavy poles, laid horizontally. And in the middle of it stood the "outlaw," pawing the ground in rage.

Through the bars of the corral, we all took a good look at the unwelcome stranger, who had been deposited on my doorstep, so to speak.

As we stood sizing him up, one of the boys turned to me and asked, somewhat dubiously, "Are you going to try to break him?"

"Why, certainly, I am," I replied.

Then, nervously, as though he were afraid I might ask him to do the job, he queried, "Who are you going to get to break him?"

To allay his fears I said complacently, "Don't worry. I'm going to put it up to the mule to break himself."

After this astonishing reply, I sent two of the men off to fetch a piece of inch rope, a hundred feet long, which belonged on a block and tackle. In one end, I made a loop with a slide knot, gave it to one of the men, a good calf-roper, and told him to sit on top of the corral fence, while another stood below him with the rest of the rope coiled in big loops.

To the other men, looking on with interest, I said, "Now, we'll go to the other side of the corral, and try to scare the mule, so that he will run round the corral and get roped as he goes by."

We didn't have much success at first, but by dint of yelling and throwing stones at the mule, he started round the fence, seeking a place to get out.

The man on the fence threw the rope, but missed so we had to do the performance all over again, not only a second but a third time, but the fourth time, the mule, in trying to dodge the loop, accidentally dodged into it, pulling it tight round his neck as he kept on going. The men held on to the rope as best they could until the rest of us could come to their assistance, and then we passed the end of the rope through the bars of the corral fence from the inside, and all five of us hauled on it. We succeeded in dragging the mule to the side of the corral, and fastened the rope so as to hold him there.

I told three of the men to get their saddle horses and saddle ropes, and we entered the corral and put two saddle ropes around the mule's neck, and the ends of the ropes were drawn tight and handed to two of the men, one on each side of the mule. They drew their ropes tightly on the horns of their saddles, in order to keep him from running sideways, while I unfastened the inch rope from the corral fence and handed it to the third rider, who started to lead the mule out of the corral.

The other two riders held him in place, while the remaining two of us drove the mule from behind, and in this way, by alternately dragging and driving, we brought him to the place where he was to be kept during the breaking-in period.

While three men on horseback held the mule, the other

man and I got a two-handled cross-cut saw, with which we sawed off a piece of log, five feet long, from a fallen tree close by. Then we fetched a team and dragged the heavy log, which weighed about five hundred pounds, to a spot near the mule. We tied the other end of the hundred foot rope, in a deep notch which we cut round the middle of the log, thus preventing it from slipping off either end.

Then came the final stage, which turned out to be the most difficult part of the job; that was, to take the rope loop on the mule's neck and tie it securely, with a tight knot, at the proper place, after which we removed the saddle ropes from the mule's neck. And then we all bolted.

The mule thought he was loose and started to run, but after running the length of the rope, it tightened on his neck, his body suddenly changed ends, and, losing his balance, he rolled over on to the ground, while the log gave a little hop.

He got to his feet, and made a run in the opposite direction, but the same thing happened again. Changing directions did not help him any, so he stopped, looked at us savagely, pawing the ground with his foot, as he had done in the corral when he first caught sight of us. And so we left him.

From time to time during the rest of the day, I returned to see how he was faring, and I found that he would run cautiously on the rope until it stopped him and then walk round the log, first one way, then the other, in a circle, the radius of which was, of course, the length of the rope.

The next day, I took him his first feed of hay and a pail of water, being careful to put it inside the circle trail, while he stood on the opposite side. Then I got out of sight.

Some little time later, he walked over and ate the hay. He was tied about a hundred yards from the house, and in full view, so I kept an eye on him during the day. I observed that while he still ran on the rope, he would always stop at the point where it began to pull on his neck.

For the first week, when I came with his hay and water, he looked at me and pawed the ground until I left, and then he walked over to the hay and ate it.

The second week, I fed him ear corn in the husk, which I

threw on the ground, and he soon learned to eat it, and to show his appreciation, he stopped pawing the ground.

At the beginning of the third week, instead of standing still when he saw me coming with his feed, he started to walk towards me, and he ate his feed quietly, while I stood by.

At the end of the week, instead of throwing all the corn on the ground as I had been doing, I just threw down an ear or two and held another ear in my hand. He ate the former, and then advanced and hesitatingly grabbed the corn in my hand, and then jumped back. But it wasn't long before he took the ears out of my hand, as any gentle horse might do.

After a day or two, he allowed me to pat his neck, and then we became friends.

When I decided to commence the second stage of his breaking, a few days later, I put a harness on him and set him to work hauling lumber from my sawmill. Though we had some difficulty in harnessing him, it was nothing like the trouble we had at first tying the inch rope round his neck.

After he was harnessed, led quietly to a waiting wagon load of lumber, and put in the wheel of a four-horse team, he never once tried to pull back.

In other words, the log, passively but effectually, had taught him to lead without pulling back. Running on the rope which held him to the log had made his neck so tender that he obeyed any pull on the rope round his neck rather than endure more pain by refusing to be led.

It was a four-day round trip to deliver the load of lumber, and I told my driver on no account to strike the mule. He was instructed, if the mule became unruly, to replace him with another horse. I asked him, on his return, how the mule had behaved.

"Well," he said, "he pulled the whole load the first day, half the load the second, and the third day he just pulled his share."

And so that was all there was to breaking Pete, as I called him, to harness for hauling freight.

After two or three trips, he was just as gentle to handle as any old workhorse.

A few months later, I was twice offered $150 for Pete, but

I refused for two reasons, one being that of sentiment, and the other was he was worth that much to me anyhow.

Strange to say, Pete was not really vicious, but if I had said this of him in his outlaw days, no one would have agreed with me. The only way by which one may find out whether an animal is really vicious or not is by treating him with kindness.

Pete looked upon me as his one and only friend during the long period he was held in captivity by the log. And he stuck to this friendship for the rest of his life.

He acquired a prejudice against roping when he was roped for the first time, a bad habit for which he could hardly be blamed, and one of which he could not be cured. He seemed to be always on the lookout, and if anyone in the corral swung a rope for any reason whatsoever, he would be out of the corral in short order. He would run off fifty or a hundred yards and stand still, allowing no one but myself to catch him. If I were not there, someone would hunt me up, and as soon as he caught sight of me, he would walk towards me, just as he did when tied to the log.

It was often a nuisance for me to have to drop everything and go off and get Pete. A man on horseback went after him two or three times, but that didn't work. As soon as he was approached, he would run away, and would not allow himself to be headed. If the rider crowded him, Pete would kick at him viciously, although he never kicked at any other time.

I might mention that Pete served me faithfully for many years, and finally died of old age.

BURRO-BUSTING

From mule breaking, it would be but a logical transition to touch on the art of burro-busting, if I might be allowed to coin the expression.

Perhaps I have been too drastic in my strictures on bronco-busting methods, so I will try to make up for it by expressing my great admiration for the efficiency displayed by one of my Mexican sheepherders, whose services were called for whenever young burros had to be broken to the pack.

This Mexican, a very powerful man, was only five feet tall, but he weighed two hundred and forty pounds and seemed to be made for the job.

I'm not sure whether Nature supplied donkeys with long ears in order to facilitate their breaking or not, but they are certainly of great help.

A young three or four-year-old burro would be caught and dragged up to the burro-buster, who would grab its ears and pull its head down and hold it between his knees. Then another herder would approach on one side with a pack saddle, and another from the other side with a roll of bedding.

During the time the pack saddle was put on, the cinches tightened, and the roll of bedding tied on, the burro would have a man in front of him and one on each side, but no one at the rear, and there the recalcitrant neophyte was graciously permitted to shadow-box with his heels.

At the next stage of the operation, he would be tied with a short rope to the tail of a gentle old burro, that had already been packed. When the other burros were ready to go, the "burrocade" was started, followed by a Mexican armed with a big stick, to keep them going.

When the old burro started moving, the bronco burro, not knowing that he also was expected to start, would stand still, with the result that the lead burro's tail would be pulled. In retaliation, the old burro, not knowing that it was his own fault his tail was being pulled, would lash out with his heels, kicking the innocent offender in the face. And to add insult to injury, the latter would be whacked from behind by the Mexican with the stick.

This novel method of dual control proved most effectual, for after two or three tail-pullings, he would put his head against the hip of the old lead burro and keep it there, to prevent any recurrence of the twin punishments.

Usually the burro would be turned loose after about two hours, and he would submissively follow along with the other burros.

I particularly liked this method of burro-breaking, for the

reason that outside of the first tail-pulling, the only mal-
treatment he would receive would be due to his own misbe-
haviour. A donkey is supposed to be stupid, but he is not too
dumb to realize the mistake he would make by pulling on that
tail a second or a third time.

CHAPTER XIV

DOG STEALING

Dog stealing is one of the many annoyances to which a man is subjected when he aspires to have a pack of hounds. As a matter of fact, my specially trained hounds would be of no possible benefit to anyone, though attempts were made to steal them from time to time.

No matter if he were a hundred or more miles from the ranch, as soon as the dog would be turned loose, he would come home. Nevertheless, the theft of any of my dogs was always a source of deep resentment to me; not in the sense of loss from a commercial standpoint, but because I regarded it in the same light as kidnapping a member of my family.

I considered my bloodhound, Sleuth, the best dog I ever owned, but as he virtually never left my side, day or night, and stayed with my wife when I was away from home, I did not fear his being stolen. Sometimes I wondered what would have transpired had a thief found an opportunity to steal him, for no one could put a hand on him, to pat him or for any other reason, without having first been introduced. It was his custom to ignore strangers, and while he never bothered anyone, if a stranger attempted to pat him, he was greeted with a low growl, and Sleuth would walk away with an air of ruffled dignity.

However, when I introduced anyone to him, saying: "Sleuth, this person is all right," he allowed himself to be patted without showing any resentment, then or later.

If a thief, by any chance, had succeeded in putting a chain on him, he would have had a fight on his hands when he started to lead him; and I can well imagine Sleuth's expression, had a stranger taken the liberty of poking a handkerchief in his face, telling him to "Go on."

But I am sorry to say, all my hounds did not seem to mind familiarities being taken with them.

In order that my dogs might be easily distinguished from others, they wore collars of a deep maroon colour. I let this be known around the country, and asked that anyone seeing a dog wearing such a collar send me word when and where he had been seen. Then, should one of my dogs be stolen, there was a chance of hearing of his whereabouts for a reason that a thief might not suspect.

In one case in particular, one of my hounds was stolen and taken one hundred and fifty miles away in a covered wagon. Presumably he had bitten through the rope with which he had been tied, as he was seen on his way back to the ranch in the main street of a little town, trailing a piece of rope, the end of which was much ravelled, as though it had been dragged a long distance.

A friend of mine, who saw him, at once recognized the dog's collar and wrote to me, which I very much appreciated, although the dog reached the ranch before I received the letter.

There was a time when one of my best hounds was stolen and I was put to much trouble in getting her back. My wife and I were absent from our Horse Springs ranch for a few days, on a trip to Albuquerque. While we were away, Tom, one of my men, took care of the ranch, one of his duties being to feed the hounds.

When we returned, the dogs naturally all rushed out to welcome us home, and I immediately missed one of them. Tom had worked for me only a short time, and when I asked him about the dog, he said he had not noticed that one was missing, especially as he knew none of the hounds by name. When I asked if anyone had been at the ranch in the past few days, he said:

"Yes, a man who said he was from one of the neighbouring ranches stopped the night. I was feeding the dogs when he came, and he asked me if I knew which you considered your leading bear dogs. I pointed to one of the hounds you told me was one of the best."

Tom let the stranger have a pound of chewing tobacco from the little commissary which I maintained at the ranch for the convenience of the sheepherders. He said he would pay later, as he had no change with him, and gave his name as that of a ranchman who lived thirty miles away and whom I knew well. That name was entered on the books.

Tom described him as a small man, and as the ranchman whose name was given was a big man, I at once suspected that the stranger was not all he pretended to be.

Attempting to recover a stolen dog presents many difficulties, for the thief would naturally be on his guard, and his friends would keep him informed as to whether you had said anything about losing a dog, and what you would be likely to do about it. The best policy was to say nothing, except that the dog had been off hunting somewhere and had got poisoned, and to see to it that such a statement reached the ears of the thief, so he would probably conclude that you would do nothing about the matter.

But I was anxious to find out the identity of the stranger, and my job, then, was to find out from my neighbours if they had seen anyone, not a resident in our locality, pass by during the previous few days, without arousing the curiosity of the person asked, as he would wonder at my motive.

There are times when even a highly conscientious person is justified in borrowing a little guile from the serpent; so, in this instance, I took an old quirt and went round inquiring of each of my neighbours whether he had lost it. At the reply "No," I said innocently that I wished to return it to the owner, and then: "Have you seen anybody riding round lately? He might have lost it, and I would like to return it to him."

Finally, I struck one fellow who said, "Yes, there was—a man named Thompson."

Casually I said, "Maybe that's the fellow who lost the quirt. I'll ask him if I run on to him." Then I turned the conversation to other things, so that the motive behind my question was not suspected.

It was about this time that I recollected an incident which had happened some months previously. I was waiting at the depot in Magdalena when the train from Socorro came in, and I noticed the arrival of two young hounds by express. They were tied to a trunk on the platform, and as I always take an interest in dogs, I had been looking at them when a man came for them. I inquired who he was, and learned that his name was Thompson, and that his ranch lay about sixty miles south-east of mine.

So this was the man to whom my neighbour thought the quirt might belong. It was, therefore, very natural for me to conclude that his object in stealing my hound was that he might have a good bear dog with which to train his two young hounds.

I then decided to make a surprise visit to Thompson's ranch. As he would never suspect that I had the least idea he had stolen my dog, it was probable that she might be found tied up openly somewhere outside, without any thought of hiding her.

When he stole the dog, Tom must have gone to get supper, leaving Thompson with the dogs. He must have taken a trace chain off one of my harnesses, and after in some way or other catching the dog, have attached the chain to her collar, dragged her off some distance to the south of the ranch, and tied her up in the brush. Then evidently, he returned to the house and stayed the night.

Next morning, after breakfast, he rode west, telling Tom he was going to visit a friend, but after getting out of sight, he must have circled round to the south where he had left the dog, and then returned to his ranch, dragging her after him.

It was difficult to know just exactly what to do about getting back my dog, Jenny, but I decided to visit a rancher about sixty miles southwest of Horse Springs, with whom I was very friendly. His cowboys knew that part of the country very well, and I hoped that one of them would go with me to Thompson's ranch. So early next morning, riding Gyp, I started out to begin my search.

On the way to the ranch, I remembered that our deputy sheriff was stopping at a place only a few miles out of my way, so in the hope of getting him to go with me to Thompson's ranch, I decided to make the detour.

The deputy sheriff, like the Canadian Mounted Police, had the reputation of "always getting his man"; in fact, he had done just that several times, in the line of duty. He was just the sort of man I would have chosen to go with me, if I should meet with any trouble.

I found him at the ranch, and lost no time in telling him that my dog had been stolen. I asked him to help me out by joining me—that I was sure my dog had been taken to Thompson's ranch—and that if I found the thief, he, in his legal capacity, might arrest him.

He listened to my sob story, and then he drawled, "I'd go with you if it was a horse or a cow that was stolen, but I ain't a-going to get into no jack-pot for jest a damn dawg!" And by way of emphasis, he expectorated a stream of tobacco juice.

So, having got his answer, I realized that further discussion was useless, and I went on my way, reaching my friend's ranch by sundown.

After supper was over, I broached the object of my visit, and while my friend and his cowboys evinced great interest and sympathy for me in what I had to say, they showed no inclination to help me. So I had to ask each cowboy, in turn, if he would go with me to Thompson's ranch, as I didn't known the way. Though I hadn't told them the deputy sheriff's reason for not aiding me, it was evident that they entertained the same view of the matter, for notwithstanding my making a liberal pecuniary offer to anyone who would go with me, there were no takers.

But I did succeed in getting some valuable information. I asked if Thompson had any enemies living near his ranch, and was told he had, especially one called Bates, whose ranch was three miles above Thompson's, both of them on the main road. Their cattle ran together on the same range, and serious trouble had arisen, which was likely to end up in a killing.

Thompson's ranch was about sixty miles away, on the other side of a range of high mountains. My plan was to make a surprise visit to his ranch early in the morning. So the logical place, it seemed to me, where I should stop the night, was Bates' ranch. I was certain he would not give Thompson advance notice of my coming to get Jenny.

Next morning the boys directed me the best way to get to

Bates' ranch. Five miles back, on the road I had come the night before, I would see a sign post, which pointed to the trail leading through a gap in the mountain range.

Then, follow the trail, and after dropping down into the valley on the other side, I would strike the main road, and going on, Bates' ranch, which had a wooden fence around it, was the first one I would come to.

It all sounded very simple when I left the ranch, and it probably would have been so had it not been that a blinding snowstorm came up. Soon the ground was covered with snow, so that I could not even recognize the road, much less see the sign post. So there was nothing for me to do but to make my way over the mountain to the valley on the other side as best I could. After a few miles of traversing a random course through the falling snow, I came to the arroyo of a big canyon, which I figured was the one which led up to the gap across the mountain. But the canyon boxed and I was forced to climb up on to the ridge at one side. It was snowing very heavily, and the mountainside became so steep that I had to get off and lead Gyp.

It must have been two hours before I reached the top of the mountain range, and though I had no idea how many feet I had climbed, I learned afterwards that I must have gone over the highest part of it.

The storm was raging and by this time the snow was several inches deep, so I lost no time in starting to descend on the other side, leading Gyp about two thousand feet down, until it was possible to ride.

The snow had changed to a heavy rain, and as it was almost sundown, the gathering darkness added to my troubles. The going was hard through dense patches of timber and brush, but at last I saw the dim light of a campfire below me on the mountain side.

As I approached, I saw that it was a sheep camp, and I dismounted and went to the fire on which was a pot of hot coffee, a cup of which the herder promptly gave me. I asked the way to Bates' ranch, and his directions were very simple.

I was to go down the mountain until I reached the valley, continue on until I came to the main road, and follow it down to the first ranch, the same way as the cowboys had told me. It had become pitch-dark, and it was impossible to see the ground, but we plodded along for miles. Suddenly Gyp stopped dead and then changed her direction, and I realized that this must be the road. Again, we plodded along for miles, till Gyp stopped once more. For the moment I couldn't think why and got off to investigate, and the first thing I knew I had run into a wooden fence, which I assumed was the one enclosing Bates' ranch. Leading Gyp, I walked along the fence and soon came to the gate.

I followed the path to the house and rapped loudly at the door. After a few seconds a voice called out, "What do you want?"

"I would like to stay the night," I answered.

Again the voice, "Where did you come from?"

And again I answered the voice, "From my ranch at Horse Springs."

Then the voice asked, "What's your name?"

The clatter of the rain on the roof made it difficult for him to hear my answer clearly when I told him.

"Tell me your name again," he called, and again I did so. Then said the invisible one, "I heard of you before, but I ain't never seen you."

"It's the same with me," I replied. "I have never seen you either."

The voice went on questioning me, which struck me as irrelevant, since I was standing in the pouring rain, waiting to be let in the house. Then came the welcome words: "Wait a minute, and I'll light the lamp."

The door was opened cautiously and there stood Bates with his left hand on the handle, his right holding a pistol at full cock. In the lamplight, he peered into my face closely, and said:

"I guess you're the man you claim to be, all right, so go on round the fence till you strike my stable, and turn your horse loose in it. He'll find the manger full of hay. I'll get supper for you while you're gone."

On getting back to the house, I rapped, and he let me in. I stood at the door, took off my wet slicker and left it outside, and feeling chilled through, walked to the stove to warm myself. My host was frying bacon, and the smell of its sizzling was most appetizing, especially since I had eaten nothing since breakfast at six o'clock in the morning. It was now midnight.

"The warmth of your stove sure feels good," I said, by way of opening the conversation.

"I expect it does," he said, "for you're in big luck to get in this house at all." At my puzzled look, he added:

"You never would have got in if it hadn't been for your English accent." Then he continued, "This Thompson outfit would like to bump me off, and there ain't no dirty trick they wouldn't play to get me out of the way without anybody suspicioning them. Thompson could get one of his gang that I didn't know to ask to spend the night. So when you rapped at the door, I wasn't goin' to open it till I was certain you wasn't one of that bunch. There was one stunt that they couldn't get away with, and that was to talk like an Englishman. So that's why I kept askin' you questions instead of lettin' you in, and by the time I got through I was dead sure that you was the Englishman you said you was."

Hitherto, I had never regarded my English accent as an asset, but this time I cashed in.

Soon I was enjoying the hot meal which he set before me. When I had finished, I sat down by the open fireplace where a cheerful fire was blazing, and began smoking my pipe. My host joined me after he had cleared away the dishes, and lit his pipe as he sat down for a confidential talk. I told him that I had heard that he and Thompson were on anything but good terms, and I had decided to come to his ranch where I felt sure Thompson would not hear of my arrival.

"You done just right," he agreed, "and if there's anything I can do to help you, I will."

By this time, he was thoroughly reassured that I was the person I represented myself to be, so he unburdened himself freely about the trouble he was having with Thompson. He said that Thompson's ranch was regarded as a robber's roost; that is, it was the meeting and hiding place of men on the dodge and other fugitives from the law. Thompson's small bunch of cattle were rapidly increasing, due to his stealing calves from his neighbours. And Bates, being one of them, had been unwillingly contributing his full share of the loot.

Also Thompson had fresh beef, supplied from the same sources, always on hand at the ranch, with which entertains his numerous visitors.

Bates said he knew that Thompson was stealing big, un-branded calves from him, from time to time, but he couldn't prove it, and he was afraid to say much, because Thompson could easily get him bumped off by asking one of his guests to accommodate him that much in return for past hospitalities.

Then he inquired the reason for my visit, and I told him of the theft of my hound, my suspicion that Thompson had stolen Jenny, and that I had come to try to get her back by making a surprise visit to the ranch of the man I suspected, before anything could be done with her.

Bates agreed with me, and we thoroughly discussed the plan for me to pursue. He advised me to approach at the back of the house at Thompson's ranch, as the windows were all on one side, at the front. If they saw me, they might suspect who I was and shoot me, or engage me in conversation while someone sneaked off with Jenny and tied her in the brush.

As it was nearing two o'clock in the morning, we decided to go to bed.

At daylight, I prepared to leave for Thompson's ranch, while I received final instructions from Bates to the effect that if there was likely to be any shooting, I had better shoot first; and that if I didn't show up at his ranch again within a reason-able time, he would notify my folks as to when and where he had last seen me. I thanked him for his kind thoughtfulness and started down the road in a none too optimistic frame of mind.

Eventually, I came in sight of Thompson's ranch, and heeding Bates' advice, I approached it at the back. When I got to within thirty yards of the house, I took my rifle out of its scabbard, laid it across the saddle in front of me, and called out: "Hello!"

Presently three men came around the house, accompanied by two hounds. Thompson was not with them, and when I inquired where he was, one man told me that he had just gone down to the pasture to bring in the saddle horses. Then I asked if they were all working for Thompson, and the man who had spoken before said that he was, but that the other two were neighbours who had spent the night at the ranch. There was an awkward pause; then I spoke to the man again.

"Didn't Thompson come to this ranch a few days ago, leading a hound?" I asked, and he answered, "No, not that I know of."

"Do you mean to say," I said politely, "that you do not know of any strange hound tied up at this ranch?"

"No," he said, "I don't."

"It ain't one of these two hounds that you claim, is it?" one of the other men said facetiously.

I replied frigidly, "No, my hounds have the habit of knowing me when they see me. These two hounds don't know me." Turning to the cowboy again, I said, "I ask you for the last time, do you or do you not know of any strange hound being on this place?"

"No, I don't," he denied. But from the guilty expression on his face, and the significant looks exchanged by the three men, I was convinced that he was lying.

I must confess that, for the moment, I was nonplussed, and at a loss to know what to do. And as they stood staring at me, I pondered, "What price your old theory of 'simple solutions.'"

Then suddenly I felt better. I always carried a London policeman's whistle attached to a leather bootlace, which I wore round my neck. Many hunters used a horn with which to call their hounds, but I never did, as it was too clumsy and awkward a thing to have dangling around one's neck, especially when riding through thick brush. Besides, I couldn't blow one anyway, but with a policeman's whistle I could hold it between my teeth and whistle for my hounds while riding at full speed.

Looking straight at the cowboy, I said, "As there is no use asking you again if you have seeen my dog, all I can do now is to ask the dog herself and, if she is on this place, she will answer me."

With that, I blew two sharp notes close together, which was

the signal when I wanted my dogs to come to me in a hurry. I had scarcely reached the second blast before there was an explosion of barks from an old stable, fifty yards distance. I shall never forget the expressions on the faces of the three men at this sudden turn of events. Now it was their turn to look nonplussed. And this they certainly did!

Riding towards the stable, I told the cowboy to come with me. The door of the stable was fastened with a chain and padlock, and I asked him for the key. He said he didn't know where Thompson kept it.

"I am sorry," I said, "I don't want to injure any man's property, but I have got to get my dog, and if you can't find the key so that I can open the door, I'll shoot the padlock off the chain."

He said that maybe he might be able to find the key up at the house, so I told him to go up to the house and get it, and I would give him a reasonable time to get back with it.

He started up to the house, and soon returned with the key, which he said he had found hanging on a nail on the wall.

Jenny was barking frantically all this time, for she had heard my voice. When the cowboy had unlocked the padlock and opened the door, I went in and found Jenny tied to a post with the trace chain, which I unfastened and tied on to my saddle.

Mounting my mule, I told the cowboy to inform Thompson that I would have him prosecuted for stealing my dog, and rode away in triumph, my hound running in circles and barking to show her delight.

Back at Bates' ranch once more, he greeted me with, "So you done got your dawg after all, eh?"

When I had given him a brief account of what had happened, he congratulated me on my luck, and added, "If Thompson had been there, you wouldn't have got away with it as easy as you did. And you ain't through with it yet. When they tell Thompson how you got off with that dawg, he ain't a-goin' to take it lyin' down.

"This road you're goin' back on goes through a pass over them mountains, and before you get to the pass, it makes a good many bends, and it goes through heavy timber all the way. Thompson and his men could cut across those bends and get ahead of you, hide in the thick brush, and shoot you as you go by. It would be a hard matter to prove who killed you, and no one would know that Thompson had had anything to do with it, because he would probably dump your body into one of the abandoned dry wells around here. Then no one would ever know what had become of you."

"And how about my mule?" I interposed. "What would they do with her?"

"That's easy," he replied. "Thompson would just get one of his 'on the dodge' men to ride her out of the country."

"But someone might recognize her," I said.

"Oh, no, they wouldn't," answered Bates, "because men on the dodge only ride by night." Then he continued, "If I was you, I wouldn't go along that road. I would cut straight across the mountains, and be sure of getting home safe."

I had to get going, so I said "Good-bye" to Bates, and thanked him for his help. As I rode along, I meditated on Bates' advice as to what I had better do. I visualized that I might suddenly come on Thompson and his gang hidden in the brush, with their rifles pointed at me. And then I thought of the unpleasing prospect of becoming a permanent inhabitant of one of those abandoned wells, so I concluded to take his advice to leave the road, only to find I had already done so. I had left the road about a mile back without being aware of it.

As this mountain range was about the same height as the one I had crossed the previous day, it was hard on poor Gyp, but I helped her out somewhat by dismounting and leading her over the steepest places, as I had done the day before.

I reached the ranch about sundown. It was Thursday evening and, on looking at the paper, I found that the grand jury was in session at my county seat, Socorro, and that they were to adjourn on Saturday afternoon. Unfortunately, my saddle horses were all at my farm ranch, thirty miles away. There was no chance for me to get a horse to take Gyp's place, so I had to ride her to Magdalena the next day, a distance of seventy miles. There was no other way out of it if I were to get to the grand jury before they adjourned, and they would not convene again for a long time.

I got into Magdalena Friday night, and Saturday morning caught the train, reaching Socorro at noon. At two o'clock I went to the court house, and the grand jury was just about to adjourn, but they kindly agreed to hear my complaint. On the strength of my story, a law book was consulted, in which it was found that, in the eye of the law, a dog was a wild animal. Furthermore, as I hadn't paid any tax on Jenny, she was not regarded as property. Therefore, stealing a dog was not a crime for which the grand jury could indict the thief.

The jurymen expressed their regret, and one sympathetic juryman went so far as to suggest that I should have Thompson arrested for petty larceny for stealing the collar and chain. I thanked him, saying that it would hardly be worth while, since the punishment for petty larceny didn't fit the crime of stealing my dog.

After expressing my appreciation to the grand jury for their courtesy, I started on my return trip to the ranch. At Magdalena, I took the mail stage home, leaving poor Gyp at the livery stable for a few days' rest. In four days I had ridden her two hundred and fifty miles, including the crossing of two high ranges of mountains. As an endurance test, I think the record she made would be hard to beat.

It was impossible to secure legal redress for the theft of my dog. Nevertheless, I did get some humorous consolation through a sort of vicarious retribution, carried out by some of Thompson's cow-stealing friends, and of which this dog-stealing incident was the primary cause.

At one time, I had a great many cattle scattered over a range eighty miles long by thirty miles wide, and in that area I had numerous cattle thieves to deal with.

Many owners, of course, had individual ranches and small bunches of cattle scattered in among my ranches. Some were perfectly honest, while others were not, and it was a difficult matter to be sure which was which.

Experience taught me, at the start, that it was no use asking one neighbour whether another would steal calves or kill beef.

If he were a friend of the man in question, and the latter were really a thief, he would deny it. On the other hand, if he were an enemy and the other man perfectly honest, he would intimate that the latter was a thief, although not actually saying so.

Then again, he might tell the man himself that you had asked him whether he was honest. If the man were honest, his feelings would be hurt, and if he were a thief, he would be resentful, and probably have it in for you from then on.

Therefore, some other method had to be found, and I stumbled on to one which invariably worked out satisfactorily.

That was to go directly to the man I suspected and ask him what he would do if somebody stole from him. If he were honest, he would usually be at a loss to reply, but he was never vindictive.

On the other hand, if the man were a thief, the virulence of his unprintable vituperation against anyone who dared to steal from him would be a fair index to the extent of his illicit operations.

Some cattle thieves operated on a much larger scale than others, and regarded the smaller thieves with a certain contempt, as being mere pikers. It is not surprising, therefore, that the former have a certain code or standard to which they are supposed to conform. In other words, the theft of horses or cattle is legitimate, but to steal a dog is beneath the dignity of a self-respecting cow thief.

Thompson had transgressed the code by stealing my dog; also, it had been swiped back from him by its owner, which was an added disgrace. So he had to offer some sort of appeasement before he could be re-habilitated and restored to his former standing among his fellow cow thieves. It seemed that the only practical way for him to offer this appeasement was to set up the drinks whenever anyone called him "Dog thief." And this proved quite expensive to him, in the long run.

He eventually reached the conclusion that crime doesn't pay, especially when that crime is dog stealing.

CHAPTER XV

BEAR-HUNTING GUESTS

DURING my many years of bear hunting, a great number of sportsmen, tenderfoot and otherwise, hunted with me. Some of my "bear-hunting guests," as I called them, were charming and delightful companions, but others, I regret to say, did not attain that high standard.

Many of them were from the East, and had never ridden in timbered mountains, where it is so easy to get lost. So taking care of my guests was a great responsibility.

In black bear hunting, I always insisted that each hunter carry a box of matches. In case he got lost, the light from his fire would serve as a beacon at night, while a column of smoke could be easily discerned in the daytime. Also, I told my guests how to strike wet matches; as most of my readers probably know, a wet match rubbed in the hair will light immediately upon striking it.

Usually one or two of my men acted as guides, so it was not often that a tenderfoot hunter got lost. In hunting grizzly, it was thoroughly understood that when we were lucky enough to strike such a trail, it was a case of every man for himself. This meant that the tenderfoot hunters, escorted by their guides, returned to camp, hunting deer on the way back, if they so desired.

Among many experiences with my bear-hunting guests, two stand out prominently, and while they were both grimly humorous, in each case the joke was on me.

On one occasion, one of my former hunting guests wrote to say he would like to hunt with me again that fall, and I wrote back, saying I would be very glad to have him.

When, at the last moment, he found he would be unable to come, he wrote again, asking if he might send a friend of his instead. I agreed to this arrangement; but his friend, in his turn, wrote that *he* would not be able to come either and asked if a friend of *his* could take his place. I answered "Yes," and this friend came. Very remote friendship, as it were.

Nature has failed to endow some people with pleasing personalities, and this man was one of them. I had nothing at all against him. I just didn't like him!

He accompanied me on a black bear hunt, and we jumped a bear but, after running a mile or so, he bayed in some thick bushes, as there was no available tree for him to climb. We approached him together on foot and, of course, my quest was to have the shot.

We glimpsed the bear among the bushes, and my conpanion left me to go where he thought he might get a better shot at him. Two or three minutes passed, and it came about that the bear was just immediately between us. Suddenly a shot rang out, missing the bear and my head by about a foot. I threw myself on the ground, and another bullet whizzed through where I had been standing. Then, here came the bear—running by me at full tilt. I shot him as he went by, and he rolled over.

Just then the irate hunter appeared, yelling, "Why did you kill him? You promised to let me have the shot."

"I had to shoot him in self-defence," I replied.

"I thought you weren't afraid of black bear," he shouted.

"I'm not afraid of black bear," I shouted back, "but I was afraid of you. Two of your shots nearly got me, and I was afraid the third one would, so I had to shoot the bear to stop you shooting." It was quite some time before he cooled down, but after the bear had been skinned, and I had presented him with the hide, he was somewhat mollified.

My second outstanding experience was on a grizzly hunt. One day, a neighbour, who lived off some ten miles, came to me and told me that a she-bear had killed one of his yearlings, not far from his ranch. He wanted me to catch the bear and her cub with my hounds, and very naturally, he wanted to join in the hunt.

I couldn't very well refuse him, though it is far safer to hunt a grizzly alone. My objections were based on the fact that you have to watch, not only the bear, but your fellow hunter, who, likely as not, will prove to be a headache before you are through.

The next day I went to my neighbour's ranch with the hounds. The yearling had been killed in a valley, fifteen miles from the heavy timber on the mountain side, and as the bear and her cub had been eating on the hill during the night, and had bedded down near it, they had to run over open ground some fifteen miles before reaching the timber. The trail, being a hot one, was followed by the hounds at full speed, but we were able to keep within hearing of them, as the ground was good going.

We caught up with them after about ten miles, and when I got within about fifty yards of the dogs, who had stopped, I proceeded on foot, leading my horse and carrying my rifle. The dogs were on a hillside, barking furiously and looking down below them.

From where I was walking I could not see the bear, who had stopped because the cub could not keep up. I walked on cautiously, expecting to see them at any moment, and just as I was passing by a big boulder, my companion pulled up his horse, and raised his rifle. Being on horseback, he could look over the boulder, and saw the bear with the cub by her side, sitting in a hollow under a fallen tree.

I had previously warned him to be sure and shoot the mother and not the cub, if he got a shot at the bear. His horse was winded, and *he* seemed to be very excited. The muzzle of his gun was going around in a circle, which was not exactly reassuring to me.

Then the rifle went off. There was a terrible squeal from the cub, and the next moment the she-bear took after my companion, who whirled his horse and bolted up the hillside. She got quite close to him, but stopped as she caught sight of me. And here she came. I waited till she got close, in order to have a better chance to give her a dead shot, and I was lucky enough to hit her between the eyes. She went heels over head, side-swiping me and knocking me down, while my rifle was forced out of my hand and fell under her.

My companion came riding up, and was very apologetic about having shot the cub instead of the bear, especially after my admonition, but promised to be more careful another time. I accepted his apology with as much grace as I could muster,

197

but vowed to myself that there would never be "another time."

While we were talking, there was a terrible racket going on, as the cub, who was not badly wounded, was fighting desperately with the dogs.

The only way he could be killed, without the risk of hitting one of the dogs, was to put a pistol to his head. As my friend had wounded the cub in the first place, I thought it only fair that he finish the job. So he put an end to the cub, a proceeding which was an added advantage to him, as afterwards, when he related his bear-hunting experience, he was able to tell his friends that we trailed up two grizzlies, and each of us got one.

There was one hunt to which I always look back with pardonable pride. It so happened that one of my former bear-hunting guests, who lived in New York, wrote to me about one of his friends, a prominent doctor, who had broken down completely through overwork. He had been advised to "get away from it all," and go to some place where he could have absolute rest and privacy. He had no desire to go to a sanitorium, nor to what is generally known as a "dude" ranch, so in talking the matter over with my friend, the latter told him he knew just the place he ought to go; namely, my ranch in New Mexico, a hundred miles from any railroad.

This idea seemed to please the doctor, so my friend wrote and asked me if I would have him for a few months, and I answered saying I would be very pleased.

Shortly afterwards, the sick doctor arrived, accompanied by a friend, who looked after him as far as Socorro. I was shocked by the doctor's appearance when I met him at the train, and still more so when he had to be practically lifted into the buggy. It was not that I minded taking care of him; it was the responsibility that worried me.

I ventured to ask him what, in particular, was the matter with him, and he replied: "Everything." A very comprehensive diagnosis. And it was not reassuring to learn that he was troubled with indigestion by day and insomnia by night, to say nothing of other ailments.

With wholesome diet, aided by our health-giving and exhilarating New Mexico climate, he rapidly improved. We got to be very good friends, and he became greatly interested in my hounds and my bear-hunting stories. I had given him a gentle pony, and he got so he could ride two or three miles at a time, at a snail's pace. After a month, he told me with great pleasure, that he could actually walk a hundred yards before being obliged to rest.

It was then he electrified me by asking if I would take him on a bear hunt. I didn't want to hurt his feelings by telling him I thought he was not up to such a strenuous undertaking, so I said I would think it over.

Some two weeks later, one of my cowboys saw the fresh tracks of a black bear at a little mountain spring near the ranch. The doctor was quite excited, and suggested that here was the opportunity to which he had been looking forward —to kill a bear. So, as I couldn't refuse, I let him have his way.

We started out the next morning, taking two of my men with us, he on his little pony, with a camera. It took us more than an hour to ride the three miles to the spring, which was surrounded by tall pines.

By this time, my guest was pretty well played out, so I suggested that he lie down under a tree and rest. Then, if I had luck in treeing the bear not too far away, I would come and fetch him. I left with the hounds, and before long they struck a hot trail, and ran it for about five miles before they jumped the bear. By an extraordinary piece of luck, the bear headed straight for the spring, and climbed a tree not over a hundred yards from where I had left the doctor.

Leaving the hounds to keep the bear up the tree, I rode down and found the doctor fast asleep. I woke him up and exclaimed, "Well, Doctor, I've got your bear!"

Rousing himself, and rubbing his eyes, he said drowsily, "What bear?"

I replied, "I don't know his name, but his address is up a tree about a hundred yards from here."

Confused momentarily, he stared at me. And then he remembered, I helped him on to his pony, handed him his camera, and we started for the tree, the doctor full of enthusiasm. We found the boys waiting for us there.

The doctor, all vestiges of sleep having disappeared, got

off his pony and took a snapshot of the bear sitting on a limb. He was quite excited, and eager to get a good picture of the bear, but he had to go back so far to get a clear view, that while it proved to be an excellent picture of the scenery, the bear was hardly discernible.

Then I handed him my rifle, with instructions to shoot the bear through the head. He took careful aim, but as he hadn't had any previous experience with a rifle, he shot him through the hips. The bear dropped out of the tree, badly wounded, but in a fighting mood. The dogs were, of course, around him, and, as I was afraid he might strike one of them, I shot him through the head with my pistol.

The doctor looked dismayed at having made such a poor shot at the bear's head, and began to apologize, but I consoled him, saying that, anyway, hitting him somewhere was better than missing him altogether.

As a fitting climax, the doctor posed, rifle in hand, with one foot on the bear, and I snapped his picture. After skinning the bear, we went back to the ranch.

The doctor suffered no ill effects from his hunt, and was so delighted with his exploit that his health mended rapidly. He frequently received letters from his friends asking how he was getting along; so, at my suggestion, copies of the snapshot were sent to them, as the best way of showing his improvement. Needless to say, this picture caused great astonishment among his friends, and evoked comments which afforded us intense amusement when we read their letters.

After three months at the ranch, he was a very different man, physically, than when he came, and for years afterwards, he wrote to me from time to time, reminding me of our hunt. He also sent me several dogs as mementos.

But, unfortunately, I was not always so successful in pleasing my bear-hunting guests.

One autumn, on a very windy day, one of these guests got lost, and when night came, he sought shelter in a deep canyon. He lit a fire all right, as I had told him to do in case of getting lost, but it couldn't be seen from the outside.

We searched for him until far into the night, and early next morning we observed a spiral of smoke in the distance. We were sure it was our lost hunter's signa., so two of us, carrying a canteen of water, a coffee pot, and a lunch box containing a good breakfast, decided to go and bring him in.

We found him sitting with his back to a tree and writing his diary, relating his experiences of the day before and the sleepless night he had passed without a blanket. I got off my horse, carrying the lunch box in my hand, thinking he would be pleased to see it, as being suggestive of breakfast. But instead, he greeted me with a look of annoyance.

"Dear me," he complained. "I've just written down, 'Breakfast, a cigar,' and now I'll have to scratch it out and say that you brought me my breakfast."

To avert such a catastrophe, I suggested that he leave the entry as it was, and call the meal that I had brought him a "lunch," and let it go at that. This two-fold recommendation seemed to meet with his approval, for he immediately began to eat with a voracious appetite and a clear conscience, and without erasing anything, he complacently put his diary back in his pocket.

There is no truer saying than "Truth is often stranger than fiction," which means, as I take it, that it is much harder to put over the truth. As an example in confirmation of this curious fact, I remember how, when sitting round the camp-fire at night, my hunting guests would beg the hired hunters I might have on that particular hunt, to tell them stories of their hunting experiences, which the latter, generally speaking, were only too pleased to do.

Some of these hunters would bore their listeners by relating stories that were devoid of interest, while others would delight their hearers with thrilling experiences that were devoid of truth. Some of these stories were so outrageous that I felt called upon to remonstrate privately to the narrators. One of them excused himself on the grounds that he was only giving his listeners what they wanted, and that was stories that they could tell their folks back home which would make their eyes pop!

This hunter, I must admit, was most successful in his efforts in this line. He called it "loading," which was the general term used for gulling tenderfeet.

Some of my guests, after they got home, felt the urge to write to their local papers, giving accounts of their bear-hunting adventures, and clippings were sent to me, as they thought I might be interested. And I certainly was.

As these accounts were based on a few days' superficial knowledge of actual hunting, supplemented by information gained from the strictly unreliable sources already mentioned, they enabled me to view bear hunting in a new light which had never before occurred to me.

Some of the clippings were masterpieces of unconscious humour, and forcibly reminded me of the old story of the foreigner who was taken to see his first game of baseball.

Upon being asked how he liked it, he was loud in his praises of the game, and was deeply inpressed by the pro-ficiency of the players, especially the pitcher, who, he said, when he threw the ball, no matter how the batter held his bat, would hit it every time.

There were rare exceptions, however, when to my know-ledge the story would be both thrilling and true. Strangely enough, these were the only stories that the listeners would not believe, unless they had ample corroboration. So they would come to me confidentially and ask me if I thought they were true. I would have to admit that they were and this was a most unfortunate answer, because it unintentionally white-washed all the other thrilling stories which were pure fiction; and these they swallowed—hook, line, and sinker, without referring to me for what I might have to say, as they deemed that to be quite unnecessary.

CHAPTER XVI

THE SELF-INVITED GUEST

On one of the many occasions when I was hunting alone, I was subjected to the visit of a self-invited guest.

With me, as usual, were Joe, my cook, who drove the mess wagon, and Telesfor, who took charge of the saddle horses, while I naturally took charge of the hounds.

After a couple of days' travel, we reached a range of mountains over which I had never before hunted. About noon of the third day, we stopped at a good camp site, and Joe prepared a hurried lunch. Leaving the dogs in camp, I made a round trip through the foothills, looking for any fresh signs of bear in the many oak thickets that lay along the base of the main mountain.

Acorns lay thick on the ground, as there was a good crop that year, and at one place I saw the signs of where a bear had been feeding the night before.

I was back at the camp by sundown, and as I dismounted, the dogs nearly knocked me down as they rushed out to greet me in their usual fashion. Then I observed a stranger sitting by the campfire, whom Joe promptly introduced as being a well-known professional trapper and hunter. We shook hands and I said a few words of greeting, remarking that any hunter was always welcome at my camp.

When supper was over, the stranger, whom I will call "Bud," asked Joe for grain, and went off to feed his three horses, and meanwhile, Joe told me what he knew about him, and why he had come to my camp. He had arrived shortly after I had left, so they had spent the whole afternoon in conversation.

He told Joe he had been out trapping for the past month, and was about to go to town to get provisions and grain, of which he had completely run out.

He had often heard of me from other hunters and trappers and of my "trick" dogs and queer ideas of bear hunting, and he wished to go on a hunt with me, in order that he might judge of this for himself. So, having been told that I was coming to this particular range of mountains to hunt, he had been on the lookout for me.

His horses were about played out, and if I would furnish him a mount and feed him and his horses he would bear hunt with me, thus giving me the benefit of his experience and advice. He also modestly asserted that he knew *"all* about hounds," and *"all* about horses," intimating that I was very fortunate to have the opportunity of acquiring knowledge about bear hunting from such an experienced hunter. Therefore, he was sure I would be very glad to accept his proposal.

All this Joe told me with a grin. Then he went on to say that Bud was a Socialist, and that they had spent the afternoon arguing about Socialism.

At that time, my knowledge of Socialism was very perfunctory, but I knew the general public opinion about it, which was redistribution of wealth; that is, share and share alike. At least, this was Bud's view of the matter, though, as there are exceptions to all rules, this did not apply to Bud's personal property, which he regarded as *sacrosanct*. He also was a firm believer in one-way generosity, provided he was on the receiving end. I do not wish to be too critical of such philosophy, but I do think he carried it to extremes when he told me he did not wish me even to pat his dogs. I assented, but told him he was perfectly welcome to pat any of mine, which, however was a Chinese invitation, since none of my dogs would let him come anywhere near them.

He and Joe, I am sorry to say, didn't get along at all, for the latter objected strongly to the "redistribution of wealth" idea, regarding himself as a capitalist, albeit a very small one. His notion of a capitalist was a man who did not have to work for his living, but had an income of his own, and Joe had a small bunch of cattle which produced enough income for his modest requirements.

He worked for me as a cook because he liked it. He would say to me, with pride, "But I don't have to." He had worked hard to accumulate enough money with which to buy his little bunch of cattle, and the idea was repellent to him that Bud should have a share in them, without working for it.

He worked for me, off and on, for several years, and I always regarded him as a loyal friend, although, from my point of view, he had one failing—to get a joke off on me, whenever possible. To gain the confidence of those who hunted with me, or even visited my camp, his technique was thus:

When alluding to me, he said he liked to work for me because I treated him right and paid him his wages, but he was not responsible for my ideas on bear hunting, which were none of his business. In this way, he naturally invited the confidence of those with whom he talked, and so they unburdened themselves of their opinions of me and of my queer notions, without reserve. And, as a rule, they were far from flattering.

Joe did not profess to agree with them, but he lent a sympathetic ear. Afterwards, when he was alone with me, he retailed all these opinions with such embellishments as he thought would make me sit up and take notice, reminding me of the quotation from Burns:

> O wad some power the giftie gie us
> To see oursel's as ithers see us.

In my case Joe represented this "power." He worked this racket on Bud, who instantly fell for it, and in no time at all, Joe commenced reporting to me the opinions being expressed by Bud.

It seemed that Bud felt quite scandalized at the behaviour of my hounds when they greeted me at my return to camp. He remarked that they behaved as though "I belonged to them," instead of the dogs "belonging to me," but this criticism I regarded as an unintentional compliment.

He also informed Joe that it was his custom to take out deer-hunting parties every fall, and as they were mostly tenderfoot hunters from the big cities, he had a great number of funny stories to tell about them. So far, he had no funny tenderfoot bear-hunting stories in his repertoire, but he hoped to make up for that deficiency by hunting with me.

Joe related all this with his usual grin, and I replied gravely that I would do my best to furnish Bud with what he wanted, but in return, I would do my best to get funny stories about old, experienced bear-hunters.

That night around the campfire, Bud regaled us with his funny stories, while I gave him a mild exhibition of what my "trick" dogs would do, such as sitting in a row, each with a piece of meat on his nose, waiting for me to say "Paid for," before tossing the meat in the air and catching it.

Bud laughed uproariously at this "trick," but failed entirely to realize its underlying significance as a fine example of absolute obedience without fear.

Next on my programme, I sat down by the campfire with a dishpan full of meat cut up in even-sized chunks, while I had all the dogs sit down about twenty feet away. When all was ready, I called out the name of one dog, who promptly left the bunch and came to me, and after receiving his piece of meat, he walked back to his place. I did the same with each dog, in succession, and if, by any chance, a dog left the bunch without first being called, a rare occurrence, dire punishment was meted out to him. He was told to sit where he could watch the other dogs get their meat in turn, while he got nothing. Two or three such punishments and the culprit was cured of his disobedience.

Bud told Joe later that he guessed it was one of my queer notions about feeding dogs, but, as in the previous case, it never entered his head that it was only another way to instil obedience.

At last, I fed the dogs by throwing pieces of meat for them to catch. If one of them missed and it fell on the ground and another dog grabbed it it was all right, but if a dog dared to growl when grabbing the meat, he was called out of the bunch and punished, as described before.

This method of preventing hounds quarrelling among themselves worked so well that I never had to try any other, except in the case of the fighting dogs.

Bud had three hounds; one about seven years old, his foot crippled by having been caught in a trap, and two young dogs about two years old. He had never hunted bear on horseback;

using his hounds only for trailing up any animal that had been caught and escaped with the trap. He had caught several black bear in that way, thus teaching his hounds to trail bear.

His method of training hounds was the usual one—to severely beat them for doing anything he considered wrong, such as running deer or rabbits. His hounds were deathly afraid of him, as was demonstrated by their cringing attitude whenever he spoke to them. I felt very sorry for these unhappy hounds, but as I was restrained from patting them, I had no way of showing them any sympathy. Having closely observed the friendly relations that existed between my dogs and myself they must have inferred that I was a friend to all dogs, for when I passed near them, instead of cringing, they wagged their tails slowly and furtively. I would have liked to have patted them, but I had to content myself by just giving them a friendly nod.

Bud and I started out on our first hunt the next morning, and I went straight to the oak thicket where I had seen the tracks of a black bear the previous afternoon.

It usually happens that when you want to show off, things have a way of not going according to plan. But on this particular occasion, they not only went well for my purpose but far better than I could have possibly anticipated. My design, of course, was to impress Bud with my knowledge of bear hunting and hounds. From what Joe had told me, Bud was under the impression that I knew little or nothing on either of these subjects.

Bud was riding one of my extra horses, an arrangement of which he approved, as he wished to give his horses a complete rest. All my dogs, necked together in pairs, followed behind my horse, with the exception of Sleuth, who was privileged to go ahead of me. Bud took in everything I did with an observing and critical eye.

When we arrived at the oak thicket we stopped, and I told Sleuth to "Go on," which he thoroughly understood to mean that he was to go ahead into the thicket and find a trail, if there was one. He had been gone but five minutes, when we heard an explosion of barks, and then a quick succession of them, as he followed the trail.

"That means a hot trail," I observed to Bud, as I got off my horse and unnecked the hounds, one pair after another. I remounted and we followed the hounds, those in the lead being some three hundred yards or more away. The ground was fairly rough and covered with brush, and the hounds rapidly gained on us, though they did not get out of hearing.

At last we reached a wide, open canyon, through which ran a much-used cattle trail. It had rained a little during the night, so all tracks were fresh. And there on the trail was a fresh bear track, going up the canyon.

We galloped for a half mile or so before we caught sight of a lone hound, following about two hundred yards behind the pack. I turned round to Bud, who was following close behind me, and called out, "They'll soon have that panther treed."

Instead of replying, he pointed contemptuously to the fresh bear tracks on the cattle trail, and shouted, "Ain't you seen them tracks?"

"Sure I have," I answered, "but the hounds are running a panther, just the same."

The hounds stopped, though the baying continued which meant that they had treed their quarry.

When a bear climbs a tree, he sits on the first big limb where he feels safe from the pursuing hounds. A panther keeps on climbing and hides in the thickest branches at the top of the tree. So when we arrived at the tree around which the dogs were barking, Bud looked perplexed at not seeing a bear on a lower limb, so I shouted, "Look to the top of the tree."

The panther wasn't visible, but its tail was hanging down in tell-tale fashion, so to speak, and as Bud caught sight of it, the look of surprise on his face was comical.

We got off our horses, and after judging where the panther's body ought to be, I shot, and he fell out of the tree, wounded, but not quite dead. To prevent the hounds being torn by his claws, I shot him again with my six-shooter.

Then Bud proceeded to skin him, and when he had finished, we started back, leaving the naked carcass on the ground.

Dogs, by the way, will not eat raw panther meat, although I have known some to do so after it was cooked. Some panther hunters, however, have told me their hounds would eat raw panther meat, so all I can say is that mine never would. Maybe they were too particular.

Returning from a successful hunt, the dogs were allowed to run where they pleased, but usually they marched proudly ahead of me, with their tails up, as though expressing their satisfaction for what they had done.

From the time Bud had started skinning the panther, he had hardly uttered a word, and from the expression on his face, I sensed that he was ruminating. At last, unable to suppress his curiosity any longer, he said, "How could you tell your dogs were running a panther, and not a bear?"

This was my opportunity to lay it on thick, so I countered by asking him with surprise, "Can't you tell what your hounds are running by just looking at them?" And I said nothing more, reasoning that it would be presumptuous to tell a man who knew "*all* about hounds," the answer to such a relatively simple question.

The fact was that some time before I had shot a panther out of a tree without killing it and one of the hounds had got badly clawed in the ensuing fight. From then on, whenever the hounds ran a panther, he would not run with them, as he would if it were a bear. So, as soon as I saw this hound trailing behind the pack, I had no hesitation in telling Bud that it was a panther.

We rode along in silence for some time, while Bud still pondered as to how I could tell what animal the hounds were running by just looking at them. Then he got another shock.

One of the hounds, without uttering a sound, suddenly started off on a run, and the others followed suit and disappeared in the brush.

"What are they running now?" Bud asked, and I replied, "Meat."

"What do you mean by 'meat'?" inquired Bud.

"Something dead," I replied, "but let's follow them."

We galloped along until we caught up with them in the brush, where they were trying to tear a deer to pieces. All at once I recognized the spot, and realized that the panther must have killed the deer at this place and evidently had been eating on it when Sleuth first ran on to him.

This explained his explosion of barks.

We drove the dogs away, and Bud skinned the deer, and tied the hide on his horse, while we appropriated the two hams for fresh meat for our own personal use in camp. The rest of the deer was cut up and fed to the dogs.

Afterwards, when we ate this deer meat, I couldn't help smiling to think that this was the first time a panther had ever inadvertently supplied me with venison.

We returned to camp with the dogs marching in front of us, as before, but this time more proudly, because their stomachs were full.

Poor Bud, however, had a new worry upon which to meditate. He could not understand how I knew that the hounds had set off on a trail for meat. The answer was very simple, though Bud, with *all* his knowledge of hounds, could not even guess it.

On many previous occasions, when my hounds were running loose, one would suddenly start off, apparently in a great hurry. The other hounds, noticing this, would take out after him, but not one of them barked, showing they were not trailing any animal. The first time this happened, my curiosity was aroused, so I followed them and sure enough, I came on to a dead cow.

It is a curious fact that dogs seem to prefer spoiled meat, for I have often thrown them two pieces of meat, one spoiled, the other fresh, and they would invariably eat the spoiled meat first. I believe that accounts for hounds being so attracted to a carcass, especially when they are hungry. In this case, of course, the meat was fresh.

To make matters worse for Bud, he had a private talk with Joe that evening, asking if Joe had any idea how I knew what a hound was trailing, just by looking at him.

Joe told him that he didn't know how I could tell. All he knew was that I could. He treated the question as if it were not worth asking, remarking that it didn't amount to anything, anyway, compared with all the other things I knew about hounds.

We started off on another hunt the next morning, and this time, Bud said he'd like to bring along his old hound, the one with the crippled foot. I said "All right," and headed straight for the place where the panther had killed the deer. with the intent of catching the bear we were to have hunted the day before, and from which we had been switched by the panther.

This bear had evidently continued to feed in this vicinity, and it was not long before Sleuth opened up on a hot trail, judging by the excited eagerness with which he barked as he started to follow it. I unnecked my hounds, as always, and the hunt was on.

Although the trail was hot, the bear had travelled a long distance before reaching the place where he decided to make his bed, and while the going was not particularly rough, the hounds soon got out of hearing.

Then it was that my slow-trail dogs came into play. Bud had apparently been watching these dogs for some time, and at last he said, "Why ain't them two dogs gone with the pack?"

I explained that they had been trained not to—that their function was to trail the pack when it got out of hearing.

From the incredulous look on Bud's face, this was evidently a new one on him. He lapsed into silence, as though it were hopeless to try to understand me.

But there was another surprise in store for him. We had gone about ten miles and were riding up a ridge on the mountain. Suddenly, Sleuth appeared, about fifty yards off, on my left. I stopped, and Bud inquired, "Ain't that the hound you call your best bear dog?"

I replied, "Yes," and then he went on, "If I had a dog that would leave a bear and come back to me, I'd take my gun and kill him."

This remark annoyed me somewhat, so I retorted, "In that case, Sleuth is in big luck that he doesn't belong to you." And then I asked, "Have you any idea why he came back to me?"

"Because he was scared of the bear," replied Bud.

"Oh, no," I said, "this bear is treed and in any case, my dog is not scared of a bear up a tree. He has left the other hounds to keep him there while he came to hunt me up and take me directly to him."

This was absolutely true, but Bud considered it an insult to his intelligence for me to try to put any such stuff over on him, and while he said nothing, his face showed that he was angry. He was at a loss to know what to do, but just at that moment his old hound, who hadn't been able to keep up with us, came up, so Bud said, "I guess I'll let my old hound stay with the bear trail and follow him."

"That's up to you," I replied. "If you should see a column of smoke going up, you'll know it's where I am, and I will wait a reasonable time for you to rejoin me before I go back to camp."

Then I called my two slow-trail dogs off the trail of the pack, and saying, "Go on," to Sleuth, I followed him, while Bud went on up the ridge with his old hound.

I had gone a couple of miles when I heard the hounds baying in the distance, and after another quarter of a mile, I arrived on the scene. I dismounted and shot the bear, then cut him open and distributed his insides to the hungry pack. As soon as they had all had their fill, I found a suitable place some seventy yards away, and built a fire.

In my saddle pockets I had brought along some newspapers and a lunch for Bud and myself, and after eating my share, I sat down in the shade of a nearby tree, and lighting my pipe, started to read.

Bud showed up in a couple of hours. His hound had followed the bear trail into a deep canyon, full of big rocks, and there he had to quit because his old hound had played out. Then he caught sight of the smoke from my fire, and decided to return to me. I gave him his lunch, and when he had finished it, he got up and said, "I guess we'd better go back to camp. It's getting late."

"All right," I replied, "but we'll have to skin the bear first."

"What bear?" he asked.

"Why, the one we trailed all morning," I answered. "It's lying in the brush up above here."

Bud said nothing, but followed me as I led him to the bear. He skinned it, and put the hide and all the meat we could carry on our horses, and rode back to camp.

On our way back, it was apparent that Bud was studying over in his mind how it was that I could have taught Sleuth to stay with the bear until he had treed, and then hunt me up to take me to the "tree."

It is hardly necessary to say that Sleuth had never been taught this "trick." He did it entirely on his own initiative but I feel sure that he got the idea when, as a puppy, he first learned to trail a man, and would get a piece of meat as a reward for finding him; then running back to me in puppyish glee, would get the second reward he knew was waiting for him. It is reasonable to suppose, therefore, that when he became full grown, he would follow the same tactics with a treed bear. At any rate, that's what he did.

Of course, for Bud's benefit, I treated the whole matter as though it were merely a stunt of one of my "trick" dogs.

Joe had supper ready for us at camp, the principal dish being bear steak smothered in onions, in the proper cooking of which Joe greatly prided himself.

After the meal was over, the dogs were ready for their "catch-as-catch-can" evening meal of "jerky" meat. I told the dogs to stay beyond the campfire in an open space of rising ground, behind which was a thick growth of bush, and Bud looked on while I threw small chunks of meat to the dogs to catch.

After I had fed the dogs for a while, suddenly I saw peering out of the darkness in the brush behind them, three pairs of eyes, glowing like live coals, and they reminded me of that imploring look portrayed in the eyes of lost souls.

Needless to say, they were the eyes of Bud's three hounds.

Though I believe in a high standard, providing that it is lived up to, I also believe that a low standard, lived up to, is preferable to a high one that is not. Personally, I set myself a certain standard that I feel I can maintain, but whether it is high or low is for my friends to judge. But there are times when, being only human, one falls from grace, and that I did on this occasion.

I assured Bud that I wouldn't pat his dogs or otherwise take notice of them, the day he arrived, and I had kept my word. But it was too hard to resist the temptation now thrust upon me. So whenever Bud, whom I was observing from the corner of my eye, happened to turn his head in the other direction, somehow a piece of meat missed my dogs and fell among the "lost souls," causing a temporay "black-out" while they scrambled for it and ate it.

The old saying, "Be sure your sin will find you out," came very near being true in this instance. The "lost souls" from then on, in evincing their gratitude for the surreptitious late suppers I had given them, wagged their tails vigorously whenever I passed by where they were tied, and not furtively, as they did when they first came to my camp. And they pretty nearly gave me away.

Their behaviour did not escape Bud's watchful eye, and as I approached the campfire, where he was standing while one of these tailwaggings was still in progress, Bud looked at me with deep suspicion, "I guess you've been a-pattin' of my dogs," he exclaimed.

I assured him, however, that I hadn't.

"Then, why are they waggin' their tails at you?" he wanted to know.

I professed ignorance, but remarked that as my dogs always wagged their tails whenever I passed them, I supposed that his dogs, on seeing them do it, had caught the habit.

Bud was not impressed with this explanation, but as there was no alternative but to accept it, he did so with bad grace. Later, in an unwary moment, he broached the subject to Joe, asking him if he hadn't seen me pat his dogs. This Joe stoutly denied, and sensing the malevolent motive back of Bud's question, to use him as a cat's-paw for convicting me of a false-hood, a tender spot was touched; which was Joe's loyalty to me. So, wilfully misinterpreting Bud's question, Joe said angrily, "So you're kicking at your hounds wagging their tails at him instead of you. Well, let me give you some advice. Just treat your dogs like he treats his, and I'll bet they'll soon wag their tails at you, too."

After this second discomfiture, Bud concluded to retire to his camp and, presumably, like Achilles, "sulked in his tent." It rained hard that night and most of the next morning, but cleared up in the afternoon. But by that time it was too late to go out on a hunt, so we put in our time by sitting around the campfire and talking. Most of the talking was done by

Bud and Joe, while I sat by as a sort of silent referee, speaking only when spoken to.

The three main subjects of conversation were Socialism, dogs, and horses. Their discussions became very acrimonious at times and I had all I could do to preserve order. No matter what Bud said, Joe held a contrary view; or if he didn't, he agreed with him in a way that was far worse than it would have been if he had disagreed with him.

For instance, Bud said that he never lent nor borrowed, adding that if people stuck to that principle, much trouble would be avoided. Joe emphatically disagreed with this view, contending that people got along much better when they helped each other out by lending or borrowing, as the case might be, but admitted that Bud certainly carried out his convictions in practice.

Joe then proceeded to tell me, before Bud, that the latter sure told the truth when he said he never lent nor borrowed, because that morning he had asked Bud to loan him his sharp pocket knife to cut off a hang-nail, and Bud had refused. So he had to go to work and do the best he could with a butcher knife.

Then he went on, "And he don't *borrow* nothing, neither. He just *takes* what he wants, and that's all there is to it. He would never *borrow* because he would never repay, so it could hardly be called *borrowing*. This morning he helped himself to enough horseshoes and nails to shoe his three horses, and also twice as much hobble rope as he needed, because, as he said, 'it's always a good idea to have more hobbles than you need on hand to offset losing them or wearing them out.' "

Bud was getting hotter and hotter, for he did not at all relish Joe's exposure of his method of avoiding borrowing. So I had to throw oil on the troubled waters by saying that as Bud had skinned a panther and a bear for me, I thought that that would more than offset the value of the horseshoes and the hobble rope. Then I advocated changing the subject and as horseshoes suggested horses, they became the next topic of discussion.

But changing the subject didn't help matters, because they fell out about horses. Joe had a saddle horse of which he was very proud. He had ridden it over from his ranch to mine, when he came to take charge of my mess wagon, and his horse was naturally brought along with my saddle horses.

Bud, also, had a saddle horse of which he was equally proud. It was one of the three he brought with him, the other two being merely pack horses.

The argument concerned the relative merits of their respective horses, each claiming that his was the better of the two. So I left them, as I had no special interest in the matter, and did not wish to take sides.

Joe was a hard worker, and very efficient in his own line of work, but he had his peculiarities, if they may be called such. We were very good friends, but he seldom agreed with me on minor matters. No matter what I might tell him to do, he always objected to any suggestion I might make as to how it should be done.

His answer would be, "Yes, but——" "Your idea is all right but I believe I would do it . . ." and then he explained the way he thought it should be done, and the argument would usually be closed by my saying, "All right, Joe. Go ahead and do it your own way. All I care about is that it be done."

But behind my back, he assumed a very different attitude. He boasted that I was an authority on any subject, and was always right, even when he personally thought I was wrong.

In this argument about their horses, Bud and Joe had finally reached a point where they thought they would leave it to a third party to decide which horse he thought was the better, so Joe suggested that I be selected. Bud objected on the grounds that he thought I didn't know enough about horses to decide such a question, anyway, and this remark got Joe's goat.

"You say he don't know much about horses," he exclaimed. "Well, I can tell you he knows more about them than you and I know, put together, and I can prove it."

"I don't see how you can do that," retorted Bud.

"I sure can," answered Joe. "Can you tell a horse to open his mouth and have him obey you?"

"No, I can't," said Bud wrathfully, thinking that Joe was trying to kid him, "and no one else can't neither."

"That's where you're wrong," replied Joe, "*he* can (referring to me) and if you think he can't, what'll you bet?"

"I can't bet," said Bud, "because I ain't got any money, but I would if I had. Anyway, you can't make me believe in any such stuff."

"Would you believe it if you saw a horse do it?" asked Joe, provokingly.

"Yes, in that case, I would," answered Bud, "but he would sure have to do it first."

"All right," said Joe. "I'll go and get one of his horses and have him show you."

The horses were grazing close to camp, so Joe brought in my horse, George, and then came to me, where I was sitting on my bed under a tree, reading. He explained how his argument with Bud had wound up, and asked me to give Bud a demonstration.

Picking up my bridle which was lying by my bed, I walked down with Joe, and said innocently to Bud, who was standing by the campfire:

"Joe tells me that you've never seen nor heard of a horse opening his mouth when told to do so." And evincing surprise that a man with his long experience with horses should have never even heard of so simple a thing, I said, "I suppose you would like to see a horse do it, so I will show you."

We walked over to where George was tied, and he looked around at us as we approached. When I got within ten feet of him, I called out, "Open your mouth, George," which he immediately did, and I put the bridle on him.

Bud's expression at this juncture can best be described by quoting Joe, who said that "it beat anything he ever saw."

However, I went on explaining unconcernedly, "As it is difficult for me to bridle a horse with one hand, my horses are kind enough to help me out by opening their mouths whenever I ask them to."

While we walked back to the campfire, Bud's expression grew still more strange, if that were possible, and then Joe broke the silence by remarking genially, "It's lucky for you that you didn't have any money to bet with, for I would sure have won it."

How to teach a horse to do this may appear to be a very difficult problem, at first sight, but as a matter of fact, the solution was very simple. At first, after I lost my arm, everyone was only too kind in trying to help me perform the ordinary tasks of life, and it was no easy matter to refuse their help without seeming ungracious, so I put it this way: if I allowed myself to be helped all the time, how helpless I would be when there happened to be no one around to help. So the sooner I learned to fend for myself, the better it would be for me.

I soon found that I could do ordinary things fairly well. There were, after all, relatively few things that presented unusual difficulties, but one of these was the bridling of a horse with one hand.

The first requisite is to have a gentle horse, who will keep his head still while you are trying to bridle him, and as my personal riding horses were exceptionally gentle, I never had any trouble on that score. So the problem consisted of getting the horse to open his mouth so the bit could be slipped into it. After that, putting the headstall over his ears was a simple matter.

I always used a curb-bit, and not a snaffle, for while I used it as little as possible, a curb-bit is essential in an emergency. In bridling a horse, I held the headstall against his forehead, raised the bridle until the bit was between the horse's lips, and then raised it with a little jerk and gave the teeth a gentle tap. After repeating this a few times, the horse would open his mouth, and the bit would slip in, thus allowing the headstall to be pulled over his ears. A horse soon learns to open his mouth to avoid the tapping of his teeth, which are very sensitive.

George, however, went a step further than the other horses, for as soon as he would catch sight of the bridle, he would open his mouth as I approached him, even six or eight feet away. This became a regular habit with him, and thus it furnished me with the idea of a good joke, especially on one who prided himself on knowing "*all* about horses."

Holding the bridle behind me, all I had to do was to suddenly show George the bridle and say "Open your mouth" at the same time. That was all there was to the trick.

It had rained heavily all night and on into the next morning, and it was too wet to hunt with the hounds in the afternoon, as all scent would be washed away, so I rode off to look for fresh bear tracks.

While I was gone, Bud and Joe got into more heated arguments which finally ended up in some sort of quarrel, and when I got back to camp, Joe came to me with a long recital of complaints about Bud. He wouldn't help with the chores around camp, such as chopping wood, or bringing in a pail of water from the creek. He would do nothing but sit in front of the campfire, smoking his pipe and talking Socialism, while he, Joe, was washing Bud's dirty dishes.

He had helped Bud for over an hour fixing up his old pack saddles, without even a "Thank you" from Bud. "And," added Joe, "I don't believe he knows the meaning of that word."

Bud's camp outfit was about fifty yards from ours, and Joe suggested that we give him food, let him cook it at his own camp, and wash his own dishes.

I had to calm Joe down and persuade him to be patient. I explained that the next morning I was going to change camp and Bud would be leaving us to go to town. I pointed out that we ought to make allowances for Bud, as from what he had told us, he had been raised the hard way, among a tough crowd and, warming to my subject, I went on, "I tell you, Joe, if I had been brought up like Bud was, I would have been a good deal worse."

Joe agreed with me, nodding his head with more approval than I thought necessary, and then went back to the mess wagon to fix supper.

Late that evening, we had our last campfire talk, and Bud was again regaling us with some of his tenderfoot stories.

It seemed that parties from the big cities liked to go on deer hunts in the fall, not that they wished to hunt, particularly, but they wanted to take a trip in the wilds and wide open spaces, just for a change. When they reached a jumping-off place for such trips, they would hire any experienced guide or hunter who might be recommended to them.

In this way, Bud secured for himself a good paying job every hunting season, and it was thus that he came into close contact with people whom he never otherwise would have known.

As he didn't burden them with a discourse on his Socialistic beliefs, he was regarded by them in the light of an ingenuous "diamond in the rough," but Bud's opinion of them was far less tolerant. Judging from his standpoint, their ignorance was appalling. Many of them had never ridden a horse and were unaware that the right side was the wrong side of a horse to get on. Nor had they ever fired a rifle before, and if they ventured to hunt by themselves, they would not get game, but only get lost.

He ridiculed them for the absurd things they did from sheer ignorance, and while enlarging on their follies, he figuratively patted himself on the back to show how much smarter he was, by comparison.

It must have been that, owing to Bud's Socialistic convictions, he was imbued with class hatred. He disliked what he called "high-toned" people, in general, and the members of his hunting parties in particular. He was not averse to being overpaid by them for his services, but instead of being grateful, he regarded them as being "easy-marks."

Many habits and customs of these "high-toned" folks met with Bud's disapproval, one of them being that they brought along servants to wait on them. This Bud considered entirely unnecessary, as in his experience, the only people of whom he had ever heard, working in that capacity, were those hired by hotels. I mention this, because subsequently, it turned out to be the chief cause of Bud's dislike of "high-toned" people, for the latter did not invite him to eat with them when meals were served. Instead, he was unceremoniously relegated to eat with the servants.

The first time this happened, Bud felt like quitting, but he needed the good pay he was getting, and concluded to take it on the chin, without reprisal. Nevertheless, this treatment rankled. But he was due for a still greater humiliation, for on one occasion, after his first meal with the servants, the latter complained to their employers that they simply would not eat with him again. It appeared that Bud's ideas of cleanliness and theirs did not coincide. As a preliminary to helping himself to butter, Bud had run his knife through his mouth to clean it. Furthermore, though fingers were made before knives and forks, that did not justify Bud when helping himself to stew, to pick out a piece of meat with his fingers, and then drop it back in the dish in exchange for another piece that had more appeal.

The whole matter, however, was easily and tactfully settled by the employer telling Bud that whenever he wanted a meal, the servants would give him one, while the servants, on their part, saw to it that when he wanted a second helping, they helped him to it.

When, later, someone told Bud why the servants objected to his eating with them, his reply was that if that were so, he thought they were far too finicky for any good use.

Bud wound up his tales of other short-comings of these affluent socialites by saying, contemptuously, "Them's the kind of folks they call 'gentlemen.'"

Here, I interposed by asking Bud what, in his judgment, from his experience with such people, constituted a "gentleman."

His reply was that his idea of a gentleman was "an educated fool with money, who thinks he's better than you are."

To give Bud his due, from the distorted angle in which he viewed the whole question, he was in a sense, correct. But I told him that in my opinion, he was mistaken, and he quickly retorted, "Then what kind of a *person* would *you* call a 'gentleman'?"

Being only too glad to have the opportunity to air my opinions on such a subject, especially to a man like Bud, I said, "A gentleman is a man who treats you better than you treat him." And then I added: "And everyone, high or low, rich or poor, can be a gentleman if he wants to be."

He thought for a few moments, and when the full import of what the definition meant had sunk into his brain, he said, "I think you're wrong, too, but if that is what it takes to be a gentleman, I'll be damned if I'd want to be one!"

"You sure said her that time!" remarked Joe, agreeing with Bud for the second time in all their acquaintance.

We started to pack up and change camp the next morning,

221

and I gave Joe a list of provisions that would keep Bud going for a few days. Joe reluctantly agreed to get these things together, meanwhile protesting, "But he doesn't deserve them."

"Maybe not," I replied, "but we can't let him leave here without anything to go on with, until he gets to town."

"Yes," remarked Joe, "but that was the fix he was in when he came here, wasn't it?" Then he went on: "I'll take them over to him, as you say, but do you want me to tell him you are giving them to him as a present? Because, I bet, if you do, he'll never say 'thank you.'"

"I don't care if he doesn't," I answered. "You give them to him, and tell him, from me, to just take them along."

He did as I asked, and when he returned, I said, "Well, Joe, did you tell him that I said to 'just take them along'?"

"I did," replied Joe, with his usual grin.

"And what did he say?" I asked, and Joe's reply was, "He said he would."

A little later, we were all ready to go, Joe with his mess wagon, Telesfor with the saddle horses, I with my dogs. Bud had his pack horses packed, and all that remained was for him to call his dogs and go. He called them, but they wouldn't come, for they had taken refuge among the dogs in my pack.

We all set to work to catch them and hand them over to Bud, who tied them up with hobble ropes, the first dog to one stirrup, the second to the other stirrup, and the third tied to the second dog. Mounting his horse, Bud started off slowly to his pack horses, fifty yards distant, and he had nearly reached them when the third dog got loose and bolted back. This so enraged Bud that he whirled round, and spurring his horse frantically, endeavoured to head off his dog before he could reach my pack, entirely forgetting that he had the other two dogs tied to his stirrups. The consequence was they were both suddenly jerked into the air, and at the second jerk they broke loose and joined the fleeing dog. So Bud had three dogs to pursue, instead of one.

In the meantime I had got on my horse, and the three hounds came straight for me and stopped under him. Then, with many curses, Bud got off his horse, untied the hobbles which had been tied to the stirrups, and came towards me to get his dogs.

Princess, my great Dane, was at her accustomed place, immediately behind my horse's hocks, and when Bud started to grab one of his dogs, Princess growled and showed her teeth, while Joe shouted. "Look out for that big dog, or she'll sure grab you!"

Bud took the hint, and had to ask me to get the dogs for him, and while I hated to do it, I got off my horse and caught hold of one of the trembling three and handed him over to Bud.

This time, Bud tied a rope round the dog's neck so tightly that he could hardly breathe, at the same time indulging in a wild orgy of blasphemy, in which he assured the dog that he wouldn't get loose again. I caught the other two, and at last he had them all tied to the stirrups of his saddle, as before.

During this time, while Bud was still cursing in a way that would excite the admiration of a marine, Joe, who was helping by holding a dog while Bud was tying the rope, kept up a running fire of comment. He told Bud that if he were training dogs, the first thing he would teach them would be to come when he called them, and other such remarks.

This only added duel to Bud's wrath, and realizing that he was not in a position to refute Joe's suggestions, he was forced to take refuge in silence. And so he rode off to join his pack horses, dragging his unhappy dogs after him. They all moved on together, while we watched them until they were out of sight.

"And that's that!" exclaimed Joe, climbing back on his wagon.

Thus ended the altercations between Bud and Joe! Both were peculiar characters, and if I had to describe Joe, I could not picture him better than by saying that, though not coloured, he was the Rochester of his day.

As to Bud, I regret to say that I had to add him to my list of "Unpleasing Personalities I Have Known."

CHAPTER XVII

WELL, I'LL BE . . . !

At our new camp, a few days later, I had an amusing experience, wherein I received four compliments—all in a row—worded in identical language, and more or less on the equivocal order.

Compliments, roughly speaking, should be divided into four classifications.

The first type come from kind-hearted people, who wish to say something they think will please you, but these compliments should be cast aside as being mostly, if not wholly undeserved.

The second kind is pure flattery, and should be discarded as insincere.

The third type is the equivocal compliment—the kind which gives you a pat on the back with one hand, and a slap in the face with the other—which, though not altogether satisfactory, is nevertheless genuine.

The fourth is the real compliment—metaphorically, a hard one to extract—and that is, dead silence on the part of critics.

One of Telesfor's duties on a hunt was to skin the bears I might kill. In case I killed a large bear at a distance from camp, he would have to accompany me the next day, with a couple of pack horses, to bring it in. But in the case of a small bear, up to three hundred pounds in weight, I could pack it on my horse and lead him back to camp, thus dispensing with Telesfor's services. This saved time, as, owing to my work, my bear-hunting time was limited, and every day I could devote to actual hunting counted.

When hunting, I rode day after day, from dawn to dark, and later, so I regarded such occasional walks back to camp as a sort of relaxation. But there was one fly in the ointment of saving a day by this method—how to pack the bear on the horse. This worried me not a little, but I finally hit on the solution of the problem.

I always carried two saddle ropes when hunting alone, one tied to each side of the horn of the saddle. Then, when I killed a small bear, I looped one of my saddle ropes round his neck and dragged him to the first convenient tree that had a limb sticking straight out at right angles, and at about ten feet from the ground. I put the second rope around the bear's neck, also, and threw both ropes over the limb. Next, I looped one of the ropes around the horn of my saddle, and made the horse pull on the rope, raising the bear until his hind feet were about a foot above the level of where my cinch rings would be if my horse were standing under the tree.

Then, with my horse holding the rope taught, I went back to the tree and pulled on the other rope, and when it was tight, I put two or three bights round any convenient branch, fastening it so it wouldn't slip. Then I led my horse forward, thus loosening the rope by which the bear had been held, and transferring its weight to the other rope.

Next, I led my horse to the hanging bear, and let him stand, while I called my dogs and borrowed four of their collars. I had a double-cinch saddle, so there were four cinch rings, and into each of these I put a collar. I cinched up the horse very tight, and then carefully loosened the rope that was holding the bear until his hind feet were at the level of the two cinch rings next to them.

I fastened the rope again, after which I strapped each of the bear's hind feet tightly with a dog collar. Then I pushed the horse side-ways until the centre of gravity of the bear was on the other side of the horse, and loosened the rope gradually until the forefeet of the bear were on the level of the other two cinch rings, and fastened it again. Going back to the horse I strapped the bear's two forefeet to the cinch rings, and when this was done, I had all four feet strapped securely to the four cinch rings.

Next, I took the loops of the two saddle ropes off the bear's neck, coiled them up, and tied them on my saddle, and lifting the bear's head, I put the horn string round his neck and secured it to the saddle-horn. My task of loading being completed, I started back to camp, leading the horse.

It is true that the bear made a very wobbly load, but he stayed put as long as the saddle didn't turn on the horse, so I didn't care how much he wobbled.

On one occasion, while returning with the bear, I struck the road about two miles below my camp, and saw a stranger riding towards me, so I waited until he drew near.

After saying, "Howdy," he asked me if he was on the right road to a certain ranch, and as it was about ten miles up the road, we went on together.

He seemed to be a man of few words, and we went on some little distance before he spoke. He had been glancing uneasily at the bear, from time to time, and presently he broke his silence, informing me that he was an old government packer, and that he had worked in one of the three pack trains used when President Arthur and General Sheridan made their famous trip over the Teton Mountains to Yellowstone National Park. He had helped pack a heavy cook stove on a mule, which was the hardest load he had ever helped to pack. It had to be tied on with a double-diamond hitch, otherwise it would never have stayed put.

Then he continued, "I've been a packer all my life, but this is the first time I ever saw a pack stay on without being tied on with ropes."

Then casting another glance at the bear, he added, "But this bear seems to stay on all right, anyway."

"Is that's all that's troubling you," I said, "get down from your horse, and I'll show you why the bear stays on."

The dog collars were not visible under the long hair on the bear's legs, but by feeling for them and finding them, he discovered how it was that the bear was fastened to the saddle. He stood back, paused a moment, and scratching his head, said, "Well, I'll be damned !"

He got back on his horse, and we went on again for quite a distance, when, unable to further restrain his curiosity, he asked, "How did you work it to load that bear on the saddle?"

As briefly as possible, I described the loading of the bear. He said nothing for a moment or two, and then:

"Well, I'll be damned!"

When we had gone a little further, he asked, "Was you alone when you packed this bear?"

"Yes," I said, "I was."

Another pause, and then he said again:

"Well, I'll be damned!"

We travelled on for another little distance, and then he looked at me and said:

"Judging by your talk, I would take you to be an Englishman."

And I replied, "I am." This was followed by another pause, and then, once more, he said:

"Well, I'll be damned!"

Nothing more was said until we reached camp, as, his curiosity having been satified, there was no need of any more bad language.

He stopped with us for supper, which, of course, included bear steaks, and he assured us it was the "best meal I ever eat," and went on his way to his friend's ranch, a fuller and a wiser man.

CHAPTER XVIII

TRAILING LOST SHEEP

THERE are certain differences between trailing domestic animals with bloodhounds, and trailing those that are wild. For some reason, as in the case of man trailing, bloodhounds do not "give tongue" on the former.

Then again, in the case of lost sheep, you cannot use the same method as for finding the trail of a man, by giving the hound his handkerchief to smell, so your only recourse is to tell your hound to hunt for the lost sheep in a way that he will understand.

In teaching Sleuth to trail sheep, when a herd had left one camp to go to a new one, I would put him on their trail at the old camp-site, and tell him to "Go on," at the same time using the word "sheep" over and over again, until finally he would reach the sheep at their new camp. Then I would pat him on the back, and give him his reward, a piece of "jerky," making him understand that I was pleased with his work.

After repeating this method two or three times, Sleuth caught on to what I wanted him to do when I said "sheep" and "Go on," and if there were no sheep trail to start on, he would go ahead until he found one.

Small bunches of sheep often strayed from the herd, generally at night, and were called "cuts." It was the foreman's business to hunt them, as the herder could not do so, since he had to watch the main herd.

My foreman would come to the ranch to ask me to help him find these "cuts," and it was natural for me to put Sleuth's services to practical use. All we knew about the lost sheep was the area in which they were lost, so we could not put Sleuth on their trail, but looked to him to find it, then follow it up until he reached them.

I knew at once when he scented sheep, because he would

change his direction, his head would lower instead of being held high, while his tail, which had been down, would raise, and stand straight out, showing that he was now on the trail. Sometimes it was several miles before this happened. Finally, on seeing the sheep, he would stop, lift one foot from the ground as a pointer does, and leave it to me to drive the sheep back to the herd.

As I had several herds of sheep at this time, there was generally a cut from one herd or another to be hunted for, so Sleuth got lots of practice in this kind of trailing.

Trailing sheep was, in a sense, trailing by slow motion, as opposed to trailing wild animals, which meant hunting at high speed. An important point was that there was no excitement about it, as Sleuth had played with pet lambs from his puppyhood.

As soon as my sheep foreman, Andres, discovered that hunting cuts with Sleuth's assistance beat hunting by himself, he made a practice of coming to the ranch to get Sleuth and me to help.

A most important point was to find the cut before the sheep became scattered. Finding a cut of, say, fifty or more sheep in one bunch is a very different thing from finding those same sheep split up in bunches of five or ten. Normally speaking, the cut would stay together for a day or so, but after that for, one cause or another, they would become separated.

My sheep-owning neighbours soon heard of this new method of hunting cuts, and one of them appeared one day, asking me if I would hunt a cut for him, which I did successfully.

Not long after this, I had an amusing experience in hunting a cut for a sheep man who was driving his herd through the country. This was during the rainy season when there were pools of surface water everywhere, and as the grass was good, this man camped in the same place for a week or so to give his sheep a rest.

One night during that time, a big cut strayed from his herd. His herder, noticing the absence of the sheep, proceeded to count them, and found that there were eighty-four missing. The owner, Jenkins by name, rode out to hunt the strays, and not finding them, decided to make inquiries at a sheep ranch in that vicinity. The owner happened to be the man whose cut I had previously found, and he advised Jenkins to see me, as I had hounds that were trained to trail sheep. He, therefore, came on to see me.

It so happened that Andres was at the ranch, and in reply to his questions, told him that he had seen no sign of his lost sheep. Jenkins then turned to me and said, "I understand you have hounds that will trail lost sheep."

I replied in the affirmative.

I would say here that Jenkins was very prejudiced against dogs, as he regarded them as the natural enemies of sheep. At different times dogs had killed his sheep, consequently he could not understand how he would be benefited by my putting bloodhounds on the trail of his lost sheep, only to get them killed when they got to them.

I explained to him that this was a rather distorted view of the *modus operandi*.

"In the first place," I said, "I only use one hound, since more would be unnecessary, and that hound will only proceed at a running walk in front of me, and as soon as he catches sight of the sheep, will stand still and raise a foot and look at them. He will then regard his part of the job as finished, and look to me to carry on from this point. As the sheep would never see him, they would not get scared, and from then on, he will stay a few yards back of me, for he has been taught not to frighten sheep by getting too close to them."

Jenkins, though somewhat appeased by this explanation, still had his doubts, but the thought of losing eighty-four sheep that might be recovered through the agency of a hound, had a strong influence in modifying his prejudice against dogs. Accordingly he proceeded to ask me what I would charge for my services, and while he was quite willing to pay a reasonable price, he indicated, by his manner, that he did not want to pay more than he could possibly help. He went on to say that he was always willing to do the "right thing," whatever that might be.

I told him I heartily agreed with that sentiment, but added modestly that I found it hard sometimes to carry out.

"Is that so," he said, eyeing me pityingly, and apparently

thinking "the poor fish." While I swallowed the rebuke in silence, nevertheless, I did not like it.

Andres and I then got our horses, and taking Sleuth along, we went back with Jenkins. After crossing some five miles of open plain, we came to the foothills of a big mountain where the cut was supposed to have wandered. Sleuth, up to now, had been following, so I said to him "Sheep. Go on."

He pulled out, as usual, thirty or forty yards ahead of us, his head raised above normal, his tail lowered, showing that he was trying to wind the scent of sheep, if possible. In this way, we went along some two or three miles, while Jenkins discoursed on his experiences in hunting cuts. He had very pronounced opinions, and didn't hesitate to express them bluntly, with little regard for other people's feelings.

He criticized Sleuth's actions, by pointing to sheep tracks that we repeatedly passed over to which Sleuth paid no attention. After about the third time that he had done so, I remarked that Sleuth was hunting sheep and not old sheep tracks, but I failed to convince him that the dog knew what he was about.

Suddenly Sleuth changed his direction, his head lowered and his tail raised. This was his signal to me that he had winded sheep, so I said to Jenkins:

"Sleuth has just winded some sheep." But this piece of news fell on deaf ears, for Jenkins immediately retorted, "How can he be trailing sheep when there ain't no tracks around?"

About a mile further on, we reached the ridge that formed one side of a canyon, some thirty feet deep and about one hundred yards wide, but instead of going on into the canyon, Sleuth suddenly turned sharp at right angles, and went on up the ridge.

I observed to Jenkins, "He has struck the trail and is now following it."

"But," persisted Jenkins, "there ain't no sheep tracks."

"That's right," I agreed, "but Sleuth doesn't need tracks to trail sheep."

This reply so bewildered Jenkins that he relapsed into silence, apparently deciding that I was hopeless.

We followed up the ridge for probably half a mile, when

Sleuth suddenly stopped, lifted up one foot, and looked across the canyon to the ridge on the opposite side. I stopped, too, and said to Jenkins, "Sleuth has sighted sheep."

We looked across to the other ridge, but there were no sheep in sight. Jenkins, who for some time back had been seething with distrust, could contain himself no longer, and blurted out, "There ain't no sheep over there, and your dawg has jest been a-foolin' of you all this time."

I ignored his remark, and merely said, "Let's go on to where Sleuth is standing. Maybe we can see the sheep from there."

When we reached Sleuth, who had not moved, we again looked across the canyon, and there, on the opposite ridge, in the deep shade of a big juniper, I saw several white spots, and I said, "Those spots look rather like sheep to me."

"Them's only white rocks," Jenkins exclaimed scornfully, but he had no sooner said this when one of the "white rocks" seemed to roll out from under the tree into the bright sunlight and stretched itself.

Then I said, "Those are sheep all right. Rocks don't stretch themselves." And without glancing at him, I rode down into the canyon and on up the other side, where Jenkins soon joined me. When we reached the sheep, we found that the rest of the bunch were scattered around among the trees beyond, and Jenkins shouted excitedly, "Them's my sheep! They're all in my ear-mark!"

The three of us rounded them up and drove them back into the canyon, and then down on to the plain below. On our way, we noted the fresh tracks these same sheep had made coming up the canyon.

Jenkins was highly elated, and kept trying to get a count on the sheep as we rode along, for he was anxious to know how many were in the bunch. The loss of even one meant much to his frugal mind. The canyon was full of brush, and it was impossible to get an accurate count, so I suggested that we wait till we reached the plain below, where we could string them out. When we got to a suitable place, he got his count, and there were eighty-three sheep, out of the eighty-four that had strayed. This was quite remarkable considering that the sheep had been lost for two days.

As Jenkins and Andres could easily drive the sheep back to the herd, there was no need of my going any further with them, so I stopped to say "Good-bye."

I should say that while we were driving the sheep down the canyon, I got to thinking things over, and it seemed to me that Jenkins' attitude had been very ungracious, considering what we were trying to do for him. His sneering and fault-finding comments on Sleuth's trailing ability were quite uncalled for, so I made up my mind that Jenkins had some sort of a reprimand coming to him. Furthermore, I do not believe in encouraging people to do wrong by letting them "get away with it," so when Jenkins again asked me what he owed me for finding his sheep, I replied:

"You don't owe *me* anything, but you have a double debt to Sleuth which you ought to pay, if you want to carry out your principle of doing the right thing, which you said you always found it 'easy to do.'"

"And what is the double debt I owe the dawg?" he inquired.

"In the first place," I answered, "you owe him an apology for all the mean things you said against him while he was working his best for you. And as he found eighty-three of your sheep, which at their present value of three dollars a head would be $249.00, I think you, at least, owe him your grateful thanks."

While I was saying all this, the expression on Jenkins' face was very resentful, and he grumbled, "So you want me to apologize to a dawg, do you?"

I replied, "No, I don't want you to do anything. The matter lies entirely between you and Sleuth. And if you think that abusing a dog, and then taking a favour from him is doing the 'right thing,' I cannot agree with you, but you must do as you please about it."

He looked undecided for a few seconds, but the relief he felt at being under no obligation to pay out his good money gilded the pill of making the apology, so he said, "Well, dawg, I'm sorry for what I said agin' you, and I shore thank you for findin' them sheep."

"That's the right spirit," I said approvingly to Jenkins.

"You've got your sheep, I am well repaid by added knowledge I have gained in successfully trailing them, and Sleuth has got what was rightfully coming to him. So everybody's happy." And then I said, "Good-bye" and wished him luck.

When Andres returned to the ranch he told me that Jenkins had expressed great surprise that a total stranger should do him such a great favour and refuse compensation for it. This was so contrary to all his previous experiences in life that he could only account for it by assuming that I must be a very queer man (*hombre muy curioso*). An opinion with which I am inclined to agree.

I never trailed horses and cattle as I did lost sheep, except in a very limited way, and then only with the object of teaching Sleuth to trail anything I might tell him to, no matter what. Therefore, when I wanted horses, I walked down into the pasture towards where they were, and kept repeating "Horses, go on" to Sleuth, and when I reached them, I would give him a piece of "jerky." After two or three such trials, he caught on to what I wanted.

The same method applied to our milk cows, and to show that he knew the difference between the words "cows" and "horses," he would go to whichever of the two I told him to, paying no attention to the others, even though he passed them first.

The secret in training dogs is based on mutual understanding and co-operation. By understanding, I mean conveying to the dog what you mean in a way that he will understand.

As a simple example of this, when I hunted jack rabbits with my wolf hounds, I would see a rabbit in the distance, sitting down, which the dogs would not see, owing to intervening bushes, and if I pointed at it, urging them to run in that direction, they would merely look at my hand, wondering what I wanted. The fact that my finger was pointed at something carried no significance.

Therefore, in order to convey my meaning to them, I would advance towards the rabbit at a walk, then quicken my pace to a run, and at that moment, the dogs would look ahead to see what I was running after, then run ahead of me till they caught sight of the rabbit, and take after him.

As a dog's vocal vocabulary is very limited, and confined to about four major sounds, such as barking when happy, howling when miserable, growling when angry, and whining when he wants something, he has to resort to some other method of expressing what is on his mind. This is done by gesture, or "sign language," as it might be called, and the dog does this with the aid of his head, body, tail, or combinations of them.

For instance, if he is angry, the hair on his back raises, as well as his tail, the latter vibrating. If he is frightened, the hair still stays up, but the tail drops and is motionless, while if he is embarrassed, the hair is only slightly raised, the tail wagging slowly and furtively.

It might be asked: "When does a dog look embarrassed?" My reply is: "When he sees a rattlesnake for the first time, he will look at it nervously, with that inquiring expression which most dogs assume when you make a low hissing sound."

As another example, I recall a time when my whole pack of bloodhounds was embarrassed. They were lying around in front of the ranch house, sunning themselves, when I took it into my head to play a joke on them. With my wife's help, I dressed like a woman, and in a woman's skirts, a garden hat, a veil, and a big shawl round my shoulders, I was quite unrecognizable. Then I sneaked out of the back of the house, and circling round, appeared suddenly before the dogs. When they first saw me, they regarded me with idle curiosity, but as I walked by, each one got up, his hair raised slightly, his tail wagging slowly, and his look of inquiry changed to a strange, bewildered expression, as though he were staring at a ghost. Then each dog, in turn, followed me slowly, until the whole pack was in line behind me, and looking at each other, not knowing what to make of it.

At last, to relieve the tension, I whirled round and shouted "Dogs!"—which was the way I always spoke to them collectively—and then they all rushed at me and after jumping up on me, ran around in circles, showing how much they appreciated the joke.

It is often said that dogs have no sense of humour, but I think anyone seeing how these dogs behaved in this instance would change his opinion.

It is with diffidence that I venture to relate two dog stories which, though absolutely true, might be regarded by many with no little scepticism. I will leave it to my readers to "belive it or not," as they see fit.

In later years I had a dog called Zep (Zeppelin), three parts police dog and one part collie, who was remarkably intelligent. My Horse Springs Ranch, at which I was then living, was close to the main country road. It was fenced, and the car entrance was some two hundred yards to the east, along the fence to the entrance gate. Any car approaching the ranch from the west had to pass the house, and after reaching the gate, turn and proceed towards the house along a road on the inside of the fence.

Whenever I came in from the west, in either my car or my truck, if Zep happened to be in the sitting-room with my wife, he would rush to the door, barking to be let out so that he could come and meet me.

Though a great many cars traversed this road, he paid no attention to any but mine, indicating that he knew the sound of their engines. To illustrate, my son took the car and was gone several days. He returned late at night, and as he passed the house, Zep, who was with my wife and me, rushed to the door to be let out. The engine was making explosions like a motor-cycle, so I said that it could not be our car. My wife replied that it must be, or Zep would not have acted as he did.

We went out to see, and sure enough, the car had entered our gate, and was now coming up to the house. When it reached us, my son stepped out, and my wife remarked that Zep had been right, after all. I inquired why the engine was making those explosions, and my son replied that he had hit a high centre and knocked the muffler off.

So I had to admit that Zep knew more about cars than I did. He could tell the sound of the engine with the muffler off, whereas I could not tell the sound of the engine of my car from any other, with the muffler on.

I had told some of my friends that Zep knew my car from any other by the sound of the engine, and the story was accepted without dispute, especially as some of them said they, too, had dogs that could tell their cars from others in the same manner. But when it came to this story, with the "muffler" addition, their credulity was overtaxed.

Sleuth played the leading rôle in the other story, and it was he who brought to my attention something that I had not thought of before.

The sense of smell in human beings is very dull compared with that of even ordinary animals, though it is not so dull but what one can easily distinguish between the scents of cattle, horses, sheep, and pigs. But when it comes to distinguishing between scents of animals of the same class, the case is different. Presumably all animals can do this, and to the bloodhound it seems an easy matter, as the following proof will show.

George and Roaney, my two horses, and Gyp, the mule, always ran together in the pasture, and were fed grain together. Whenever I wanted them, I would take my bridle and say to Sleuth "Horses,' 'and he would walk ahead of me into the pasture until he found them. Usually they would be fifty or more yards apart, and Sleuth would always stop at the first animal we would come to. I would then bridle it, jump on its back and ride back to the ranch, while the other two would either follow or run ahead, kicking up their heels.

On reaching the stable, if it were feeding time, I would fill the nose bags with grain, and put them on their heads. As the heads of each of the three were of different lengths, the headstraps of each nosebag had been adjusted accordingly, and the name of each animal was written in large letters on the nosebags, or morels, as they are called in the South-west.

One day, I was carrying George's nosebag, which had just been repaired, in my hand, and without thinking waved it towards Sleuth who was walking behind me, and said "Horses," before hanging it up on a peg in the stable where it belonged.

I then followed Sleuth, as usual, into the pasture to get the horses, but when we got to them, Sleuth, instead of stopping at the first animal we came to, went on to George, who happened to be the furthest away.

For a moment I didn't understand why he did this, and then it struck me that it was George's nosebag I had waved to him when I had said "Horses," and he had gone to him, supposing that he was the horse I wanted!

I got to studying over this, so the next day I took Roaney's nose-bag and waved it at Sleuth when I said "Horses." Sure enough, this time he went straight to Roaney! After this, to make doubly sure, I would wave one or the other of the nose-bags at Sleuth, and each time he went straight to the animal to which it belonged.

To Sleuth, therefore, belongs the credit as far as my experience goes, for furnishing proof that a bloodhound can tell one horse from another by his individual scent.

Practically everybody believes that a bloodhound can easily distinguish between the scents of one human being and another, but many refuse to believe that he can draw the same distinction between animals of the same class!

It seems curious that some people should draw the line between the two, but I have found they do, and they will stick to their erroneous beliefs, even after being furnished ample proof to the contrary. This is a good illustration of the old saying, "A man convinced against his will is of the same opinion still."

To digress for the moment I recall one time when I accomplished this feat. In 1885, when Geronimo and his renegade Apache Indians were depredating in my section of the country, I happened to be returning to my headquarters ranch, which at that time was thirty miles north of Alma. There were four other men riding in the same direction, so I joined them. Our road went up the Frisco River, but after leaving Alma a couple of miles, we decided that it would be safer to ride through the hills instead of on the road where the Indians might ambush us. We split into two parties, one man and myself riding to the left, while the other three rode to the right of the road. My companion and I reached the ranch all right. Next morning I decided to ride to a small settlement, now known as Reserve, where there was a store and saloon, to find out the latest Indian news. As I rode along I happened to look back and saw a man riding behind me. I stopped for him to catch up, and naturally asked what news he had. He told me a party of five had left Alma the morning before, and that one man had returned that afternoon and said the Indians had ambushed them. His horse had been shot under him, but he had escaped while his companions were all killed. He then gave me their names which included mine. I told him that there must be some mistake, as I knew positively that one of those mentioned was still living. He was quite annoyed at my doubting him, and offered to bet me that what he had told me was true. I replied that I would not bet as I did not bet on certainties. This annoyed him still more and he said: "I guess you are afraid to bet."

"Oh, no, I'm not," I replied, "but I'll tell you what I'll do. I'll bet you the drinks, and the saloon keeper I know will be able to decide the bet for us."

When we reached the saloon I asked the bartender to introduce me to my companion. He looked very surprised and said:

"It looks like you are already acquainted, since you rode in together!"

"Never mind," I said, "just introduce me by name." He did so, thereby unknowingly deciding the bet in my favour, much to the astonishment of my companion who was thus convinced of my identity. After finishing our drinks I set up the cigars, in order to soothe any ruffled feelings and incidentally to celebrate the first time I had ever convinced a man against his will.

The above instances, of course, are only a few examples of dog language expressed by gesture, and after studying the reaction of dogs under varying conditions, you finally acquire a knowledge of what is in their minds and this means that you understand your dogs.

After mutual understanding has been established, then comes co-operation, and that means helping hounds in ways that are not possible for the hounds to help themselves. But be careful not to try to help them where your help is not needed, such as helping them to trail, which is not co-operation, but is that form of pernicious activity which, in these days, is know as "back seat driving."

It seems strange the dogs should distrust their own eyesight, but by their actions they show that they do. Every dog owner must have noticed that after a brief absence from his dog, the latter, while fully recognizing him, will, nevertheless, generally sniff at his clothes in order to reassure himself that he had made no mistake as to the identity of his master. I recall a striking example of this distrust when I was living at one of my ranches known as the N. H. Ranch. The house was set back from the road some thirty yards and was surrounded by tall pines, and in front of it by the side of the road was a small knoll from which you could see down the road for a quarter of a mile. Generally speaking, I returned to the ranch from my work about sundown, and my hounds being well aware of this would gather on that knoll just before sundown and wait patiently for me to show up. When I didn't return, and it became too dark to see, one of them would throw his head back and howl, while all the others would instantly join in, and after a minute or two of howling they would slowly retire to their respective sleeping places. But when I came back before dusk and they could see me coming along the road, when I got within about a hundred yards and they could fully recognize me, it would be supposed they would come straight to me. Instead, they would leave the knoll in a running walk and circle round with their heads held high in the air until they winded me, and then instantaneously they would all rush at full speed to meet me, baying their loudest, and making a deafening chorus that could be heard a mile away.

It reminded me of two lines I had read in Byron:

How sweet to hear the watch dog's honest bark
Bay deep-mouthed welcome as we draw near home.

And even to this day, whenever I think of my hounds, I can still hear, in fancy, their deep-mouthed welcome.

CHAPTER XIX

THE LAVA COLD TRAIL

As I have already explained in another chapter, I put in a great deal of time on the study of cold trails. A lapse of forty-eight hours was the most that I had thought necessary in studying cold trails, with relation to bear hunting, as after even twenty-four hours, the chances were that a bear would be so far away as to make it a waste of time to try to trail him up.

But, if a man were lost, you would naturally want to trail him up, no matter how cold that trail might be. The same, of course, applies to hunting a lawbreaker.

An incident, as an example of the latter, whereby identification could be proved by trailing with bloodhounds, was an experience that was thrust upon me.

On a Sunday morning, about ten o'clock, two men shot into my sheep camp, killed three sheep, and fired a few shots close to the herders, in order to scare them into taking the sheep away, and keeping them permanently from that section of the range.

Some of my ranches were adjacent to those of a cattle man named Brown, and while I had a perfect right to range my sheep around my own ranches, Brown thought differently, and regarded it as an infringement on his range rights.

My sheep foreman came to his particular herd on Monday evening, and found out what had happened. As this sheep camp was twenty miles from Horse Springs, where I was then living, he decided to wait over until the next day, Tuesday, to tell me about the shooting. He reached the ranch about noon, but I happened to be away and didn't get back until late in the afternoon.

While the two herders recognized one of the men who had shot at them, my foreman thought that further identification, if it were possible to get it, would help greatly to corroborate their testimony. Consequently, what would furnish better proof to that end would be for my hounds to trail the two men to the place to which they might have gone immediately after the shooting, and thus identify them as the culprits.

It so happened that there were several neighbours waiting to see me at the ranch when I arrived, and of course, they heard what my foreman had to say about the two men who had done the shooting. They all agreed that I ought to try to trail them, but when I reflected that the trail would be three days old the next day, Wednesday, the chance of succeeding seemed rather remote.

Three of my enthusiastic neighbours cheerfully accepted my invitation to go with me, so the next morning they came to the ranch, and with my sheep foreman and a herder, making six of us in all, we started off together. I took four of my best hounds with me, Sleuth, Psyche, Rufus, and Rudolf.

This all happened in the middle of January, and while there was very little snow on the ground, it was zero weather, with a cold wind blowing. Otherwise, the day was fine.

We reached the spot where the shooting took place about eleven o'clock in the morning.

We found the empty shells that had been thrown out of the rifles when the sheep were shot, and also two sets of footprints, and, as the ground was soft when the tracks were made, they were very plain.

A strange thing, however, about these footprints, and one we couldn't understand, was that the prints of one pair of boots were so small we concluded that they must be those of a small woman or a child. Those small footprints could not possibly have been those of Brown's wife, as I was acquainted with her and knew her to be a large woman.

We paid especial attention to their horses' tracks. One horse wore No. 1 shoes, and the other, a pony, wore No. 00 shoes, one of which was missing, that of the near hind foot.

As I walked to the place where the two men had left their horses, I called the hounds to me and told them to "Go on," and then we all mounted and followed them.

They took the trail without difficulty, as they went along

at a gait of about four miles an hour, and did not zig-zag to amount to anything.

Except for cold winds, the weather had been fine from the time the trail had been made three days before, and the scent that was retained by the grass or by the leaves on the bushes seemingly had not been affected. Only the scent which had been floating in the air had been dispelled by the winds. This was obvious, as the hounds did all their trailing with their noses close to the ground, and this they would not have done had there been any scent left in the air.

We followed the trail for about three miles, the hounds apparently scenting it easily for they kept close together. But occasionally, where there were patches of barren ground, they would separate, and then come together again where the grass was thick.

I was much pleased at the apparent ease with which my hounds were running such a cold trail, and my three ranch-men companions were congratulating me on that fact.

Then, suddenly, the unexpected happened. We reached the edge of a lava bed, or "malpais," as it is locally known. This lava bed was two miles wide where we had to cross it, and it consisted of nothing but loose black lava rocks, some of them round and others flat, with sharp edges. This rock could not retain scent for any appreciable length of time, but there were a few tufts of grass here and there, growing in the crevices between them, which afforded the only scent left for the hounds to trail by.

The two men we were trailing evidently rode over the lava bed, knowing that they would leave no footprints by which they could be trailed.

I confess I was much bothered, because I had never run into this kind of a cold trail before.

I watched the hounds closely to see what they would do, and they did what one would naturally expect; that is, separated from each other, often being forty yards apart. While each one seemed to be trailing individually, he kept his eye on the other hounds, and when any one of them struck the scent on a tuft of grass, instead of barking as he would do when trailing a wild animal, he would give a convulsive start, at the same time quickening his pace.

The other hounds would instantly notice this, and run to the same tuft and act exactly the same as the first hound had done, showing, evidently, that they, too, had struck the scent.

They would go along a little way together, and then scatter, until one of them would again strike the scent in another tuft of grass, and then they would go through the same performance all over again.

It was now that my previous experiments in cold-trailing helped me out. I fully appreciated the fact that in attempting to take a trail that was three days old, and over lava rocks, the trailing capabilities of my hounds would be taxed to the utmost. Also, I could rely on the fact that as long as the hounds kept going, no matter how slowly, they were still trailing. Had they come to the conclusion that they couldn't follow this trail any longer, they would have returned and stood and looked at me as if to say, "What next?"

We were all on foot, leading our horses, partly because the malpais was very rough to ride over, and partly to keep warm by walking. Notwithstanding the best efforts of the hounds, our pace did not exceed a mile an hour. This was not fast enough to keep us warm, and my ranchmen friends showed signs of wanting to quit. They didn't think the hounds were still on the trail, and while I assured them they were, I knew jolly well they thought me a victim of wishful thinking.

Finally, after about an hour of this sort of slow trailing, they were only too ready to return home. I didn't feel justified in asking them to stay any longer, as I could give them no definite assurance that we could keep to the trail over the lava until it connected with ground where it could again be easily followed.

However, I did persuade them to continue a little further with me, and again the unexpected happened, but this time it was in my favour.

I suddenly saw on a lava rock a glint of light, shining like a piece of mica does in the sand, and drawing attention of the others to it, we all walked over for closer scrutiny.

Sure enough, a horse's hoof had slid on the rough lava rock, and a tiny fleck of iron had been scraped off the horseshoe. It was this that had glittered in the sun.

This tiny speck of evidence proved that we were still on the trail, and I had no difficulty, now, in persuading these near-quitters to stay with me a while longer.

There was another mile of lava bed to cross, but we made it in about another hour. Then we struck soft ground again, and ran on to the tracks of the two horses we were trailing. We all mounted and followed the dogs for some five miles, until we reached a ranch belonging to a man who had worked for me, off and on, for years.

He had seen us coming, and invited us in to have coffee, which was very welcome to all of us. At the first opportunity, I drew him to one side and asked him, confidentially, if he could remember what visitors he had had on the previous Sunday. He said he had had two, who had come to dinner, about two o'clock in the afternoon. I inquired whether one of them was not a woman, to which he replied that they were both men, and gave their names, Brown and O'Neill. I then told him that one of them must have been a woman or a child, as the footprints of one person were so small that they could not possibly belong to a man. When I asked him if he had noticed the size of O'Neill's feet, he said he had paid no attention.

We finished our coffee and started home, for we had about thirty miles to go, and it was now late afternoon.

When we got to within about five miles of Horse Springs, we passed a ranch, the owner of which I was well acquainted with. He had heard us coming and looked out to see who was riding by so late at night, for it was now eight o'clock and quite dark. We could see him and one of his cowboys standing in the doorway, their forms sharply silhouetted in the light of the open fire in the room behind them.

I recognized the cowboy, and curiously enough, he was the brother of O'Neill, the man who was with Brown. I talked to the ranchman for a moment, and then turned suddenly to this cowboy and said:

"What size boots does your brother wear?"

"He don't wear no size," he replied. "There's no regular size small enough to fit his feet, so he has all his boots made to order."

I thanked him and we rode away, leaving the two men wondering why I had asked such a question.

The next day, I went to our county seat, made a complaint against the two men, Brown and O'Neill, got out a warrant for their arrest, and had a date set for their trial in the justice of the peace court, the object being to have them bound over to the grand jury.

The day of the trial, I had my two Mexican sheep herders, who had been shot at, as my star witnesses. I also had one of the ranchmen who accompanied me on that trail prepared to swear to watching the bloodhounds trail the two men from the tree that they shot from to the ranch where they had dinner.

Just before we went into court, Brown drew my two sheep herders aside, telling them he wished to speak to them. I do not know what he actually said, but I do know that when they went on the stand, not only did their testimonies conflict, but they knew nothing about the shooting except that they had been shot at by "someone" from "somewhere." This sort of evidence didn't help me any in the prosecution of the case.

Then my ranchman witness and I went on the stand, and swore to trailing the two men in the manner which I have described, and to the fact that the tracks of the two horses, ridden by the men just after the shooting, were the identical tracks of the two horses which Brown and O'Neill rode to the ranch house at which they stopped for dinner on the day the shooting occurred.

We also swore to the small footprints of one of the two men, and then drew the attention of the Court to O'Neill's excessively small feet, in substantiation of the evidence which we had sworn to in that regard.

Brown and O'Neill were acquitted on the grounds that there was not sufficient evidence to convict them. The justice of the peace said further that he was certainly not going to bind them over to the next term of court on the strength of evidence based on the mere trailing of the hounds. And thus the case ended.

I cannot say that I was altogether pleased with this verdict, and I could not help thinking to myself that Shakespeare, when he said, "Every dog has his day," overlooked the law courts.

I think I should add that Brown said he had mistaken my herd of sheep for that of another man who had no ranches in that section, and therefore had no range rights. As he had been imposing on Brown for some time past, he considered it his own recourse to shoot into his sheep.

Brown said he was sorry for the mistake, but after he knew that he had shot into *my* sheep, he felt that it was too late to apologize. Also, he had no idea that I would ever know who had done it, and to obviate the possibility of anyone trailing him, he crossed that lava bed, where horses' footprints would leave no impression. But he reckoned without my blood-hounds.

From a sporting standpoint, losing the case was quite unimportant. Personally I had no feeling of animosity towards the defendants, and the scare they got of getting into serious trouble afforded me ample satisfaction for their misdeed. What was important, however, was that they had inadvertently set my bloodhounds the most difficult cold trail that they had ever been called upon to follow. I regarded this as a favour for which I was truly grateful. All the facts in connection with the trailing were sworn to publicly in court and their accuracy was never challenged, and, although the evidence furnished by the hounds was not admitted, that did not cast any reflection on its validity.

Incidentally this three-day-old cold trail was thrust upon me and while no one thought the hounds had any chance of success I did think that they had, so I welcomed this opportunity of showing what they could do. While the outlook seemed hopeless I felt that it was only fair to the hounds to stay with them as long as they showed signs that they were still able to trail, but had it not been for the accidental scraping of a horseshoe on a rough lava rock I am afraid I would have given up the chase as an impossibility. Nearly all sportsmen prefer a close finish to a walk over. Horses have won races by a nose, golfers by one stroke, boxers by a hair-line decision, but I think that my bloodhounds could justly claim the unique distinction of winning a cold trail content by a "speck," so to speak.

CHAPTER XX

GRIZZLIES—A CLOSE-UP

THE discovery of the grizzly is credited to Lewis and Clark, who were the first to draw attention to this animal as being a distinct species of bear.

On their expedition, 1804–6, crossing the Rocky Mountains over the Continental Divide, they ran on to grizzlies, who in those days roamed around in the day time. According to their report, the party shot one grizzly ten times, four of the bullets going through the lungs, and two through the heart. Notwithstanding this handicap, the bear lived for twenty minutes, during which time he swam half a mile. As it is generally conceded that the grizzly is more tenacious of life than any other animal, it is very likely that the above authentic story was the basis upon which that claim has been made.

Whether bears are smarter than other animals or not is debatable, but there is no question that they are highly intelligent, which the following incident will confirm.

On a mountain thirty miles south-west of Magdalena, two grizzlies had been killing a good many cattle, and a generous bounty was offered to anyone who would kill them. Two trappers, therefore, decided to try to catch them with a big grizzly bear trap, so they camped near a place where the tracks of these bear seemed to show up the most, and set their trap. But presumably the grizzlies were trap shy, as they refused to touch the bait that was in it, although their tracks showed that they had been around it. Incidentally, all big grizzlies are trap shy, as they would have been caught when they were young if they were not.

After about a week without success, the trappers concluded to try some other way. That night, a deer which they had killed and hung up to a tree at their camp, was dragged down and taken off by these bears, and this gave the trappers an idea.

They built a small cabin, about eight by ten feet, with big logs in walls and roof. A trap door was placed at one end of the cabin, and at the other end they hung up another deer, fixed so that if it were pulled, the trap door would be sprung. When all was ready, the trappers went back to their camp, with the hope that at least one of the grizzlies would be caught during the night.

The next morning they found that the door had been sprung, but there was no grizzly inside, and they saw that he had dug his way out. The curious thing about it was that the dirt which had been removed on the outside of the cabin had been scratched away from it, showing that the hole under the cabin wall had been dug from both sides. This was proof that one grizzly had been trapped, and that his mate had helped out by digging a hole on the outside of the cabin to connect with the hole dug by the grizzly on the inside. This remarkable example of co-operation demonstrates a high order of intelligence.

By the way, the canyon which was the scene of this bear-trapping incident is called "Bear-Trap Canyon" to this day.

I have often been asked which is the best place at which to aim when shooting a grizzly, but as there is a divergence of opinion on this question, I can only venture to express my personal views.

If a grizzly is facing you, with his head down, and not moving, a shot in the centre of the forehead will kill him instantly; but if his head is up, it is best to shoot him straight through the throat, breaking the neck-bone. A shot at the body is inadvisable, as it will only wound and infuriate the bear. To shoot him through the heart is a difficult matter, first, because it's hard to tell just where the heart is; second, even if you knew where the heart was, the chances are that the bullet would strike a rib and be deflected. A shot through the heart would not prevent him from attacking you, although he might survive but a short time.

If the bear has his back to you, and if his head is still, shoot at the back of the ear in the direction of the brain. But if he is moving, take a line shot for his backbone, and if you hit that anywhere, he will fall over, paralysed. If the bear's side should be towards you, the best crippling shot is to shoot through the point of the shoulder, which will down him and render him practically helpless.

What is of the most vital importance is to keep cool, for, at close quarters, a man who is an indifferent shot, but keeps his head, is better than a crack shot, who gets rattled.

The grizzly, to give him his due, is not often the aggressor, and he will seldom attack a man unless the latter first molests him. As a matter of fact, he would rather run away than fight. On the other hand, if he is wounded, even if he doesn't see you, he is likely to hunt you up to attack you.

On one bear hunt, I remember riding along a mountain ridge, while a hundred feet below me, a grizzly was running along through brush and timber with the hounds behind him. I crowded my horse, so as to get ahead of him, intending to dismount and shoot him as he went by. This I succeeded in doing, except that I only wounded him. He must have winded me previously from a little, fitful gust of wind, for he stopped, raised himself on his hind feet, and moved his head round in a semi-circle, with his nose in the air, evidently endeavouring to get my scent again.

I shall always think that, had he scented me, he would have hunted me up, but in this case, I killed him with the next shot, so I'll never know what he really would have done.

As a rule, when a grizzly is struck by a bullet, he will snap at the place, with a snarl, but on rare occasions, when he is painfully or seriously wounded, he will "bawl." This is the expression that trappers use for the sound made by a bear when caught in a trap.

I do not wish to emulate the cub reporter, who said that a certain scene was indescribable, and then proceeded to describe it, but I will endeavour to give my conception of what the bawl of a big grizzly sounds like.

I was riding along a four-strand, barbed-wire fence, which went through a belt of timber, when suddenly the deep silence was broken by the most extraordinary, heartrending sounds. Urging my horse to a gallop, to find out what was up, I came on to two stallions fighting over the fence. The horse on the far side of the fence had got his hind legs entangled in the two middle wires, and had fallen down sideways against the fence. He was screaming in agony, for the other horse was kicking him unmercifully. As soon as I got to them, I dismounted, picked up some rocks, and threw them at the aggressor, in the hope of stopping him from kicking. Instead, he whirled round and lashed out at me, and I realized that this attempt to stop him didn't work, but only caused him to turn his attention momentarily to me, for he continued his kicking, so I had to try something else.

I took a cartridge out of the cylinder of my six-shooter, and with some difficulty extracted the bullet, then replaced the cartridge in the cylinder, so that it would go off at the next pull on the trigger. I then walked up to the horse, whose head was near the ground, because his heels were up in the air, and fired into his face, point blank. As I stepped aside, the horse sprang into the air, pawing it with all four feet as if he were trotting, and then when he struck the ground, without a perceptible pause he trotted on and disappeared into the timber.

Meanwhile, the other horse was continuing his screams, so something had to be done, and quickly. As I had nothing with which to cut the fence wires, I fell back on my versatile six-shooter, and shot through the two wires that were holding him. Being thus released, he hurriedly got to his feet and ran off, trailing a leg.

As I replaced my six-shooter in its holster, I could not help smiling at the thought that this gun had, twice in succession, acted in the role of a life saver, instead of fulfilling its intended destiny as a death dealer.

The first time I heard a grizzly bawl, it reminded me of the agonizing screams of this horse intermingled with the roar of an enraged lion, this combination resolving itself into the most terrifying, blood-curdling sound that it is possible to imagine. And it is especially impressive if one happens to be standing alongside the bear, as I did on two occasions.

So far, I have neglected to mention "spoilt" bear, the term used by hunters to designate the bears that could not be caught either in traps or by hounds.

When a bear becomes suspicious, and is too wary to be caught in a trap, he is "trap-shy"; that is, spoiled for trapping.

When a bear has been trailed by baying hounds, having once escaped them, he is most anxious to avoid a repetition of that experience, so whenever he again hears the baying of hounds, he promptly decamps for parts unknown. Consequently, one of the chief objections to young hounds running after deer is the fact that by their baying they scare away all the bear within hearing. This especially applies to grizzlies, who, because they live at the tops of the mountains, are more apt to hear a hound baying below, since there is nothing to obstruct their hearing the sound. But black bear, living at the lower elevations, would not hear the hounds as well where sound would be shut off by intervening timber and low hills.

Here, I must confess that I contributed to the "spoiling" of a good many grizzlies during my "hit or miss" period of hunting with ordinary hounds, as they nearly all got away, and each one that did so was spoiled that much more than he had been before.

There were, therefore, only two ways to catch a "spoilt" grizzly, apart from running on to him by accident. One way was to locate a dead cow, killed and still being eaten on by him, for as I have mentioned, he will bed up close to his kill, instead of returning to his mountain-top bed, as he usually would.

The other way was by paying a surprise visit; that is, going direct with your hounds to the grizzly's home on the high mountains, around which he is supposed to be "using."

"Using" is hunting vernacular, denoting that the bear is temporarily frequenting certain areas in search of food.

No matter on which side of the mountain he happened to go hunting for food the day before, he would come back to his bed, and though he would vacate his bed on hearing or scenting your approach, you would strike his hot trail somewhere in the vicinity of his bed.

In hunting the old way, with ordinary hounds running loose, you would be likely to cross a black bear trail, which the hounds would take. You would be forced to follow them, and while you might catch that particular black bear, you would be apt to scare away the grizzly you wanted to get.

But with my new way, it was entirely different, because my bloodhounds were all necked in pairs, and kept together as one unit, until my lead hound, Sleuth, struck the hot trail of a grizzly, and it was not until then that I would turn the others loose.

I may say here, that once a grizzly begins killing cattle, he will continue doing so, as it is the easiest method by which he can get his food supply. In that trait he resembles the man-eating tiger, especially an old one, who finds it easier to catch a man than a wild animal, and once he contracts the habit of eating human beings, it becomes permanent.

As a rule, cattle that have been killed by grizzlies are found close to water. The reason for this probably is that the bear finds it easier to wait for a bunch of cattle to come to water, and then pounce on one of them, than it would be to hunt them up and pursue them through the hills.

It is easy to tell when a cow has been killed by a grizzly, because its neck is always broken. A bear has to be a big one to be powerful enough to kill a cow in this way.

Consequently, when a cow has been killed by a bear, it must have been a grizzly, not a black bear, the latter being so much less powerful. Therefore, when a black bear is found to be feeding on a dead cow, it does not mean that he killed it.

The size of a bear is best determined by the size of the feet, for they remain the same whether the bear is fat or thin. To determine the weight of bears I killed, I bought a spring scale that would weigh up to two hundred pounds, and on it I weighed a bear cub of less than that weight, first in its entirety, and again when he was stripped of his entrails. I found the difference to be approximately 10 per cent.

As a check, I weighed another cub, and found the difference to be proportionately the same so I took this as a basis for weighing larger bear.

In weighing the latter, I had them cut in pieces of less than two hundred pounds each in weight. Then, by adding up the weight of the pieces, plus the 10 per cent, I got an approximate estimate of the actual weight of the bear.

By this method, I determined the weight of each of the largest grizzlies I have killed to be around eight hundred pounds, which I believe is as heavy as any grizzly gets to be in the Rocky Mountain region. By the same token, the tracks of these bears measured as big as any tracks ever previously seen, being a little over eight by twelve inches.

Grizzlies have attained far greater weights than the above, as measured by the "guess" system; and I must admit, that if wishful thinking be taken as a basis for estimating the weight of heavy bears, my spring scale method made a very poor showing by comparison.

Curiously enough, grizzly bear hunting on horseback, with hounds, was the only thrilling sport that I know of where there were only amateurs, and no professionals. Ordinarily a professional, as I take it, is a man who makes his living out of his particular sport, but if he tried to do that out of the sport outlined above, he would go broke before he had got well started. So it is small wonder that there should be a dearth of professionals, thus leaving that sport as a monopoly for amateurs.

There are, of course, professional grizzly bear "trappers," although there are not many of them. But trapping a grizzly, and then shooting him in the trap, from a sportsman's point of view, is not "cricket."

Two very important points that I must mention in connection with catching grizzlies are mountain top trails and closed seasons, the former being greatly to the hunter's advantage, and the latter decidedly the reverse.

Mountain top trails, as I called them, were trails used by grizzlies for getting round the tops of the mountains in the easiest way, and it was many years before I realized their full significance. Roughly speaking, these trails were about three hundred feet below the crests of the mountain ridges, the reason being that the heads of the canyons that surround the mountains usually peter out at about that level; and usually it is easier to go round the head of a canyon than to cross it, that is, if you are near the head.

These trails are hard to see, unless you are on the lookout for them, as, seemingly, they are not continuous. This is because, in one part of the trail, they are merely tortuous tunnels through dense brush or quaking aspen thickets. In

255

another, rocky ground leaves no evidence that the soft, padded foot of a bear has ever passed over it; while in still another, which is the only part of the trail which is visible, the soft ground shows up a bear track here and there, if not continuously.

It was only natural that in the course of years, I became familiar with the different mountain ranges I hunted over, and that, when I became aware of the importance of knowing the exact locations of these mountain top trails, I made a particular study of them.

A grizzly usually makes his bed alongside the brush tunnels, so that no matter what part of the mountain he may be ranging over during the day, he will come back to his bed at night. These beds, as I have mentioned before, are round holes scratched out of the ground, about three or four feet in diameter, and six to twelve inches in depth, big enough for the bear to curl himself up in comfortably. A curious fact I noticed about these bear beds was that they were dug on the upper sides of big trees on steep mountain sides. The roots of a big tree will raise the ground on the upper side, so that the water from heavy rains will run down on each side of the raised ground, leaving the bear bed high and dry; while if the bear bed were dug below the tree the water would run into it and fill it up. It is reasonable to suppose that the bear fully realizes this, and thus he furnishes another proof of his intelligence.

So when I received word that fresh grizzly tracks were seen anywhere on a mountain range, at a time that I could spare to hunt, I would take my pack and make a bee-line for any bear beds that I knew of on that mountain, and thus have a good chance of getting a hot trail of that particular grizzly right away.

In the study of bear trails, I was greatly aided at different times by snow that had fallen two or three days previously, but had not melted off. Bear tracks over snow in one direction may not mean anything in particular but when there are tracks going both ways, you may be reasonably sure that it is a bear trail. Under such conditions, whenever time permitted, I would tell the hounds to stay with my horse, and I would follow this snow trail for long distances if necessary. It mattered not what kind of ground I went over, or how dense the brush through which I went, the snow trail guided me just the same, and in this way I learned to know the location of these trails when there was no snow to aid me. Thus, I ran on to bear beds that I would never have found, had I not followed the snow trail, previously.

Another great advantage in knowing exactly where these mountain top trails are is that when the bear is running along on one, while the hounds are pursuing him, and you are riding on the top of the mountain just above him, you can ride some distance ahead, dismount, and after reaching the trail, select some safe spot from which to shoot him as he comes by.

Should he, however, decide to stop in a dense thicket, your only recourse then is to go to him, which has its drawbacks, one being he may scent or hear your approach, and thus, is likely to see you first. Should he then attack, you will have to fight him with your back to the wall, so to speak, for you cannot escape from him, if he should decide to run after you, as he could easily outrun you. While this adds greatly to the thrills of the sport, one is gravely impressed by the fact that one can have too much of a good thing.

Of course, when I had Twist with me, I had a certain self-confidence that was lacking when he got lost from me, and on such occasions, it can be realized how keenly I deplored his absence, for by barking in the bear's face, he would not only tell me where he was, but would, also, by distracting his attention, give me a fine chance to get in a fatal shot.

The second point was that of closed seasons. It is true that in those days, unlike to-day, there was no legal closed season for bear, but in its stead, nature took upon herself the task of prescribing one.

Bears begin hibernating about the twentieth of November, and do not leave their dens until the beginning of March, and in the high mountains, where the grizzlies roam, the snow is so deep, or the ground so boggy from melting snow, that it is impossible to ride after them until the end of May. From that time until the end of September, the weather is so hot during the daytime that it is both inadvisable and impracticable to hunt with hounds, because of their getting so thirsty. When they reach a certain point, and can stand it no longer, they will leave the bear trail to go off and hunt water, and after finding it and satisfying their thirst, rather than return to the trail, they are apt to prefer to call it a day and return to camp.

Consequently, the season for hunting grizzlies would be restricted to about six weeks in the year; namely, in October and the first half of November. Even assuming that I could leave my business for six weeks at a stretch, that would be far too short a time to make much headway in training hounds; and then it would be nearly a year before their training could again be resumed. During this time they would get entirely out of hand, and obviously it would take several years before a pack of reliable grizzly bear dogs could be sufficiently trained to be of real practical use, if ever.

In the case of man trailing, conditions are entirely different, for barring bad weather, you can trail a man any day in the year, and thus give your pack continuous training which is exactly what I was able to do.

Whenever I had the time to spare, I would take the pack out for a run, sometimes for a mile or so; other times for several miles, as my time permitted. The pack consisted normally of four or six bloodhounds, necked together in pairs, Princess, my great Dane, with one slow-trail dog necked to her on each side, and my fox terrier, Twist, while Sleuth either went ahead, or ran behind with the pack as I might tell him to do.

On my way out, until I reached the point where I decided to return home, the pack was under the strictest discipline. But on the return trip, the hounds were all unnecked and allowed to run along as they pleased. Under this method of training, it was not long before they took it all as a matter of course, and the knowledge that they were going to be turned loose after a while reconciled them to accepting discipline in a cheerful spirit.

Is it any wonder, then, that due to being able to train my pack continuously and unhampered by closed season restrictions, I finally had a pack so obedient that I could handle it as though it were just one dog?

Sometimes we unconsciously do things that we think at the time seem trivial, but which turn out to be of great importance later on. Many times, especially on the longer runs after unnecking the hounds for the return trip, I would call out loudly, "Home," which they thoroughly understood to mean that we were going back to the ranch. Out of curiosity, to see what they would do, I just followed them to see what course they would take to get there. I noticed, without thinking much about it, that they invariably took the shortest way back, too short in fact, as they would start to cross deep canyons or go through thick timber where I could not follow on horseback! I would then whistle to them to follow me, and after I had ridden round such impassable places, I would again call out "Home," and they would run ahead in the right direction as before.

It was not until later when I hunted grizzlies with them that I realized the value of their guidance at times when I was uncertain myself whether I was still in the right direction. Whenever I did get a grizzly, it would be near sundown, and the distance from camp might be twenty miles or more. This would have to be ridden through timber and brush, to say nothing of deep canyons that had to be crossed. As long as the weather was fine and I had the light of the moon or stars, there was nothing to bother about, but there were other times when the case was quite different.

After running a bear many miles a heavy rain would come on, which would wash away all scent in the air, or on the ground, which forced the hounds to quit the trail and come back to me. I would start for camp with them following me, but as soon as I said, "Home," they would run ahead as they were accustomed to do when on practice runs. They seemed to take it for granted that "Home" meant camp when we were camping out.

After sundown it would become so dark that I had to get off my horse and lead him, partly because he could not stay on his feet on steep hillsides, because the ground was so wet and slippery, and partly because of my head running into branches of trees that I could not see. From time to time I would feel uncertain as to whether I was still in the right direction to the camp, and if I could not see the hounds I would call them to me, and by listening I could judge the direction from which they came and then go ahead with renewed confidence. The going, of course, was very slow, but I would finally get to camp, although I might not get there until two or three o'clock in the morning. Such experiences are most unpleasant, but they are not dangerous.

But with blizzards, it is a different matter. They come up sometimes very suddenly, and what with blinding snow and an icy thirty-mile wind, the temperature at eight or nine thousand feet elevation is apt to fall to below zero. Under such conditions, if you cannot make camp, you are likely to get frozen, for you cannot make a fire in a blizzard. I have known of many deer hunters being frozen to death, although they were at much lower elevations, and only a few miles from their camps when the blizzard started.

I was lucky enough not to be caught in more than one bad blizzard, and when finally I reached camp all I could do, as it was impossible to light a fire, was to crawl into my blankets, boots and all, and while getting warm I had ample time to meditate on the joys of grizzly bear hunting before falling asleep. Incidentally, I would mention what I have found relatively few people know, and that is what to do in case of frost-bite, or frozen fingers and toes. The general custom is to rub the frozen part with snow, so that it will thaw gradually, and also to keep the patient away from the fire. The remedy I have always found best was to soak the frozen part in kerosene oil, which is generally obtainable even in the most remote places. It alleviates the pain in a very short time, and there are no after ill effects, such as swelling and blisters. Also, that rubbing chilblains with kerosene will take the itch out of them.

The illustration facing page 81 shows a fox terrier, a bloodhound, and a bull terrier, sitting in a row, each with a piece of bread on his nose and, having been told that the bread was "on trust," are awaiting patiently the words "paid for," before tossing the bread into the air, and then catching and eating it.

When this snapshot was taken, one of the onlookers remarked, "That's obedience, all right, but you are standing in front of them. Would they be as obedient if you were absent?"

"I don't know, but we can find out," I replied.

With that, I called two of the bloodhounds, and putting a piece of bread in front of each, I said "On trust," and walked away, out of sight.

After a full two minutes, I returned, and after photographing them, said "paid for," and they instantly seized their pieces of bread. Neither dog had moved while I was away, and after such an example of obedience, it can readily be believed that they would be equally as obedient in all other respects. This implicit obedience proved to be of great practical convenience to me, as I could continue their training without its interfering with my work in the least.

For instance, part of my work consisted of riding from one of my sheep herds to another, to find out if the herders needed any supplies, or if they had anything to report. While the pack would not bother the sheep in the least, the sheep would be scared and run at the sight of so many dogs, so that when I would get within a quarter of a mile of the herd, I would look around for a big shady tree, and tell the dogs to "stay there," which they did. I would often be absent two or three hours at the sheep camp, but not a single dog would ever leave that tree until I came back or called them away.

It was the same thing in bear hunting. I could leave the pack at any place I wanted them to stay till I came back or whistled for them, as the case might be; or if I wanted to go off on foot, they would stay with my horse.

I would often take Sleuth with me on such trips, but that made no difference to the pack, as they regarded him as a privileged character. As a matter of fact, it was Sleuth who had trained the pack when they were puppies, so that when they became grown, they fully understood that whatever he might do was no concern of theirs until they were unnecked, and then they would run to him and whatever animal he trailed, they would trail, also.

With this in mind, it was very natural that I should look to Sleuth to settle, in my favour, the question of whether or not a pack of reliable bear dogs could be created without ever having had any previous training in running bear. After all, it was difficult to see why a pack that had been trained to trail anything they were told to should suddenly draw the line at trailing bear.

It was even more difficult for a bear hunter, after having spent years training a hound to become a reliable bear dog, to believe that such a hound could be obtained, ready made, so to speak, without ever having had any previous experience in hunting bear.

It seemed to me that this controversy could only be settled by actual demonstration, and I was convinced that Sleuth, by reason of his unprecedented mode of training, was the logical medium by which my contention could be substantiated.

That the killing of "spoilt" or "outlaw" grizzlies, as they are often called, is no easy matter, I think it would interest my readers to hear what Enos A. Mills wrote on this subject. He wrote many books on wild life in the Rockies, and among them, one entitled *The Grizzly*, published by Houghton, Mifflin Company in 1910. He hunted the grizzly many years, not with the rifle, but with the camera, and he is generally accepted as one of the leading authorities on the habits and characteristics of that animal.

From page 13 of that book, I quote the following, viz.:

"A Utah grizzly killed about one thousand head of cattle in fifteen years. During this time there was a large reward for his death. Numerous attempts were made to capture him. Old hunters and trappers tried with rifles and traps, expeditions of men, horses and dogs pursued him. All those years he lived on as usual in his home territory, made a kill every few days, and was seen only two or three times.

"Another grizzly, eluding pursuers, slaughtered live stock freely, and managed to survive thirty-five years of concerted efforts to kill or capture him. There was a rich reward on his head.

"There are similar accounts of Clubfoot, Three-Toes and other outlaw grizzlies. All of these bears slaughtered cattle by the hundreds in their home territory, lived with heavy prices on their heads, and for years outwitted skilful hunters and trappers, escaping the well-organized posse again and again. Knowing many of the hunters and their skilful methods and the repeated triumphs of other grizzlies over combinations and over contrivances, I am convinced that the grizzly is an animal who reasons."

CHAPTER XXI

SUSIE
QUEEN OF THE "SPOILT" GRIZZLIES

At long last, I had my pack of bloodhounds ready for their first bear hunting trial. The pack I started out with consisted of five bloodhounds, Sleuth, Psyche, Rufus, Rudolf, and Inveed. The latter got his unusual name because, as a pup, he had distemper, so we called him the "Invalid." This was shortened to "Inveed," and he knew this name so well that by the time we wished to change it, he refused to answer to any other.

Then there were the two slow-trail dogs, Panther and Wolf. Incidentally, I started in by calling them "liaison dogs," which is exactly what they were, in that when the pack got out of hearing, these dogs, by trailing them, restored the contact between me and the pack. However, I stopped using the term "liaison dogs," because I found it too highbrow for local consumption, and for that reason I was forced to use the term "slow-trail dogs," though, technically speaking, a slow-trail hound is one that trails on a leash.

Also, there was Princess, the great Dane, whom I regarded as a sort of "mother ship" to the pack, any dog who misbehaved being put under her care by being necked to her, as punishment; three bull terriers, Grip, Nap (Napoleon), and Biz (Business), which I took along, not that they were of any particular use, but because I didn't have the heart to leave them behind, as I knew how they loved a scrap; and finally, Twist, my fox terrier, whose invaluable and unique services have already been described.

I have often been asked why one or two bloodhounds would not have been enough, instead of the five, or more, which I always took with me. There are several reasons, one being that the baying of a number of hounds is continuous, and therefore can be heard much more easily than the sporadic barking of one or two.

Another reason is that hounds seem more encouraged to do their best when there are several of them; and still another reason is that some of them may get crippled or tender-footed, so that if I depended on only one or two hounds, I might suddenly find myself without any hounds at all.

When I started out on this first bear hunt with the bloodhounds, which was in October, 1898, I fully realized that what I had learned through years of hard experience in bear hunting was to be brought to a final test, and whether it would be a success or failure would be determined by the events of the next few days.

While it was generally admitted that I had a well-trained pack of hounds, doubts were frankly expressed that it would be possible for hounds to catch bear, without any previous experience in hunting them.

The point to be decided was whether a pack of blood-hounds that could trail a man with success could be switched over to trail a bear with equal success. If this could be done, and if my surmise were correct, I would then have a ready-made pack of trained bear dogs without further ado.

However, as I wasn't too cocksure of the outcome, I decided to hunt alone, with just Joe for camp cook, and Telesfor in charge of the saddle horses, as usual.

The first day, when we started on this momentous trip, we made our camping place on Alamocito Creek, along the banks of which there were many oak trees and thickets, and as it had been a good season for acorns, the ground was strewn with them. I left the dogs in camp, and rode off to hunt for signs of where bear had been feeding on these acorns, and finally found fresh tracks in a big oak thicket, about three miles from camp.

The next morning, bright and early, I started off, taking Telesfor with me, with all the hounds following. Sleuth, on this occasion, was not allowed to run in front of me, as was his usual custom. I felt sure that I would get a hot trail when I reached the thicket where I had seen the bear tracks the evening before, and on reaching it, I called Sleuth to me, and told the other dogs to stay with my horse. I went into the thicket, and soon found where a bear had been feeding the night before.

Sleuth was showing signs of uneasiness, and looking at me inquiringly, so when I found the tracks, I told him to "Go on." This he instantly did, baying at the same time, while I ran back to the pack and unnecked the hounds, who bolted after Sleuth the moment they were loose. I unnecked Wolf and Panther, who had been necked together, turning Panther loose, and necking Wolf to Princess.

I then got on my horse and followed them, the other dogs following me, with the exception of Panther. He ran just ahead, trailing the pack, but staying with me on account of Wolf, as I had hoped he would do, and as he had done before when running bobcats.

After about a four-mile run, the hounds jumped the bear, who soon climbed a tree around which the hounds were baying furiously as I came up. I dismounted, and taking careful aim, shot him through the head, killing him instantly, and he fell down among the dogs, almost hitting one. I was particularly careful to kill the bear, as the hounds had never fought one before, and if he were only wounded and full of fight, some of them might have got hurt, in which case they probably would have become "bear-shy." On the present occasion, as the bear was dead, the dogs were all able to "wool" him good, without fear of reprisal, a plan calculated to inspire them with confidence in tackling their next bear.

Telesfor skinned and cut up the bear, after which I filled up the dogs with entrails and meat until they could eat no more.

We packed the bear meat and the hide on our horses, and started back to camp, and it was a proud bunch of dogs that ran ahead of us. But I think none of them was prouder of their success than I.

The next day I hunted in a different direction, and ran on to the fresh trail of a bear, which Sleuth took this time of his own accord. Everything went off as it had the day before, with the exception that I turned Wolf loose, instead of Panther, but as both dogs behaved the same, the two hunts were strikingly similar.

266

That afternoon I changed camp to a new site a few miles distant, and the next two days I caught a bear each day, with Panther and Wolf exchanging places, as before. I moved camp again, and the following day caught my fifth bear, which was a large one, and we ran him some fifteen miles before he treed.

Now that my pack had caught four bear in as many successive days, thus showing what they could do, the mere fact of catching this fifth bear was relatively immaterial. What was of the utmost importance, however, was that it was on this hunt that my two slow-trail dogs, Panther and Wolf, were turned loose simultaneously for the first time. It was with grave apprehension that I watched them, wondering if they would run with the pack or stay with me. They started out after the pack, but after they had gone about seventy-five yards, they stopped, and one of them ran back to me, as if to urge me to hurry up, and then the other did the same.

It seemed to be too good to be true. When the first one reached me, I shouted to him, "good dog," and then "go on," to encourage him to go back and take the trail of the pack. I followed the same tactics with the other dog as soon as he reached me, and from then on, they ran to and fro alternately, continuously passing each other, like two animals in a cage.

This "back and forth" method of trailing the pack was done entirely on their own initiative. In places where the timber was thick and my horse could not follow the trail, I would have to make a detour, and the dogs would leave the trail at my call and run ahead of me, side by side. But as soon as they struck the trail of the pack again, they would run back and forth, as before, thus enabling me to tell, for sure, whether or not they were trailing the pack.

On this particular hunt, on account of the deep, rocky canyons that could only be crossed by making detours, either above or below where the bear and pack had crossed, the pack finally got out of hearing. So I was dependent on Panther and Wolf to bring me back within hearing of the hounds, until I reached the place where the bear was treed.

I need hardly say how delighted I was at the behaviour of

my slow-trail dogs, which surpassed my most sanguine expectations.

After getting these five black bear in five consecutive runs, it was reasonable to suppose that my hounds were now ready to tackle the highest phase of bear hunting; that is, catching grizzlies.

Only a few days previous, a ranchman, whose range ran along the west side of Crosby Mountain in the Datil Range, sent me word that a grizzly had been killing his cattle, and to bring my hounds and try to catch this bear. I moved my camp over to Crosby Mountain, then went over and visited the ranchman, who told me that the bear had killed a cow at the Crosby Springs a couple of days before, and was supposedly still eating on it. This was most welcome news to me.

He went on to say that this grizzly was known as "Susie," sometimes "Big Susie," because she was a very large bear, and was known to have run on Crosby Mountain for a great many years.

It was then that I realized that this was the same bear that Dan and I had run three years before, when Miss Agnes Morley (Mrs. Cleaveland) was with us, an episode which is so well described in her *No Life for a Lady*. I well remember that hunt, and Susie winning the round by getting away from us.

It happened that Dan and I were camping at the Morley Ranch, and we had been told that this grizzly and two cubs were "using" on Crosby Mountain. By a great piece of luck, it had snowed a little during the night, and early next morning, Dan and I started out on our hunt, joined by Miss Morley. As the snow had obliterated all old tracks, any that we might run on to would not be more than a few hours old. On the north hillside, where the sun did not strike, the old snow was still deep.

In the afternoon, we struck the trail of Susie and her cubs. The ground was still thinly covered by snow, and we could easily follow by sight, while as it was thawing, the hounds had no difficulty in trailing. They soon got out of hearing, but this, for once, made no difference, since the bear tracks in the snow were easy to follow. After running some ten miles, we heard the hounds baying at some place where the bear must have stopped, and which turned out to be a cave, probably the one Susie had picked out in which to hibernate with her cubs.

The cave was on a steep north hillside, and had been dug out under a flat ledge of rock that skirted the hill. A big, dead pine had fallen up hill, the roots sticking up in the air about ten feet below the cave. The hounds were baying furiously in the space that lay between the cave and the roots of the tree. We approached a spot about fifty feet above the cave, and dismounted, tied up our horses and held a council of war.

I knew that Miss Morley was very anxious to kill a grizzly, a feat that no other girl had ever accomplished, so far as we knew. Our problem was to figure out a way in which she could do this without any risk. Miss Morley suggested that we should all go down to the cave together, but I remembered the responsibility I had assumed when I promised her mother that I would look out for her safety. Under such circumstances, it seemed to me preferable to face a wounded grizzly rather than an irate mother whose daughter had got hurt in spite of my promise that she would come to no harm. So Miss Morley's suggestion was politely declined.

About thirty feet from the cave, and facing it, stood a young pine, and one of its sturdy branches, some ten feet from the ground, was a suitable place for a person to sit and shoot at the bear. So we decided that Miss Morley should climb the tree and await developments. Dan loaned her his rifle, keeping his six-shooter as his only weapon, and then climbed another tree close by.

While the vantage points of Miss Morley and Dan were strategically correct, as was also the bear's in the cave, I realized that the continuation of such a procedure would be very inconclusive; that is, it would only lead to a bear-hunting stalemate. In order to avoid such a contingency, I thought it was best to go to the cave and investigate.

Stooping low, I approached the fallen tree at a point facing the mouth of the cave. I then pushed my rifle on to the trunk of the tree, and raised my head slowly, to look over. Unfortunately, the cave was between me and the setting sun, whose rays shone directly into my eyes, and I was obliged to pull my hat down and peer into the cave from under the brim.

For the first few seconds I could see nothing. Then, in the semi-darkness of the cave, I saw the outline of Susie's head and her glinting, beady eyes, looking straight at me. I moved my rifle slowly to aim, and I needed only one more second for a perfect shot. But Susie didn't grant me that second. She bolted out of the cave straight at me—as Dan subsequently expressed it: "Like a bat out of Hell"—and as I moved the sun's rays blinded me, and all I could do was to thrust my rifle forward in the hope that it would go down her throat.

Unluckily, I missed my aim, and the rifle went off, kicking itself out of my hand on to the ground, sideswiping her neck, and inflicting only a slight flesh wound.

I bent over to pick up the rifle, but at that moment, Susie appeared around the roots of the tree, and took after me. I ran up alongside the tree trunk, and realizing she was gaining on me, took a cartwheel header over the log into the snow on the other side, and rolled on to the ledge of rock which was just above the cave.

At the same instant, Miss Morley fired, and Dan, thinking that she had hit me, shouted, "You've killed him! You've killed him!"

These remarks were hardly calculated to induce her to act in a normal way, especially as Dan kept yelling repeatedly, "Kill the bear! Kill the bear!"

Though, perhaps I should say that, in his excitement, he didn't express himself in exactly those polite terms. It is not surprising, therefore, that Miss Morley should have continued snapping her rifle at the bear without putting in a fresh cartridge.

Meanwhile, I picked myself up and pulled out my six-shooter, while the two cubs came running out of the cave to where I was, and, standing up, one on each side of me, their heads being even with my shoulders, grunted like scared hogs.

All this time, Susie was milling round under Miss Morley's tree, while the dogs kept baying at her furiously. The cubs and I were looking anxiously at the tree trunk, expecting Susie to come over it, but with entirely different emotions. The cubs were looking forward to a family reunion, which I certainly was not.

It was one of those moments when you have to think quickly, and I concluded to vacate the conspicuously undesirable spot on which circumstances had placed me by jumping down off the ledge and running into the cave, leaving it up to Susie, in her turn, to get *me* out. Fortunately, I was not called upon to take this course, as the baying of the hounds began to recede, indicating that Susie had decided to retire from the field of battle.

As soon as the full import of this dawned on me, I plucked up courage, and shoved my six-shooter into the ribs of one of the cubs and fired. He fell forward into the snow, kicking, but the other one disappeared before I could treat him the same way. I then ran around the roots of the tree to where my rifle lay and, picking it up, climbed the hill to where I had tied my horse. Scrambling on to his back, I pulled out after Dan, who had already started off after the hounds and Susie, whose trail was marked with occasional drops of blood on the snow.

We had not pursued her very far until it became dark, so we called the dogs to follow us, and returned to camp the way we had come, passing the cave, but we found that Miss Morley had already left.

And now the time had at last come when I was to hunt Susie for the second time. Having been told exactly where I would find the cow that Susie had killed at Crosby Springs, I started out the next morning to hunt her. I headed straight for the dead cow, with all the dogs, including Sleuth, following close at my horse's heels. When I got within about fifty yards of the cow, I dismounted, leaving all the dogs, except Sleuth, to stay with my horse. Sleuth ran ahead of me, and at once scented a bear trail and started to follow it, baying excitedly, while I, after observing several of Susie's big tracks, ran back, unnecked the dogs, and started after the pack.

From the lively way the hounds bayed, I knew it was a hot trail, and it was not long before they got out of hearing. After some five miles, with my slow-trail dogs pointing the way, I again got in hearing of the hounds, but this time the baying remained in the same place, from which I knew the bear was either bayed, or up a tree. Listening on, I noticed that the hounds were barking alternately, which meant that they had treed a black bear. If they had been baying Susie, a grizzly, she would have made an occasional run at them, which would have caused them to bark simultaneously, with a sort of scared bark.

This was an unexpected blow to me, as I had felt sure that the hounds were running Susie. But there was nothing I could do about it, except to ride to the tree and shoot the bear out of it.

After the dogs had had their customary meal, I rode back to camp and sent Telesfor out with a pack horse to bring it in.

The reason for the hounds taking the black bear's trail, instead of Susie's, was because it was the hotter of the two. Susie had come in first, and had eaten on her kill, and after she had left, the black bear came along and took his turn at eating, thus leaving the stronger and later scent.

Ordinarily, the catching of this black bear would have had no special significance, but in this case it was different, for I was much worried over the fact that Susie might have heard the hounds baying this bear, in which case it might have resulted in her leaving Crosby Mountain, like any ordinary "spoilt" bear would have done. I presume the reason she didn't was that as she had been run by hounds before and, having got away successfully, she must have developed a certain contempt for them. She would have got away this time, had it not been for my double-header trailing stunt, one that she could never have figured on.

Early next day, I started out and, like the day before, as soon as Sleuth reached the cow, he started off on a hot trail, which this time really was Susie's, although at first I was afraid that it might be that of another black bear.

The hounds soon got out of hearing. For the first few miles the going was good, until I reached a deep canyon, the side of which was too steep for a horse to go down. I decided to go to the left to find a place where I could cross, which was the wrong choice.

Panther and Wolf had already started down into the canyon, so I had to blow my whistle to call them back to me. With these dogs ahead of me, side by side, I rode down about a mile before I could find a place to cross the canyon. I went up on the other side, and when I reached a point that was opposite to where the bear and pack had gone down into the canyon, Panther and Wolf continued on, showing that the bear and pack must have changed their direction. I went on for another mile before I could again drop into the canyon, and then I went down it with the expectation of striking the trail at any moment. I had gone but a quarter of a mile when, on passing the mouth of a side canyon, Panther and Wolf suddenly took up it, and sure enough, on its sandy bed were Susie's tracks, with hound tracks occasionally showing up in them, proving positively that we were on Susie's trail, and not that of another bear.

We followed the trail up this side canyon until it headed up on the mountain, through the usual thick timber and quaking aspen thickets, which grew profusely around the northern end of the mountain top. There were, however, places where the timber was not so thick but what I could ride through it. So calling Panther and Wolf off the trail to join me, as I could no longer follow the dogs, it was through one of these gaps that I rode to the top of the mountain.

All this time I was out of earshot of the hounds, but I knew the general direction in which they were headed, so I followed along near the edge of the timber until finally I did hear them.

Susie had evidently stopped to rest, because the sound of the baying was stationary. I rode on to a point about five hundred feet above where she had stopped in a quaking aspen thicket. The wind was in her favour; that is, there was no steady wind from any one direction, though had there been one, I could have directed my movements in such a way that she could not have winded me when I tried to approach her.

While this particular day might be called a "still" day, the air was not motionless. Little currents of air would start up from somewhere, and after a brief but erratic existence, end in the same place, confirming the Biblical saying that "The wind bloweth where it listeth." This gave Susie a great advantage, because no matter from what angle I might

273   T

approach, these tell-tale, fitful gusts of wind would give me away, causing Susie to get a move on.

As she dashed straight away from me, I could only infer that she must have winded me, which was the last thing I wanted her to do. When I left my horse and wormed my way down the mountain side to within about fifty yards of her, she would then suddenly bolt, and every time I decided to follow her, she wouldn't stop long enough for me to get a shot. I would follow her until I got temporarily exhausted, and then I would have to give up and wend my weary way back to my horse, George, who, by this time, was half a mile or more away. Then I would clamber into the saddle and leave it up to him to continue the chase, while I would rest and get back my wind. This was my advantage.

But Susie also had an advantage, aside from the wind. Though contrary to the rules of war, while she was on the defensive, she still held the initiative, and by forcing me to make detours most of the time, I was compelled to travel two or three times as far as she did. But to offset this, George and I could chase her on a sort of double shift basis; that is, when I had to make these quaking aspen excursions on foot, George would have a good rest, and when I would get back in the saddle, it was my turn to take it easy.

It was a sort of game of hide and seek. Hour after hour, all day long, I had chased her from one quaking aspen thicket to another, and it was now mid-afternoon. It began to sink into my brain that if she could wind me every time I came near her, and run away before I could get a shot, keeping up those tactics until dark, she would win this round.

So far, the battle had been even, in that while I had never caught up with her, she had never got away from me. Luckily for me, she took this latter view into consideration, and decided upon some other method of giving me the slip.

Instead of continuing to dodge back and forth between the quaking aspen thickets, she suddenly left them, and ran towards the southern end of the mountain, where there was little timber or brush. I was at least a half-mile away from George, and the time it took to get back to him gave her a good start.

I galloped in the direction in which the baying of the hounds showed she had gone, and it was not long before Panther and Wolf again picked up their trail.

The southern end of the mountain was a big, rocky, flat mesa, about nine thousand feet high, around which was a rimrock, or wall of rock, some eight or ten feet high, in which there were a few gaps.

Susie went across this mesa, and going down through a gap on the east side, she ran along the wall to the south side, and then on to the west side to a big gap immediately above a rock slide, which descended abruptly for about a thousand feet. This rock slide was some two hundred feet wide, and was composed mostly of flat, sharp rocks sticking up in all directions, with some roundish rocks of various sizes scattered about here and there.

As I rode over the mesa, I heard the hounds baying after Susie, who was running along the foot of the rock wall, so I made straight for this gap, and got there the same time she did, neither of us seeing the other until we were only about thirty feet apart. She stopped, raised up on her hind legs and looked at me, then whirled round, and bolted down the rock slide. She very soon lost her balance, and went heels over head, but when she caught on her feet again, she was going so fast that she was unable to stop until she reached the bottom. She had loosened a lot of the roundish rocks, and they pursued her all the way down, a few of them hitting her square on the back. This would have caused her to increase her pace, if that had been possible.

Little did I think, as I watched her plunge down, that this rock slide would be the determining factor in giving me the decision in this second, and what proved to be final round with Susie.

The hounds, of course, followed her down the rock slide, stepping very gingerly over the sharp rocks, and they were only about one-third of the way down when Susie reached the bottom.

Meanwhile, I had to dismount and lead George to one edge of the rock slide before we could start down the mountain. The descent was so steep that I had to step aside, from time to time, to let George slide by me when he lost his balance, but as soon as I got to where I could ride, I remounted and followed the hounds, who were by this time a mile away.

I had with me Panther and Wolf, Twist, the three bull terriers, and Princess. Susie was evidently heading for one of the big caves on a rocky peak, known as Sugar Loaf, and if I didn't reach her before she crossed the narrow valley between Crosby Mountain and Sugar Loaf, my chances of getting her that day were very slim indeed.

After galloping some two or three miles, I again heard the hounds baying. I could hardly believe my ears, because the way in which they bayed indicated that Susie had stopped. When I got to within about fifty yards of her, my bull terriers rushed forward to attack her. I jumped off my horse and pulling my rifle from its scabbard, ran to a tree about ten yards from where Susie was bayed, and stood behind it, ready to shoot at the first opportunity. I didn't have to wait long before she came rushing out from under a big juniper tree into a small open space in front of me.

Grip had her by the throat, Biz by the left ear, and Nap by the right ear. At first she tried to shake this weird canine pendant and earrings loose, but that didn't work. Then she turned her head to the left, trying to get hold of Biz; then the other way to catch Nap. But like apples bobbing out of reach of a boy's mouth, they stayed out of reach of her jaws. After several such vain attempts, she decided to confine her efforts to catching Biz. She turned faster and faster, in order to grab him, but the only result was that the three bull terriers, by centrifugal force, revolved at a tangent. After about three revolutions, Susie concluded that this wouldn't work, so she stopped and sprang into the air and shook herself. But that didn't work, either. So when she struck the ground, she lowered her head, and rubbing the ground with it, she literally scraped the dogs off her ears, flinging Biz to the left and Nap to the right.

Grip, however, was still hanging tenaciously to her throat, her head being just under the bear's lower jaw, which prevented Susie from biting her, so Susie raised up on her hind legs, and with her forepaws tried to push Grip's body into her mouth.

At that moment, Nap, who had got back on his feet, sprang at her to renew his hold on her ear, but quicker than a flash, for I never saw it, Susie struck him in mid-air. He went hurtling through space, body and tail wiggling, as he tried to regain his balance, until he struck the stump of a pine about seven feet up from the ground, and about twenty feet away.

With all his ribs on one side caved in, he fell to the foot of the stump, limp and helpless. Susie then repeated her attempts to bite Grip, but at that moment I shot her through the brain and she dropped dead.

Incidentally there is a general impression that bears hug, not amicably like human beings, but aggressively. What basis there is for this belief I do not know, but as far as my experience goes I have seen numberless bear and dog fights, but have never seen the least tendency on the part of the bear to hug his opponent. On the contrary, when Grip had Susie by the throat, the latter, not being able either to bite or strike her with her paws, raised up on her hind feet and tried to push Grip's body which was hanging down over her breast, into her mouth. If a bear's natural instinct was to hug, she would never have passed up such an opportunity as this to have hugged Grip to death.

Grip kept on biting her as though nothing had happened, and then all the dogs piled on to the luckless Susie, "woolling" her, with the exception of Princess, who, remembering her previous experience with a seemingly dead grizzly, took no interest in the proceedings.

When I thought that the dogs had "woolled" Susie enough, I drove them off, and then it was that I discovered why Susie had stopped when she did. Upon looking at her front feet, I found that the pads had been cut to pieces, leaving shreds hanging from the side. Owing to the great momentum forced upon her by the steepness of the rock slide, she was unable to control her pace, and thus prevent the soles of her feet being cut up as they were. The pain must have been so excruciating that it was impossible for her to continue her flight on the raw flesh of her front feet.

Had it not been for this, she would have got into one of the large caves on Sugar Loaf without my having had a chance to get a shot at her; and even if she didn't, with night coming on, it would soon have been too dark to shoot.

I often have been asked how hard a blow a grizzly can strike. While this is a very difficult question perhaps I can give some idea of how it might be answered.

Poor Nap weighed forty-five pounds, and when Susie struck him, he went through the air for twenty feet, and I am sure he would have gone another twenty feet had he not been stopped by the pine stump. While I do not feel competent to estimate how hard a blow that would represent, it is possible that some astute mathematician might be able to figure it out.

As a further possible estimate from another angle, I would add that I once came across one of my bulls who had been killed by a grizzly. This bull weighed at least twelve hundred pounds, but nevertheless, his huge neck had been broken as easily as that of a cow by a blow with one paw, while in addition, his whole face had been bashed in, evidently by a blow from the other.

The defeat of Susie was the red-letter day of all my hunting experiences. It marked the gratifying culmination of years of hard work and painstaking mental effort, and proved that bloodhounds could be trained to trail any animal successfully, without having had any previous experience in hunting that particular animal.

CHAPTER XXII

THE JEWETT GAP GRIZZLY

WHILE I killed many more grizzlies in the next few years, I did not purposely hunt any more black bear, unless it were a very large one, and in this effort to hunt only grizzlies, curiously enough, I was greatly aided by the grizzlies themselves.

Every time one of them was imprudent enough to kill a cow, I was promptly informed, and I would sally forth with my pack, and go straight to the cow, thus getting a hot trail avoiding the usual loss of time before finding one. But there was nothing unusual to record, with the exception of one big fellow, known as the Jewett Gap grizzly, a photograph of whose head, with its mouth open, appears in the illustrations, as well as on the jacket.

I had known this bear by sight; that is, by his footprints, for some ten years, during which time he killed a great many cattle and sheep. Large bounties had been offered for him, and many trappers had tried to catch him, without success.

Then, one day, I received word that on the previous night he had run through a herd of sheep, slapping them right and left as he went through, killing about forty, and carrying one nearly two miles before eating it.

The next day, I hurriedly left home with my hounds, and went to the place where the remains of the dead sheep lay. Sleuth, who had been running ahead of me, scented the trail, and pulled out, baying excitedly although the trail was more than thirty hours old.

Five miles beyond, we ran on to a freshly killed cow, and as its neck was broken, I knew that this grizzly had done it. From there the trail was very much hotter, because he must have been eating on the cow during the night.

After going about another five miles, the hounds jumped him out of his bed, and the chase was on. The bear, as usual, headed for the heavy timber and rough places around the top of the mountain. I chased him all day, making detour after detour. At the places where it was impossible for a horse to follow, I had to call Panther and Wolf off the trail, and skirt around until they again struck the trail of the pack, and then follow it until I was forced to make another detour.

It was not until late afternoon that I caught up with them, and by this time, the bear was pretty well played out, and had stopped on a steep hillside, just below the top of the highest peak of Fox Mountain. He was sitting up on his haunches, with his tongue hanging out, while the pack was baying him from a safe distance, about thirty yards below. As I approached the ridge just above him, I got off my horse and, taking my rifle, climbed down the hillside among the bushes to a place about twenty feet above him, from which I could get a clear shot.

I was just raising my rifle to shoot, when my two bull terriers, Grip and Biz, whom unfortunately I had brought along, ran forward and attacked him from behind. He turned and, jumping up, stood on his hind legs, raising one paw in readiness to strike, while Grip and Biz were barking at him furiously on the ground just above him.

It was at this moment that I had a clear shot at his throat, and fired, with the object of shooting through it, and breaking the neck bone. But instead of dropping, he lunged forwarp on his front feet and came at me, and I didn't fully realize this until he had got half-way to me. This was one of those not infrequent emergencies, when I had to stand on one foot and rest the muzzle of the rifle on the other, in order to reload.

By this time, the bear's head was so close to me that I couldn't shoot at it, so I poked the rifle against his back, between the shoulders, and fired, breaking his backbone. He rolled over and over down hill, and although he could not rise, his demeanour was so aggressive that I had to finish him hurriedly with a shot in the head with my six-shooter.

How I could have missed such a relatively large target as his throat at so short a distance as twenty feet, was hard to imagine, but since there was no bullet hole in the neck, the evidence that I had missed was indisputable. However, it was not until I felt over the throat several times for the bullet hole that I was fully convinced of this.

I returned next day with two men and two pack horses to pack the bear back, and I asked the men if they could find a bullet hole in the throat, but they met with no better success than I had. But when they started to skin the bear, one of them held up one forefoot, saying, "Here's your bullet hole."

Sure enough, the soft-nosed bullet had splintered into little pieces, breaking both bones in the wrist, and leaving a hole you could put two fingers through. Evidently, the bear struck at a dog the instant I fired at his throat, and his paw must have intercepted the bullet.

Such a strange coincidence would probably never occur again, and while one must figure that anything may happen, the chief objection to such incidents as this is that they have a tendency to undermine one's self-confidence, and self-confidence is an indispensable requisite in hunting grizzlies.

CHAPTER XXIII

MEMENTOS

I HAVE often been asked what I did with my grizzly hides. Many of them I presented to relatives and to intimate friends, who, recognizing the suggestion of a close personal element, appreciated them more than they would ordinary gifts of greater intrinsic value.

However, certain individuals sometimes offered to buy the hides, and I recall one man who proffered several times the commercial value of a green hide, increasing his offer when I refused to sell.

As he seemed to feel offended when I refused his second and larger offer, one of my ingenious excuses flashed into my mind. I explained that if I were to sell any hides, my status as an amateur bear hunter would be lost, and I would be placed in the professional class, a contingency to which I would strongly object.

The would-be buyer accepted my unfavourable reply with ill-concealed disapproval, and later commented freely that I was a poor business man for refusing an opportunity to sell something for more than its value, when I had the chance.

This criticism, coming from him, struck me as odd, as, if *he* were a business man, why should he offer me several times the value of the hide? So I was driven to the uncharitable conclusion that what he really wanted was the hide of a freshly killed bear to take back with him to his home in the East, to exhibit to his friends as undeniable proof of his hunting prowess. Needless to say, he didn't get the hide.

Among the best of my grizzly bear hides which I gave away was one which I presented to the Wyndham Club, St. James Square, London. This was an eight-hundred-pound grizzly, mounted standing up, with his mouth open, and the natural skull was used in mounting his head, thus displaying his huge canine teeth. He was placed on the first landing of the main staircase of the Club.

I gave another to the Commercial Club, of Albuquerque, and others to General Nelson A. Miles, George J. Gould, Harold C. Wilson, of St. Andrews, Scotland, and Jonathan Darby, my brother-in-law, of Leap Castle, King's County, Ireland. The latter hide was Susie's, and was hung up in the main hall of the Castle, but I regret to say it was burned up, when Leap Castle was destroyed by fire during the Irish riots.

And my largest and finest black bear hide I gave to my sister, the Dowager Countess Castle Stewart.

The Jewett Gap bear hide I kept for myself, having selected it through sentiment, in the remembrance of our brief, but all too close acquaintance.

In addition to this bear hide, I have a memento that I treasure highly, one which I'm sure deserves mention, and that is a collection which I think is unique. While it has no intrinsic value, mere money could not buy its duplicate.

It consists of a lot of misshapen pieces of lead that can be held in one hand. Each piece of lead was a bullet that had killed a grizzly, and I often wonder, when I look at this collection, whether it was worth all the energy and risk expended in getting it.

Personally, I think so.

CHAPTER XXIV

MY LAST HUNT

In this closing chapter, I grieve to have to recall the fate of my best hounds. It came about on my last hunt, and to me, it's such a painful subject that I can only dwell on it briefly.

I had been sent word that a grizzly was killing cattle in a certain range of mountains, about seventy miles from the ranch, and on arriving at my destination, I made camp a few miles from a spring around which this bear had been operating.

I left the hounds in camp, and went to the spring to find out whether a cow had been recently killed there and upon returning to camp, I found Rufus, who the cook told me had just come into camp, having a fit from the effects of poisoning by strychnine. After another spasm, he died. My cook told me the direction from which he had come. I rode out to hunt up the other hounds, and had not gone over a half mile before I came on to a dead cow, around which were Psyche, Rudolf, and Inveed, all having fits.

There was nothing I could do for them, so I sat down beside one, while the other two crawled to me. Between convulsions, they would lick my hand and look in my face pathetically, expecting me to help them. But I couldn't. There was nothing left for me to do except watch them die, one after the other, while I stroked their heads, as the only way in which I could express my sympathy.

After this, I went back to camp to get a shovel, and to bring the cook back with me. We dug a grave, in which we put the dogs, and covered it over with a pile of rocks, and then returned to camp.

The next day we went back to the ranch, and that was the end of my last hunt. I felt sure that Sleuth must have, also, met the same fate, though I never found his body.

As to those who put out poison indiscriminately, under the impression that they will poison coyotes, I can only say that coyotes are too wary to be poisoned that way; that the only animals they do kill are an odd skunk or two. I do not wish to be vindictive against those who so ignorantly put out poison, but I have to admit that I find it very hard to forgive them.

I also had a keen disappointment due to the death of my hounds. In November, 1896, while I was in New York, Frederic Remington took me down to Mulberry Street to meet his great friend, Teddy Roosevelt, who was, at that time, police commissioner of New York City.

Remington had previously told him about the bear hunt he had had with me, and which he had illustrated in *Harper's Magazine* for August, 1894, and Mr. Roosevelt had expressed a desire to meet me, if I should ever happen to come to New York. So he took this opportunity of introducing me, and after discussing bear hunting for some time, Mr. Roosevelt said he would like to come on a hunt with me, but feared he never would be able to afford the time. He then went on to say that killing a black bear held no particular interest for him, but hunting grizzly! That was something else! He said that if I could guarantee him a grizzly, he would temporarily chuck up any job he might have and go on that hunt.

I replied that I was sorry that I couldn't guarantee anything more than a black bear at that time, with the hounds I then had, but that the day might come when I would be able to do so.

Then he said, "Well, if that day comes, promise to let me know." And I promised. We then shook hands over it, and he said, "Well, that's a go."

I little thought, at the time, that I would ever be in a position to justify myself in guaranteeing a grizzly, nor did I ever think that had Mr. Roosevelt come on a grizzly hunt with me, the job he would have been chucking up, temporarily, would have been that of running the United States.

It was just at the time that I was about to fulfil my promise to Mr. Roosevelt that my hounds were poisoned. In fact, I had already picked out a certain grizzly that I was keeping in reserve for him.

So it can well be imagined what a sad blow it was to find myself suddenly unable to carry out my agreement, as he, of all sportsmen, would have most keenly appreciated the bear-hunting abilities of my bloodhound pack.

As soon as I became resigned to the loss of my hounds, I began to think things over, and derived some consolation from the fact that there were very few grizzlies left to hunt in the section of the Rocky Mountains over which I had hunted, and feeling that I had already had my full share of them, from that time on, I became a zealous convert to their preservation, to prevent so noble an animal becoming extinct.

So, hanging up my rifle on the wall, with this paraphrase, sorrowfully I exclaimed:

"Ichabod! The glorious sport of hunting grizzlies with bloodhounds has departed!"

"FRONT NAME" DICK

The frontier bred some strangely independent characters. For this third printing of Meet Mr. Grizzly *we are adding a story by Montague Stevens wherein he recalls an unforgettable hireling who came to work on his ranch. Ms. Nancy Coggeshall of Reserve, New Mexico, brought this tale to our attention. The story was first published in* The Cosmopolitan Illustrated Monthly Magazine, *March, 1897, illustrated by Frederic Remington. "Front Name" Dick is a classic account of rough, cowboy humor, and proof that truth is not only stranger than fiction, it is funnier too.*

Some years ago I had a cook who was certainly a most original character. When he first made his appearance, he rode up to where my outfit was camped and said he understood we were in need of a cook and that he would like to get the job. I asked him if he had ever cooked for a cow outfit before and he answered that he "guessed he had right smart," so I said, "Well, there's the wagon and the cooking tricks; just turn yourself loose."

As no one had asked him his name, the boys had been calling him "Cooky-come-lately," but as I could hardly address him in that manner, I inquired of him what his real name was. "Well, the front name I goes by nowadays is Dick," said he, "and as I ain't got no partic'ler use for no more name, jes' call me Dick. Yer see, my mother got marr'd several times, I disremember jus' now how many," said he, reflectively, "for she had awful bad luck with her husbands. I b'longed in the second batch of kids, but when I got to be about fifteen years old I had a difficulty with the stepfather I had at that time, so I pull'd out from home one day, for to earn my own living for myself and I never thought to ax my mother a'fore leaving what my own pa's name was. My folks giv' me the name of Silas, and the boys back in Texas, where I used to work, would call me Si for short, but ther' was another feller in that country that went by the name of Cyclone Bill and they used to call him Cy for short too. Well, this yer Cyclone Bill had a very hard reppytation and that was a-sayin' a whole heap, 'cause even the decent folks in that country in them days was mighty tough. He was allus adoin' some dibilment or other, was Cyclone Bill, and there was considerable reward out for his captur', so there was allus depp'ty sheriffs out a huntin' for him, and wunst in a while some of them depp'tys, as was smart-allecky, would arrest me just 'cause my name was Si. It didn't do me no good to kick, and when I would say I warn't the man they was a-huntin', they'd say 'that's all right, you will have to 'splain that in court, but you'll jus' naturally have to come along with us right now anyhow.' Well, I was tried more'n wunst for Cyclone Bill's divilments, but I allus come clear by provin' what these 'ere lawyers calls a alibi. But then it was mighty unpleasant bein' arrested for 'nother man, and as the hoss stealing was a-gettin' wuss all the time, the depp'tys was a-gettin' so as they warn't so partic'ler about takin' a man to jail at all, and I got afeared that maybe some time, when I warn't a-suspicionin' nothin', I might be tuk' off in the brush somewheres and never given no show to prove my allibi, so I concluded I'd change my name and I tuk' the name of Dick for Silas."

For the next few days he worked incessantly, cleaning up everything there was to clean around the wagon and arranging and re-arranging its jumbled contents in a manner that finally seemed to meet with his entire approval. His cooking was excellent, and called forth the remark from one of the boys that "it was the slickest hash he ever had throw'd up to him, and as to the puddin's they were jes' larruping truck."

Things went along smoothly for a time, until one morning Dick drew me on one side and said, "Well, I guess I'll have to quit yer."

"Why, what's the matter, Dick," said I.

"Oh, I ain't mad at you," he said, "you ain't done nothin', but you see I don't feel as I can do justice to my perfesh the way things are agoin'. You're a-payin' me good wages to cook for you, and I calc'late to give you good valyer received in return, and when I feel I ain't able to give it, why I'd rather quit. Ye see, since I have been workin' for you I have fixed up everythin' in the waggin in good shape, but them boys is allus a-pullin' things around everywhichways, so I can't find nothin' when I wants to, and this mornin' one of 'em spilt a lot of horse-shoe nails in my sour dough kag, and 'nother one upset the axle grease over the dried apples; of course it ain't my property, and maybe I ain't got no right to kick, but I kan't he'p it jus' the same."

"Well, Dick," said I, in a conciliating tone, "I appreciate your feelings, but I wouldn't wish you to leave me on that account."

"Well, in my 'sperience there ain't but one way to fix it," said he, "and that is for you to give me leave to run this yer waggin as fer as the grub and all the other truck that's in it is concerned."

"Why, certainly, Dick," I said, "go ahead and run it to suit yourself, and as long as you do your work right, you need never fear I won't back you up whenever necessary."

"All right," he said, "I'll go ahead, and I b'lieve I kin give you good satisfacshun, but I'll jus' speak to them boys afor' you at dinner to-day and tell 'em what you've told me." That day at dinner, Dick made his little speech. "Boys," said he, "the boss here has give me leav' to run this yer waggin, and I'm a'shure a-goin' to run it. I have fixed everythin' in the waggin in good shape and jus' know where everythin' is, and if any of you wants anythin' out of it at any time, I'll git it for you. Now, I ain't got no hard feelin's agin anyone of you, but I want to tell you right now, that the fust man I ketch a-munkin' in my waggin from this on, I'm a-goin to kill right then and there. Maybe some of you thinks I'm a jokin', but I ain't, and if any of you wants to find out what a rough joke is, jus' go and git somethin' out of the waggin' without konsultin' me. Then, agin, I don't want no horses tied to the waggin wheel, and when yer ridin' up
to camp and the wind's a-blowin' I want you to look out not to kick up the dust so that it falls into the chuck I'm a cookin'." Having delivered himself thus, he took his six-shooter out of his belt and laid it quietly

on the mess box in front of his clock, and then with a conclusive wave of his cooking spoon, which he always used to emphasize his statements, he said, "Well, I ain't got nothin' more to say, boys."

Dick was most methodical in his habits, but he had no opinion of any man who didn't have a watch or clock to work by. He was very taciturn by nature, but when I would be alone with him in camp sometimes, he would open up and reveal the curious workings of a quaint mind. He was most careful about his clock, and when we moved camp would always wrap it up in dish-cloths and pack it away in a box that just fitted into one of the smaller compartments of the mess-box. "Well," he remarked to me sententiously one day, as he was, what I was impious enough to call, "unswaddling his clock," "there ain't many men that thinks as much of a clock as I do, or takes as much care o' one as I does; now I have had this yer clock for many a year and she's never gone wrong. O'course I allus wraps her up careful when we moves camps, 'cause I would be afeared, if I didn't, that the jostlin' o' the waggin over them rough roads might discomplicate her innards, but she has never gone back on me so fur. Now I used to pack a watch, but in my business of cookin', a watch ain't much use compared with a clock. Ye see, a man's hands is often covered with dough makin' bread, or wet and greasy washing dishes, or all bloody handlin' meat, so he kan't be a-fumblin' in his pocket for his watch to see the time, but you take a clock and she's allus a-talkin' to you all the time. Whenever I looks at my clock she's allus a-sayin somethin', maybe it's, 'Dick, are yer buckets full o' water?' or, (here he happened to glance at the clock) why she's tellin' me to grind the corfy right now," and he hurried off, while I waited patiently until the coffee had been ground to resume the conversation.

Dick certainly loved his profession, what he called his "perfesh," and nothing pleased him more than an opportunity to exhibit his skill. It was very seldom under any circumstances that he showed any emotion, but whenever we would happen to have a few extras to our usual bill of fare to cook, such as fresh fruit or vegetables, he would get positively excited, and when dinner was finally ready to serve, he would call out with a complacent wave of his spoon, and as near an approach to a smile as he would ever allow himself to indulge in, "Boys, come a-runnin'." On the other hand, when the grub was "slim," he would call out dolefully, "Well, here's h-ll, fellers."

One day, when Dick was in one of his reminiscent moods, he confided to me a good deal of his past history. "Ye see," said he, "I was wunst in business myself, and thought I was a-goin' to make my pile, but it didn't pan out, somehow. I tuk up a minin' claim in

290

Colorado, in a camp as was boomin', and sold out fur a thousand dollars even. The feller as had the claim along aside o' me sold out to the same parties as I did and for the same price. We used to trade work with one 'nother whilst we was a-doin' assessment work on them claims, and so we got to be partners like, and when we both sold out we thought we'd go into business together. My pard's name was Pete, but they used to call him 'Surly Pete', 'cause when folks would ax him questions he warn't allus perlite in his answers. To give you an idee, one time, when he was a-comin' out from town to camp, he met a feller on the road as axed him how fur it was to town. Now Pete was one of them fellers as never got blind drunk, but he liked to take his drink pretty reg'lar. Well, this trip I'm a-tellin' you of, he had his bottle of whiskey in his pocket, and when this feller axed him how fur it was to town, Pete, he pulled the whiskey bottle out of his pocket to see how much there was in it, and see'n there was two thirds gone, he says, 'Stranger, the distance is about two-thirds of a bottle o' whiskey.' The other feller says, 'Beg pard'n, but I don't know as I quite understand yer;' and Pete, he says, 'Oh, go to h--l; I ain't got no time to waste talkin' to fools as kain't understand nothin'.' And then he whips up his team and drives on, and o' course the other feller thought that Pete was a bit surly. But Pete, he was a good man just the same, though at times he took spells of being queer and notional. His perfesh was bronco-bustin'; and at that kind o' business he was hard to beat. So when we got paid for our minin' claims, he got me to go into the hoss business with him. We come down into New Mexico and tuk us up a ranch, and Pete he went around buyin' hosses, while I fixed up the ranch and built us a cabin. I tell yer, we thought a heap of ourselves in dem days, 'cause we was capitalists and could do as we liked. But it didn't last very long," added Dick, dolefully. "This yer business of bein' a bloated capitalist ain't what it's cracked up to be. A man keeps a-payin out good money for work and one thing and another, and when he gets his stuff ready to sell, the market's allus off, somehow, and he don't get nothin' fur it. Well, Pete, he paid out all the money we had for a dandy bunch o' mares and colts. He calc'lated on breakin' the colts and sellin' 'em for cow ponies, and we thought as it wouldn't be no time afore we would both be rich. We run them hosses for two years, and tho' we lived awful hard, we was allus cheerful, 'cause we thought we was a-makin' big money.

APPENDIX

"We was a livin' mostly on credit tho', but we only owed at the store in our town, which was thirty miles from the ranch. The storekeeper was very friendly at fust, when our credit was good, and would tell us to jes' help ourselves and git anythin' we wanted; but we found out arterwards that this was only 'cause he thought we was capitalists. He would introdooce us to these yer drummers, fellers what's all dressed up and talks a whole heap, altho' I don't know as they ever says much," said Dick, contemptuously; "and the storekeeper, he'd say, 'Lemme introdooce to you Mr. Dick, who is one o' our most prominent hossmen,' and they'd say, 'Proud to know you, Mr. Dick;' and then I'd feel kind of big like, and treat 'em to a drink. But when we began to get slow about payin' our bills, that there storekeeper would get insultin' like and would say he allus thought we was gen'l'men, and gen'l'men allus paid their debts. So we thought we'd jes' hurry up and sell some of our hosses and get shett of him. Well, we was jes' about thro' breakin' our first batch of bronks, and was a-gettin' ready to turn 'em over to a party as had agreed to buy 'em, when Pete's saddle turned with him one day, and he was throwed off and got a kick in his ribs what caved some of 'em in. He was sick for a long time, and I had, o' course, to take care o' him. It was jes' about this time that a feller came along and wanted to know if he could stop with us, as he was busted and cudn't get no work. He called hisself 'Ike,' but it warn't till some time arterwards that we found out his real name was 'Wanderin' Ike,' one of the wust hoss thieves in the whole country. Pretty soon 'nother feller come along, claiming he was in the same fix as Ike, but he didn't let on that he know'd Ike; but they didn't stop but a few days afore they both pulled out and tuk off all o' our hosses as they could git aholt o'. Ye see Pete, was still abed and I couldn't leave him, besides which, they tuck off the only hoss I had been keepin' up, so I was plum afoot. We jes' couldn't do nothin' at the time, but o' course we couldn't help havin' hard feelin's agin this yer 'Wanderin' Ike' in partic'ler, an' I jes' swore that as soon as I could I'd get onto his trail in good shape, so I puts Pete onto the fust waggin as passed our ranch goin' to town, and I went with him, as I wanted to 'splain the circumstances to that there storekeeper afore leavin' to hunt fur Ike. Well, I 'splained the matter to him, but he said he couldn't axcept no sech excuses, and wanted a settlement right off; so as we couldn't pay no cash, we concluded we was busted. We didn't have no receiver nor no assignee, nor nothin' of that kind; we just busted, and that was all there was to it. I give him a bill of sale to what hosses as was left--them, I means, as Ike failed to take with him--and we called the thing squar'; and then I pulled out of that thar seckshin with nothin' to show for all my money and work but a reppytashun for fair dealin'. I had heered that Ike had skipped to the Indian Territory with my hosses, but it was some months afore I caught up with him.

"It come about in this way: I was a-workin' in a liv'ry stable, when one day a depp'ty sheriff come along and put his hoss up in the barn, and while I was tendin' to it we got to talkin', and he says to me, 'I'm arter a noted hoss thief of the name of Wanderin' Ike, and I've heerd he's in a little town some ten miles off,' and then he axed me if I knowed him. 'You bet yer life,' says I, 'and I sure got it in for him too.' 'Well,' says he, 'I've got papers for him, but the parties as has got the warrint out told me, on the quiet, that while they was satisfied that Ike had done the stealin' they didn't know as they had quite sufficient evidence to convict, so they told me they would give me a hundred dollars if I bro't him in alive, but they would make it two hundred dollars if I could furnish good evidence of his death. So I believe I'll work for the two hundred,' said he, with a wink. This depp'ty went by the name of 'Shorty,' 'cause he was a small man, I s'pose, but he was most generally known as 'Shootin' Shorty,' 'cause when he had to 'rest bad men he allus believed in 'shootin' fust and then sizin' up the situation afterwards. 'Well,' says Shorty to me, 'seein' as you got it in for Ike, too, you had better come along with me, and I'll make it right with you, for I may need some help.' So the next day we saddled up and went over to the town where Wanderin' Ike was a-stoppin' and, sure 'nuff, we located him in one of the saloons there, a-havin' a high old time with some of his gang. As we was afeard Ike would remember me, Shorty proposed to wait until he come out of the saloon to go to his hoss, which was tied outside, and for me to hide behind a waggin as stood in the street and cover Ike with my Winchester, and to shoot if he showed fight when Shorty 'rested him. Shorty then tied his hoss up in front of a store opposite the saloon and waited for Ike to come out. Pretty soon Ike come out and walked to'ards his hoss, and then Shorty he crosses the street and goes to'ards the saloon, as though he was a-goin' there to get him a drink. Jes' as he was passin' near Ike, he says, 'Hello, pard, have you got a chew of terbacker about yer?' and Ike says 'Yes,' and was puttin' his hand to his side pocket and a-gittin' it out, when Shorty he pulls his gun and shoots Ike through the head. Ike fell all of a heap and his plug of terbacker rolled to one side, and Shorty he picked it up. O' course every one as heard the shot come runnin' up, and Shorty says, drawin' some papers out of his pocket, 'I've got these yer papers for this man, and when I told him to hold up he started to pull his gun, so I had to kill him in self-defense;' and with that, Shorty bit a big chew off the plug of terbacker. The crowd seemed quite satisfied at Shorty's explanashun, and o' course I couldn't say nothin', but when Shorty offered me a chew off that there plug, I says, 'No, thank you; I doan know as it would taste jes' right, Shorty.' 'Oh, pshaw!' says he, 'you're fullish; this is all jes' a matter of business with me.' We then went to the hotel and got us our dinner, while some of Ike's friends tuk him to the back end of the saloon. It appears Ike had some friends in that town, 'cause there was quite a number of them as chipped in to have him buried decent; and I chipped in a dollar, too," said Dick, modestly, "'cause I didn't feel that I had any more hard feelin's agin him. They had laid him out in state," said Dick, "like one sees in the 'Perlice Gazette' when they lays out one of yer big-bugs back East what gets killed by an-archests. They got the barber to shave him and wax out his mustash, and they bought him a fine suit o' black clothes, and a dandy pair of boots which cost eight dollars, 'cause I remember," said Dick, earnestly, "seein' the price chalked in big figgers on the soles, 'cause his feet was a-settin' up straight like. They sure fixed him up in fine shape," continued Dick. "O' course his boots was several sizes too big," he added, critically, "but then yer see it's a mighty hard matter to git new boots onto a dead man."

"What became of Shorty?" I inquired.

"Oh, he skipped out of that town mighty quick," replied Dick, "jes' as soon as he got through with his dinner, and then he started home for to git his money. But he never got it, tho', for the parties as told him they'd give him the two hundred dollars claimed that they had since found out that it was 'nother feller as had done the stealin', and it warn't Wanderin' Ike at all. They said they was mighty sorry for Ike, but o' course they couldn't pay out good money for the killin' of the wrong man, so they give Shorty his expenses and told him they didn't want to hear nothin' more from him on the subject."

Dick was looking very despondent one morning, so I said, "what's the matter, Dick?"

"Well," said he, "I'm out of sorts-like -- down on my luck, I s'pose. I used to have friends at one time, and it seems as though there warn't none o' them left, and it sure makes me feel lonesome."

"Why, what has become of them?" said I, sympathetically.

"The most o' them is dead," said he, sorrowfully, but with a certain touch of pride he added, "but they sure all died with their boots on. Why, there was 'Bad Luck Bob' that got hung by mistake for 'nother man, and then, there was 'Charley,' who got shot 'cause he wouldn't allow hisself to be bulldosed, and the man what murdered him got off scott-free, 'cause he had a wife and family. Oh, I tell yer, there ain't no sort of justice out West here; a man's got to take the law into his own hands if he wants to git justice," added Dick, significantly. "Take the case of 'Bad Luck Bob,' he was as fine a man as I ever knowed. He was one of them fellers as had the kourage of his own convikshuns, 'cause he never got drunk, and he warn't even ashamed to say so," said Dick, with great admiration.

"He allus 'tended to his own business and tried to leave other folks alone as much as he could, but in this world a man who has to make his own livin' has jus' naturally got to have dealin's with other folks wunst in a while. Well, this here Bob was a miner, and had some prospex which he was a-doin' his assessment work on, and one of 'em begun to show up pretty good. Well, ther' was 'nother feller in that ther' minin' camp where Bob was, of the name of Smith. He was a depp'ty sheriff, and part surveyor, and part minin' expurt, but mostly no account," said Dick, with great sarcasm. "When he seen Bob's prospec' was a-pannin' out well, he tuk up a claim right alongside o' it, and then claimed that the lead was mostly on his land. Bob, he paid no attenshun, but jes' continued developin' his lead, but this yer Smith told Bob one day he must git off what he called his claim, but as Bob still went on a-workin' and a-sayin' nothin', this yer Smith come up on him one day with a dubble-barr'led shot-gun, and told Bob he would kill him if he didn't quit working on that ther' claim right then and thar. As Bob was unarmed, and didn't want to git into no shootin' scrape no how, he jus' put on his coat and went back to camp, and then he went to town to see a lawyer for to git an injunshun out agin Smith from a-comin' onto his claim, and to git him put under bonds to keep the peace in the future."

"Well, Bob, he was as good a shot with a six-shooter as ever I see, and when he'd be a-drivin' along the road and see a prairie dog, he would most allus shoot at him for practice, and on this yer partic'ler trip, when he was a-drivin' back from town, he tuk three shots at prairie dogs, so he happened to have three empty shells in his six-shooter when he got back to the minin' camp. It was dark when he got in, and after leavin' his team at the liv'ry stable, he started to walk back to his cabin. He had his dog along with him, and as he was passin' Smith's house, which happened to lie between the liv'ry stable and his cabin, Smith's dog came a-runnin' out o' his back yard and jumped onto Bob's dog. Bob started to separate the dogs when Smith, hearin' the fuss, come a-runnin' out o' his house to find out what was the matter. He left the door behind him open, and as he was a-standin' in the light which streamed out from the house, suddinly there was three shots fired and Smith he fell down, shoutin' out 'I'm shot, I'm shot.'

Bob didn't know what to make of it quite, so he jumped behind a barrel as was a-settin' out in the yard, and draw'd his six-shooter ready to defend hisself. Then some of Smith's friends that was in the house come a-runnin' out and goes up to Smith, who tells 'em he's a-dyin', and that the man who shot him was over ther', pointin' to where Bob was a hidin'. Then Bob he steps out with his six-shooter in his hand and says, 'Gen'l'men, I ain't done this, and I don't know nothin' about it, exceptin' that ther' was some feller close to me as done the shootin', and then skipped out into the darkness.' And then Smith, he says, 'Boys, he's the man as has done me up, don't believe none of his lies,' and then they 'rested Bob and took his six-shooter away from him, and when they unloaded it, and found them three empty shells, they said Bob's story about 'nother feller doing the shootin' and skippin' out in the darkness was mighty thin. Then they axed Bob what he was a-doin' in the back yard anyhow, and Bob, he says, it was on account o' the dogs a-fightin',' and they said that that was about as thin a story as the other one, so Bob he wouldn't say nothin' more, seein' as he didn't seem to mend matters by doing it. That night Smith died, jus' a-cussin' the whole time, and a-swearin' he would sure git even with Bob. Then they tried Bob before the justice, he said, it was the wust case of cold-blooded murder he had ever heered of, so he sint Bob to jail to wait his trial at the next term of court, and the judge wouldn't give him no bail.

"Poor Bob, he tuk everythin' very quiet, and behaved hisself like a man, and when his trial come up I went to the town where it tuk place, and went to visit him as much as I could to brace him up. Bob didn't have no money to hire a lawyer for to defend him, but Smith's folks, they hired a lawyer as was a-workin' hard for a big rep, and promised him an extry big fee if he got a convickshun. I kin remember well what that ther' lawyer said, too," said Dick, fiercely, " He told a hole lot o' lies about poor Bob to the jury, right afore Bob's face, as he was a-sittin' in the dock, and, o' course, Bob he looked mad, and would move uneasily in his chair, and he'd look at that ther' lawyer in a way as would make him feel he was mighty glad there was other folks present. And then the lawyer would tell the jury to look at Bob, and axed them whether they didn't think he had murder in his eye. And then the lawyer told the jury that it was high time that the country was cleared o' desperadoes, and that it would be a stain on the country if a honorable man like Smith, who was a depp'ty sheriff and a officer of the law, should be shot down like a dog in his own back yard and his murderer go unhung. 'Why,' he yelled at the jury, 'it is your duty to find that man guilty o' murder in the first degree, jus' look at 'im, he's a bad man. Jus' think o' him a-skulkin' around honest citisen's back

297

yards night-times just in order to do 'em up, and in the day time, I warrint you,' he said, 'he prowled around like a lion ram-pant, a-skeerin' the little children a-playin' in the gutters.' Why," said Dick, with suppressed emotion, "that was a awful lie, 'cause at that time there warn't no children in that ther' minin' camp, and there warn't no gutters. But the jury believed it all, and they warn't out no time at all before they come back with a verdict of guilty o' murder in the fust degree, and poor Bob was sentenced to be hung.

"I talked to one o' them jurymen afterwards," said Dick, "and axed him how it was they was so quick in decidin' the case, and he told me as how the foreman of that jury said to 'em, 'Gen'l'men, this yer case seems mighty simple to me. Anyway, there's a whole lot o' killin' a-goin' on in this country right now, and it's got to be stopped. There ain't been no man found guilty of murder in the fust degree in this yer court for a long time, and it's high time there was, so we had better make an example of this yer feller. Anyhow, we can't have officers of the law shot down in their back-yards and desperadoes a-rampantin' around minin' camps like a roarin' lion and skeerin' the lives out o' our little ones. I'm a father, myself,' said he, 'and I kin feel for the parents of them little children. Shall we say "*guilty*," gen'l'men, and then we can all go home to our families and feel as though we had done our duty to our country?' Then the foreman he sat down and mopped his head with his handkerchief, and then a juryman got up and said, 'That after a elokent speech like that, there was nothin' to do but cast in his vote for "*guilty*;"' and the other jurymen said they guessed they'd do the same, and that's how it was poor Bob was found guilty unanimously in short order. I felt awful sorry for Bob," said Dick, "and I went every day to the jail to see him. He tuk his medicine, though, like a plum gen'l'man and a man. He said he didn't min' bein' hanged in partic'ler, and he might jes' as well hang then as at any other time, but what he objected to was being hanged for nothin'. He didn't have enough hard feelin's agin Smith to have killed him, but he said he wished now he had done the killin', as then he'd be hanged for somethin'. Every one in the jail was plum stuck on Bob," added Dick, "and even the sheriff as had to hang him thought a whole heap o' him. Why, when the day came when Bob was to hang, the sheriff come to Bob and says, 'Bob, I've got to hang yer to-day, but there's no partic'ler time set for the hangin'; so would yer rather be hung before breakfast, or after?"

Here I interrupted Dick by saying that I didn't quite understand how a man could be hanged before breakfast, since he couldn't very well eat his breakfast afterward.

"That's so," said Dick, waving his spoon meditatively, and then he added, with some slight irritation in his voice, "Well, it was mighty perlite in that ther' sheriff, anyhow." Then he went on to say, "I tell yer, I never felt so broke up in all my life as I did that mornin' when poor Bob was hung. The sheriff, after he had fixed the rope round his neck, axed him if he had anythin' to say, and Bob said, 'Yes,' he would like to say a few words. He wished to say good-by to us all and to thank us for our kindness. 'It's no use my sayin' I'm innocent of this yer killin', I s'pose, but some day you'll sure find out I am. I've allus been unfortunate all my life, and, even as a boy they used to call me "Bad-luck Bob," and they'd say, "There warn't a mule in the country as could kick, but what I'd be standin' around somewhar within range of his business end and get hurt," and then he said, 'I don't want to detain yer, gen'l'men, any longer, so please, Mister Sheriff, let her go.' Then the sheriff sprung the trap, and I pulled out," said Dick, "for it made me feel mighty sick."

"Why, Dick," said I, "was that the first time you ever saw a man hanged?"

"Oh, no," he replied, in a somewhat injured tone, "I've been to lots of hangin's but these others was different, 'cause they was all bad men as needed hangin'. I've helped to hang 'em, too," said he, very significantly. "I remember the fust time I ever helped to hang a man I was told to climb a tree and tie one end o' the rope to it and then let the other end, with a noose on it, hang down over a limb. Then the crowd they lifted the feller up and put his head thro' the noose and then they let go o' him. But the feller's weight stretched the rope so that his toes touched the ground, and then they shouted to me to untie the end of the rope as was fastened to the tree and tie it up shorter, but the knot had got draw'd so tight I couldn't undo it, so they shouted out, 'Never mind,' and then four o' them hung onto the feller and took their feet off the ground and the feller got hung that-a-way, and they luked for all the world like bees a-hivin'. They call hangin' 'stretchin' a man's neck,' and that ther' feller's neck was sure stretched when they cut him down-a swan wouldn't have been in it. Ain't yer never heard o' a swan-like neck," added Dick, as though he thought I did not properly appreciate his simile.

"Why, yes, Dick; certainly," said I, reassuringly, "but I don't know that I ever heard of one in that particular connection, exactly."

"Well, perhaps not," replied Dick, somewhat mollified, and then, after musing a while, he said, "I forgot to tell you that, sure enough, we found out afterwards that poor Bob was proved innocent, after all. It appears that there was a big minin' suit on at the time that ther' feller

Smith was killed, and Smith was the only witness that the other side
was afeard of, so they hired a feller to kill Smith, and it jes' happened
that poor Bob come along as this feller was a-hangin' round, waitin'
for a chance to kill Smith, and that's how Bob got into it. After the
killin' this yer feller skipped out, and as ever' one knowed that there
was hard feelin's between Smith and Bob about that ther' minin' claim,
no one ever suspicioned that it was this yer other feller as done it, until
he tuk sick and was about to die, and give the whole thing away."
Then the clock told Dick it was time to get the supper ready, and
further conversation was postponed.

The next day, when Dick was through washing up his dishes after
breakfast, and was filling his corn-cob pipe for his post-prandial
smoke, I asked him to tell me how Charley met his end.

"Ah, poor Charley," said Dick, "he got killed by 'Bull-dose Bill.'
Ye see it came about in this way: Charley was implicated in business
with a feller by the name o' Jack. They had a small bunch o' cattle and
was a-doin' fust rate, when this feller Jack tuk sick and died. He didn't
leave no will, and as this yer Bull-dose Bill was a sort o' cousin o' his,
he claimed Jack's part in the outfit, as he said he was the nearest of kin.
Well, this yer Bull-dose Bill was a reg'lar hog about everythin'. He
was one of them fellers as thinks what's his'n's his'n, and what's yours
he's ready to divide with you; and then, if you did give him half of
what was all yours, he'd kick if he didn't get the biggest half. No one
can get along with a man like that, so Charley proposed that they
should divide what stuff ther' was--and he was just willin' to git the
wust of the division, jes' so long as he could git away and run his own
business by hisself. But Bull-dose Bill wanted to take everythin' for his
share, and finally Charley couldn't stand it no longer, and he told Bill
in plain words what he thou't of him. Bill was a awful coward and was
a-feard to say anythin' back, so he kept quiet, but a few days after, he
and Charley went out to drive in a bunch o' hosses which they was a-
goin' to divide, but, to'ards night, Bill he come back alone and said as
how he and Charley got to quarrelin' about them hosses, and that
they'd got to shootin' at one 'nother, and that Charley had shot at him
twice fust, and then he had shot at Charley, and Charley had fallen off
his hoss, dead, he supposed--anyway, he left him in a rocky cañon, and
'splained to us about where it was, so as we could go out the next day
and bring him in. So the next mornin' I and 'nother feller called Jim
saddled our hosses and took a pack-hoss along for to bring Charley
back on.

"Finally we come to the place where Charley was. His hoss was
still a-grazin' near him, and there lay Charley, shot through the back o'

the head, with his arms stretched out and his six-shooter layin' in his hand, which was open. I told Jim that, from the luks of things, I was satisfied that Charley had been murdered. I picked up the six-shooter and, sure 'nuff, there was two empty shells in it, but when I held up the barrel to the sun and looked through it," said Dick, with great solemnity, "it was as bright as a dollar. Then I remembered as how Charley had been cleanin' his six-shooter the day before, and then I felt sure that Bull-dose Bill's story was all a put up job, and that he had put in them two empty shells hisself. But," continued Dick, "we had to do somethin' with poor Charley. It was mighty hot weather at that time, and he was too fur gone to pack on a horse, so we concluded we'd bury him right thar. As we hadn't calc'lated on buryin' him thar when we started out, we didn't have nothin' to dig with but our pocket knives, and as the ground was mighty rocky, we couldn't dig the grave but about six inches deep, so we conkluded we would jes' lay him in it and cover him over with rocks. Then Jim said as we couldn't fix him up a Christian burial 'cause we had no preacher along, he would make a cross instead and set it up at the head of the grave. So I says to him, 'All right; you go ahead and make you a cross, while I hunt around for rocks to cover him with.'

"Finally Jim got his cross fixed and we set it up, and then we lay poor Charley in his grave and covered him up with them rocks. I had tuk off his hat and coat and shaps (Chaparajos), tho', and laid them to one side, and Jim he says, 'What do you want with them things?' And I says, 'Don't you see how his feet's a-stickin out thro' them rocks?' And then I went and got a hoss-shoe nail out of my saddle pockets and put the hat on top of the cross and fixed it on with the nail. Then I put the arms of the cross through the sleeves of his coat and then fastened his shaps below that; and when I had it all fixed, I tell yer it made a dandy skeer-crow for to skeer away the kiyotes. Jim looked sort of dissatisfied about it, and I says, 'What's the matter with it, Jim?' and he says, 'Oh, nothin'; I guess the skeer-crow is all right, but it seems to me it ain't altogether usual-like to have one.' Then we pulled back to the ranch, and when we got there we found that Bull-dose Bill had gone to town to give hisself up for what he called 'killin' Charley in self-defense.' It appears Bill had a wife livin' in that town and he had friends there; anyway, he didn't have no trubble to get bail--and then to think of the gall of the feller!" said Dick, with great disgust. "Why, he was wantin' to get made administrator for poor Charley, 'cause Charley didn't have no relatives that he knowed of, and as he had a half-interest in what stuff there was, he thought he had a better right to the 'pointment than any one else. However, some of his folks told him

301

he had better keep quiet about it till after the trial. So he said he would, as he guessed it would be the best pol'sy.

"Jim and I was both witnesses at the trial," said Dick, "but shucks, the jury didn't believe nothin' we said, for that ther' lawyer as was defendin' Bill axed the jury as he was a-cross-examin' us whether we luk'd like respectable citisens whose words could be believed, or whether we luk'd like desperadoes. The jury didn't say nothin', o' course, but I think they thought we luk'd like desperadoes," said Dick, with great humility, "but I don't know as we could help that. I've allus had to lead a hard life, and it tain't unnatural that I should look tough," he added, apologetically. "The trial tuk three days, and then come the final wind up, when the lawyer for the defense made his speech to the jury. The court-room was full, and everyone seemed excited. Bull-

302

dose Bill was at his usual place in front of the jury, but he seemed all spruced-up like, and he had a big bokay in his button-hole, and right near him set his wife, all dressed in black like a wider, and three little children dressed like orfins. One of 'em was Bill's kid, but them other two was only borrowed for the occashun," said Dick, waving his spoon deprecatingly. "Then the lawyer, when it come to his turn to speak, he got up and jest a-pranced up and down in front of the jury without a-sayin' a single word. I guess it must hav' been to show off his fine clothes," said Dick, "for he had on a boiled vest, what they calls a white weskit," he added, diffidently, "and a red necktie. Then he started in on the jury in great shape, and talked about the killin' as though Bill had done the country a benefit in riddin' it of one of its wust karacters. Then he axed the jury to look at the bokay Bill had in his button-hole, and then he told 'em 'he was a-wearin' it as an emblem of innocence.' Then Bill's wife and the children commenced to cry like everythin', and he told the jury to look at them, and then he axed 'em if they could ever go back and face their own families after making a widder of that pore defenseless woman, and orfins of them three little children. Then when he had finally got through he sat down and luk'd as tho' he hisself would die of grief if they brought in a verdict of guilty. Then the jury went out, and we waited about an hour when they come back with a verdict o' 'not guilty.' I had seen how the thing was a-goin' all along and didn't expect nothin' else," said Dick, "so I pulled out of the court-room and stood outside and watched them all come out. Pretty soon I seen Bull-dose Bill a-comin' down the steps of the court-house, just a-smilin', with his wife on his arm, and with that ther' bokay in his coat; they looked for all the world like a bride and bridegroom a-comin' out of church arter ther' weddin', and them three little children was a-cavortin' around, and Bill's kid was a-telling them other two as how 'Paw warn't goin' to be hanged arter all,' while the lawyer, he was a-pattin' them on the head promiscuss-like, and I heerd one of his friends a-congratulatin' him on the big contingent fee he was a-goin' to git, but all that time," said Dick, lugubriously, while he slowly stirred some hash he was cooking, "I was wonderin' why Bill, if he thought so much o' his fam'ly, couldn't have thought o' 'em when he was a-murderin' Charley, and then I thought o' that ther' lonesome grave up that rocky cañon, with Charley's feet a-stickin' out o' them rocks, and that ther' skeer-crow a-skeerin' off the kiyotes, and I thought o' Charley's old mother, whom he allus supported, when I fust told her about the killin' and how we buried him, and how she never got over it since. I tell yer," said Dick, shaking the drops of gravy off his spoon ominously, "a dead man's got no friends, and ther' ain't no

303

sech thing as justice. But ther' is times when I thinks over these things, and that ther' Bull-dose Bill had better not come around where I is or one o' us would sure get hurt." And then at that moment in came trooping several hungry cowboys to get their dinner, and Dick excused himself on the score that he had to attend to the duties of his "perfesh."

Some days after, when Dick and I were alone again, I ventured to ask him if any of his friends had ever succeeded in escaping an untimely end. Dick pondered for quite a while, and then he said:

"Why, yes, I kin remember one, but he's away up in the world now. He's got him a fine house and a wife what visits with high-toned folks, and dresses just irregardless o' expense, and then he hisself is a banker and teaches Sunday school," said Dick, with a comprehensive flourish of his spoon. "I don't know as I ever liked him, tho'," said Dick, "tho' I kain't say as he ever done me any harm."

"Why didn't you like him?" I interposed, inquiringly.

"Well, for one thing he warn't skruplus in business, not as I kin claim to be over partic'ler myself," said Dick, modestly, "but for downright crookedness, this yer' feller beat any man I ever knowed. His name was Phil, but we boys used to call him 'Fly Phil' cause he was mighty foxy in everythin' he done or said, and then he could tell sech lies, and then look so innocent like, that a man would as soon rob a pore blind widder as disbelieve him. He was a dry komic, too," added Dick; "he could imitate anyone, and keep a crowd a-laffin' by the hour. I remember the time he made his fust raise out o' a smart-alecky tenderfoot from the east, who thought folks didn't know nothin' out west, 'cause they used hoss sense instead o' pens and paper for to run ther' business. He was one o' these yer fellers with a three-storied eddicashun and a one-story brain. I remember Phil a-comin' to me one day with this yer tenderfoot in tow and introdoocin' him to me as a capitalist from the east as was lookin' for a good business investment. I disremember his name just now, but Phil used allus to speak o' him to us as Budget, 'cause he was allus a-figurin' out his business on paper and making what he called 'budgets.' You've seen them kind o' men, ain't yer?" asked Dick, and on my replying in the affirmative, he continued: "Well, that figurin' on paper ain't no good in the west here nohow. If a man can't carry his business in his head and act accordin' he will sure get left sometime, 'cause he might mislay his figgers some day and then he wouldn't know where he was at. Ye see," said Dick, confidentially, "if a man can work a thing out in practice, what's the good o' his workin' it out on paper, and if he can work it out on paper but can't do it in practice, what good does it do him? Anyway, what's the use o' being able to figger how to do somethin' that you can't do?"

said Dick, and as his logic seemed incontrovertible, I begged him to continue his story about Budget.

"Well, as I was a-tellin' you, Fly Phil was a-fixin' to put up a job on this yer Budget. At that time Phil was a-runnin' a little one-hoss saloon, but he warn't makin' no money, but he told Budget that he was a-doin' a way-up business, and that he was a-savin' the profits he made in order to use them in developin' a mighty fine prospec' he claimed to have up in the mountains. Then Budget, he got kinder excited over them profits, and he axed him if he would sell his saloon, and how many drinks did he sell every day, and Phil said he might sell the saloon, but he never kept no count o' the drinks, but that Budget might find that out for hisself if he wanted to. So Budget said he would, and he sat in one corner o' the saloon and pretended he was a readin', but he was really a-keepin' account o' the number o' drinks that Phil sold. Well, Phil, he told me on the quiet that he didn't want to have Budget disappointed, so he give me two dollars and told me to come into his saloon in the evenin', just casual-like, and drink it up. After supper I went into his saloon, and there I found all the other boys jes' a-treatin' one 'nother like British lords, and they whispered to me that they was a-doin' it all on Phil's money, and for me to drink with 'em, which o' course I did," said Dick. "We'd look 'round wunst in a while at Budget a-keepin' tab on our drinks, and we'd all holler, but Budget, he was too interested in his figgers to ketch on to what we was a-laffin' at. The next day I met Phil, and he told me that he'd sold out his empty beer and whiskey kegs and his good will to Budget for five hundred dollars, and that he was a-goin' to leave town to start in business somewheres else, 'cause, as he said, winkin' one eye, in his agreement with Budget he had agreed not to start a opposition saloon in that ther' same little town. I went into Budget's saloon a few days arter," continued Dick, "to see how he was a-gittin' along. He was a-standin' behind his bar waitin' for customers, but he had a awful long face on him, and he said 'as how business had fallen off dreffully.' I can't say as he got much sympathy from the boys," said Dick, "'cause he was one of these yer clost-fisted fellers as would make the eagle on a dollar squawk afore he'd let go of it, and them kind of men's never pop'lar out west.

Another day, when Dick appeared to be in one of his conversation moods, I said to him, "Dick, how is it you have never got married?"

"Well," said he, "I have come pretty close to it wunst, but it ain't subject as I keer much to talk about."

Thinking that perhaps I might have unwittingly hurt his feelings, I went on to say that I was very sorry I had mentioned the subject.

"Oh, that's all right," said he, "no offense taken;" and then, after a

305

while, he continued: "But I don't know as I mind tellin' you about it anyway. Ye see, the boys laff at me a good deal at times, and I don't know as I altogether likes it, for I don't quite know jus' what they are a-laffin' at, but," added Dick, almost gratefully, "I never see you laff at me, but then maybe it's because you're English, and they say Englishmen never see a joke."

I admitted apologetically that I was an Englishman and presumed that that must be the reason. Then he continued: "Yes, I was wunst in luv, I believe. The boys said I had it mighty bad, but then, I was only a kid at the time, not more than twenty-two years old. I don't know jes' how it affects yer," said he, "but I know that whenever I used to go to see Mary I'd feel awful queer. I'd feel sorter ashamed o' myself, and I didn't know what to do with my hands nor my feet nor my hat, until she tuck it away from me, and I couldn't say anythin', and then I'd be a swallerin' great chunks o' nothin' the whole time."

"You mean you had a lump in your throat," said I, with some hesitation.

"Yes, that's about what they call it."

"How long did you exist in that condition," I asked.

"Oh, it wore off as we got better acquainted, and come to an understandin' about the matter, but jes' after that her Paw said 'he didn't want me to be a-callin' on his girl any more,' so I axed the old man what he had agin me. 'Well, for one thing,' says he, 'you're the blasphemiousist man I ever heered, and I don't want my dawter to marry that kind of a man.' "Ye see," said Dick, by way of explanation, "a short time afore that I was a-crossin' a creek with a four-mule waggin that was heavy loaded and I got stuck in the mud, and I had to talk to them cussed mules in the only language they could understand, and when they finally pulled the waggin out, I luk'd around and ther' I see the old man and Mary in his spring waggin in the road right behin' me, and he had been a-waitin' for me all that time to get my waggin out o' the creek, so as he could cross. I said to him, 'Good mornin', but he jes' drove on and never paid no attention. Ye see, he was one of these yer religious cranks as is mighty hard for a feller o' the likes o' me to please. He never worked on Sundays, and didn't allow no one nor nothin' else on his ranch to work neither, not even his windmill," said Dick, earnestly. "But the girl was sort o' stuck on me, all the same," continued Dick, proudly, "and we would have got married, too, if it hadn't been for my own fullishness. As I couldn't visit her any more, we had to write to one 'nother, and that warn't satisfactory, as I ain't no scribe," said Dick, sadly. "I had to git 'nother feller as was clerk in the store to write for me, and I'd tell him what I wanted to say, and

306

he'd fix it up in fine shape."

"I don't want you to think me unduly curious," said I, "but what sort of letters did you 'fix up' between you?"

"Well, I don't know as I kin just remember, although I think I kin remember the last letter we wrote. Ye see there was a-goin' to be a big dance given at Christmas, and all the folks in the country was invited, and Mary and her folks was a-goin' to it, too. Well, Mary and I had concluded that we would skip out together the fust chance we got, and git married, and I thought that we would get a good chance at that thar dance. So I got the clerk to write to her fur me. The letter was like this: "'Friend Mary--Yours received and contents duly noted. There's going to be a dance at Shaw's ranch Christmas night, and we can skip out together and get married by a justice of the peace while your folks is a-eatin' supper. So be sure and be ready. No more at present. Yours respectfully, Dick."

"That was a very well expressed letter, Dick," said I; "but why did you commence with 'Yours received and contents duly noted?'"

"Well, I don't know as I know exactly myself," said he; "but that thar clerk said he allus commenced his letters that way, 'cause his boss told him it looked business-like, and he thought Mary would think the same. Well, we all went to the dance, and I told Mary as how I had everythin' fixed for skippin' out at supper time, for I had two hosses saddled and tied to a tree some three hundred yards off. There was quite a lot of timber 'round that ther' ranch, and some o' it had been chopped down for to build the house, so there was a lot o' stumps 'round, and jes' as it was a-gettin' dark I pointed out one o' them stumps to Mary and told her that as soon as supper commenced she was to go to that ther' stump and I would meet her ther', and then we'd go to where the hosses was tied and ride off to a ranch where a justice of the peace would be waitin' for to marry us.

"Everythin' was all fixed," said Dick, "but I was so excited and nervous-like that I couldn't help tellin' some o' the boys about it, and they was jes' tickled to death; and some o' them went off and got some whiskey from a store near ther' for to celebrate my weddin', and o' course I had to drink with them and thank them for their kind feelin's. But I had to drink with so many o' em that when the time come for me to go out and meet Mary I warn't feelin' jest right. I went out to that ther' stump and waited and waited for her, but she never come, and finally I fell asleep, and when I woke up I was almost froze. I went back into the house, but it was all dark, for every one had gone home and the folks in the house had gone to bed. Next mornin' I went around to see Mary and she was sure hot. She wouldn't take no explanations, and said, 'If a man couldn't keep an app'intment as important as that one was, she didn't have no use for him.' Then I told her as how I had gone to that ther' stump and waited for her, and she said she had waited a full half-hour at that stump, too, and had caught a drefful cold a-doin' it. And then we come to find out that I had made a mistake about the stump and had waited at the wrong one. Then I told her as how the boys had been treatin' me to whiskey for to celebrate the weddin' and that I s'posed that that was how it was I had got mixed up on the location of that ther' confounded stump. But that only seemed to make her hotter, and jes' then her paw come in the room and axed me how I dared come into his house agin after he had warned me not to; so I guessed it was healthier for me to pull out, so I went off and I never spoke to Mary no more after that, and since then," said Dick, "I've never had no ambish to get married. I don't like settlin' in one place no way; I jes' like to drift aroun'; and then I hates towns," he continued, with great asperity.

"What is your prejudice against towns?" said I.

After some little hesitation he said, "Why I went into a little jim-crow town wunst where I warn't acquainted any and I got 'rested by the city marshal for a tramp!" said Dick, with great indignation. "Ye see this here town was on the railroad, and there was a good many tramps a-beatin' their way through on the freight trains all the time, and these tramps would break into houses and steal things when the folks was out; and the folks complained to the mayor, who told the city marshal to 'rest any man on the streets as was a stranger and didn't appear to have no visibul means o' support. Well, I was a-standin' on the sidewalk a-watchin' the folks a-passin' up and down the street, when suddenly the city marshal comes up and 'rests me. I says to him, 'What's this fur? I ain't done nothin'.' And he says, 'You come along with me and you can settle that with the justice of the peace.' Well, when we got into the court-room the justice said to the marshal, 'What's the charge aginst this prisoner?' And the marshal, he says, "Loafin' around the streets without no visibul means o' support, your honor.' 'No visibul means o' support?' says I; 'Why, I've got ten dollars in my pocket right now;' and I drew it out to show 'em. 'Oh! you have, have you?' says the justice, 'then I fine you ten dollars and give you half an hour to get out o' town.' You bet I got out o' that town mighty quick, fur I didn't want to have any more truck with any sech people."

Dick worked on for me for several months, until one day one of the boys rode up with the mail. On looking it over I found a letter addressed to "The Cook of the S. U. Outfit." I passed it over to Dick and told him I supposed it must be meant for him.

After reading the letter, he told me he would like to speak to me a minute, so I stepped to one side with him.

"Well," said he, "I've got to quit yer this time, sure, and I sure hate to go, but I can't help it. Bein' as you allus treated me as a gen'l'man, I know you wouldn't take advantage of a pore man what's on the dodge, so I guess I'll tell you why I'm quittin' you, or you might think hard on me for quittin' you so sudden-like. Ye see, I was a-cookin' wunst for a cow outfit back in Texas, and I had to make 'em jes' sech a talk as I made to your boys that time you remember of. Well, the boys down ther' treated me all right, except one, who talked around to the other boys that he proposed to git whatever he wanted out o' the waggin whenever he tuck a noshun to.

"One mornin', when all the other boys had left the camp, he was a-munkin' around as usual and started towards the waggin for to get somethin' out. 'Hold on!' says I, 'what is it you want to git out o' ther', and I'll git it for you.' He says, 'You jes' tend to your cookin' and leave me alone.' 'That's all right,' says I, 'but you kain't touch nothin' in that waggin, jes the same,' but he paid no attenshun and got up on the waggin brake. 'Jump off o' ther', says I. 'You go to h--l', says he, and he called me some hard names. So I picked up my gun and let him have it right a-tween them cross eyes o' his," said Dick, in a somewhat nonchalant way, "and o' course he died. I hated to do it," he added, apologetically, 'but I jes' naturally had to. Yer see, a man ain't no man at all if he don't keep his word.

"But I did the best I could for him," continued Dick, by way of extenuation, "for I wrapped him up in the waggin sheet--the one we usually wrapped up beef in," said he, emphatically, "for to keep the flies off him, and then I put him under the waggin in the shade, and then I tacked up a notice on the mess-box, tellin' the boss that I done it, and for him to take what money was a-comin' to me for to bury him decent, and then I pulled out, and," added Dick, sorrowfully, "them pore boys had to cook their own dinners for theirselves that day. Since then I've been a-hidin' out and a-makin' me a livin' a-doing odd jobs, but in this yer letter my old pard tells me that the sheriff o' that ther' county, where this little fuss tuk place, has jes' got onto where I is, and is jes' a-gittin' out rekkysition papers for me, so I guess I'll pull;" and with that he saddled up his private horse, rolled up his clock in his blankets, tied them behind his saddle, and rode off, and that was the last I ever heard or saw of "Front-Name" Dick.

* * *

A few days after, the officers of the law appeared at camp and inquired of me as to where I thought Dick had fled to. My answers as to the direction he had taken were so definite and so explicit that they never caught him!

CPSIA information can be obtained
at www.ICGtesting.com
Printed in the USA
LVHW030136211222
735627LV00001B/94